Classic Game Programming
on the NES

MAKE YOUR OWN RETRO VIDEO GAME

TONY CRUISE

FOREWORD BY
PHILIP AND ANDREW OLIVER

MANNING
SHELTER ISLAND

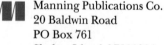
Manning Publications Co.
20 Baldwin Road
PO Box 761
Shelter Island, NY 11964

Development editor:	Doug Rudder
Review editor:	Radmila Ercegovac
Production editor:	Deirdre Hiam
Copy editor:	Kari Lucke
Proofreader:	Melody Dolab
Technical editor:	Dan Weiss
Typesetter:	Tamara Švelić Sabljić
Cover designer:	Marija Tudor

ISBN 9781633438019
Printed in the United States of America

Get the eBook FREE!

(PDF, ePub, Kindle, and liveBook all included)

We believe that once you buy a book from us, you should be able to read it in any format we have available. To get electronic versions of this book at no additional cost to you, purchase and then register this book at the Manning website.

Go to https://www.manning.com/freebook and follow the instructions to complete your pBook registration.

That's it!
Thanks from Manning!

brief contents

contents

foreword

As pioneers in the exhilarating era of the Nintendo Entertainment System (NES), we are delighted to introduce *Classic Game Programming on the NES*. This book is not just a retrospective glimpse but a vivid re-exploration of an epoch where creativity blossomed amidst technological limitations. As the authors of 10 NES titles in the early 1990s, including the *Dizzy* games, *Firehawk, Super Robin Hood,* and *DreamWorld Pogie,* we faced these challenges head-on, transforming our innovative ideas into engaging gameplay and captivating visuals.

Our developmental journey was one of innovation and adaptation. We utilized an IBM PC equipped with an Intel 286 processor, 32K RAM, and a 30 MB hard drive. Programming involved using a DOS editor, running a 6502 compiler, and using a PDS board to connect the PC to an NES development kit. For graphics, we employed DPaint3 on an Amiga, later converting these creations into NES-compatible formats. This book guides you through the evolution of such methodologies to the best modern tools and pipelines available today. In our early careers, the NES was a source of inspiration, teaching us to navigate and transcend its limitations.

The NES, despite its modest 1.66 MHz CPU, was a marvel in its time, ingeniously designed for pixel mapping, hardware sprites, and scrolling. This allowed the creation of smooth, visually stunning 2D games that were just 256 × 240 pixels (organized as 32 × 30 tiles of 8 × 8 pixels) displayed on CRT TVs. With more than 60 million NES consoles sold worldwide, its phenomenal success and influence on the gaming industry and culture was, and remains, undeniable.

Classic Game Programming on the NES transcends being a mere guide; it is a tribute to the ingenuity and fervor that epitomized game development in this iconic era. The book diligently unravels the complexities of programming for a console that profoundly influenced the trajectory of the modern gaming industry.

This book is crafted for both enthusiasts and aspiring developers, offering an unparalleled blend of technical insight and historical perspective. It extends an invitation to delve into both the "how" and the "why" of NES game development, celebrating the NES's legacy as a hotbed of innovation and creativity in video gaming.

Our foray into the world of the NES during the 1990s was transformative, shaping not just our careers but our very lives. This book pays homage to a time when programming was as much an art form as it was a technical skill, demanding not only expertise but also a flair for creative problem-solving within stringent technical constraints.

Classic Game Programming on the NES is a comprehensive educational resource that meticulously deconstructs the unique programming challenges and solutions intrinsic to the NES. More than a programming manual, this book offers an in-depth exploration of the technical intricacies that will deepen readers' understanding of game development. It is an indispensable read for anyone intrigued by the intricacies of game design and programming on one of history's most iconic gaming consoles.

Each chapter melds technical detail with practical advice and insights into the creative process that underpinned NES game development. This book is an invaluable asset for those aspiring to master the art of programming in a context that profoundly influenced a generation of games.

—PHILIP AND ANDREW OLIVER, ALSO KNOWN AS THE OLIVER TWINS

I have been programming computers in Australia for more than 40 years.

Starting in the early 1980s with the purchase of a secondhand TI-99/4 computer in partnership with my father and then progressing to a Spectravideo SV-318 a year later, I loved playing games, mainly in the arcades and on the two main home consoles of the period, the Atari 2600 and the Intellivision.

Having little money to spend on games, I decided to make my own versions for the Spectravideo. Some early game listings were published in the local Australian user group publications and were received well at the time.

Then the entrepreneur in me thought, why not put some of these games on tapes and sell them locally and via the user groups? Thus the Program Pack series of titles was launched with the initial pack containing one utility for drawing sprites and three simple games. This was soon followed by more and more titles and program packs, with more than 50 games being released in a short period.

After dabbling with enhancing some of the early games with add-on machine code routines, I decided to program my very first 100% machine code title, *Meteor Swarm*. Heavily inspired by the arcade game *Asteroids*, this was very well received and, along with a cover designed by a local artist and a second B-side title, *Birds of Orion*, was the very first release under the Electric Adventures name (the Program Packs were subsequently rebranded as Electric Adventures).

Around the same time, the ColecoVision was launched in Australia. Coming with *Donkey Kong* packed with the console, the systems practically flew off the shelves.

I worked in the local games store that Christmas and can remember opening the store in the morning to receive a huge palette of ColecoVision systems, stacking them around the store, and then selling them well before closing each day. So my first experience with the console was demonstrating the system in store to customers and watching lots of lucky people take them home for Christmas.

My efforts, both working in the store and selling my own titles, paid off a few months later, with enough money to upgrade to a Spectravideo SVI-328 Mark II and, most importantly, a SVI-603 ColecoVision adapter—along with a ColecoVision joystick from a broken system and several actual ColecoVision titles on cartridge.

Soon I was playing *Mouse Trap, Q*bert, Frogger,* and *Popeye* at home and learning more about great games. In the years that followed, ever more complex machine code games were released (*Munch Mania, Pyxidis,* and *Video Grafitti*). All of the titles were ported to the MSX systems after the purchase of an SVI-728, itself followed by an SVI-738 X'Press.

Next, I turned my hand to writing, starting with tutorial articles on enhancing basic games with machine code (Beyond Basic), the Micro's *Gazette* magazine, and finally the book *Spectravideo and MSX Complete User Guide*.

Moving on from retail, I embarked on a career in the software industry, writing complex data-driven business applications; I ran a company selling a market-leading point-of-sale solution; and I spent many years in the financial planning, banking industry, tourism and gaming, resources, and now the manufacturing sector.

In the past 10 years, with a renewed interest in all things retro, I converted several of my titles from the Spectravideo/MSX originals across to the ColecoVision and the Nintendo Entertainment System (NES), and created a video series on making retro games. My interest in developing games for the NES comes from its Japanese origin and part of its graphics chip design inherited from the TMS graphics chips found in the Spectravideo and MSX computers (and many others).

The first title I developed for the NES was the NES Championships cartridge for the inaugural Game On Expo in Arizona, where it was used to re-create the excitement of the original Nintendo World Championships held in the console's heyday. It contained three mini-games: *Sydney Hunter, Pedal to the Metal,* and a conversion of my existing *Meteor Swarm* game that had to be played within a 6-minute and 21-second time frame (just like the original). I developed this in three months, learning both 6502 Assembler and the NES hardware at the same time. I later released an enhanced version of *Meteor Swarm* and *Sydney Hunter and the Caverns of Death* (converted from the Super Nintendo game of the same name).

I like the challenge of developing games for limited systems, especially an 8-bit system like the NES. It allows you to completely control the underlying hardware and see how far you can push it. I have always liked teaching and mentoring others and have written this book to provide a platform for newcomers to produce their own ideas and creations for the NES. I truly hope this book allows more people to start making games for one of the very best 8-bit home consoles.

acknowledgments

This book wouldn't exist without the support of my family, especially my loving wife and my four beautiful and talented girls who are themselves making their way in the world.

I would also like to thank the many friends I have met around the world with a passion for retro systems, for playing, collecting, or creating new games, and for seeing how far various systems can be pushed. Thank you to Philip and Andrew Oliver for their generous addition.

I would also like to acknowledge the help and support of the team at Manning Publications for working through the process of creating this book with me: development editor Doug Rudder, review editor Radmila Ercegovac, production editor Deirdre Hiam, copy editor Kari Lucke, proofreader Melody Dolab, and technical editor Dan Weiss.

To all the reviewers: Andrew Bovill, Andy Pasztirak, Christian Sutton, Cicero Zandona, Dave Corun, David Li, Deborah Mesquita, Fabien Sanglard, Gary Bake, Geoff Barto, German Gonzalez, Greg Wagner, Gregor Zurowski, Jens Christian Bredahl Madsen, John McNew, Jonathan Reeves, José Alberto Reyes Quevedo, Laud Bentil, Maciej Jurkowski, Martin Tidman, Mattia Di Gangi, Michael Kolesidis, Michael Petrey, Mike Wall, Nick McGinness, Nicolas Modrzyk, Paul Silisteanu, Rahul Modpur, Ray Georges, Rick Bunnell, Rob Lacey, Yan Guo, and Zbigniew Curylo, your suggestions helped make this a better book.

about this book

Classic Game Programming on the NES is a comprehensive guide to developing your first retro game for the Nintendo Entertainment System. It brings together the scattered secrets of NES development, distilling them into clear instructions on how to get started, what your game needs to work, and what tools you'll need to use. Learn about the NES's awesome and unique architecture, the surprisingly simple 6502 Assembler language, game logic, and more.

Throughout, all concepts are illustrated with a simple space-based shoot-em-up that's based on the awesome *Astrosmash* game reminiscent of games from your childhood.

Who should read this book

For anyone interested in building their own retro games! No programming experience required.

How this book is organized: A roadmap

The book is divided into 16 chapters and 3 appendixes:

- Chapter 1: Let's program games—An introduction to the NES console and what we will be aiming to achieve.
- Chapter 2: Getting set up—What tools will be needed to develop games for the NES on modern systems.
- Chapter 3: Starting 6502 Assembler—A look at the basics of programming in 6502 Assembly language.
- Chapter 4: Math, loops, conditions, and bits—We cover more 6502 Assembly language concepts.

- Chapter 5: Starting somewhere—First we look at what is needed to make a "Hello World"–like demonstration on the NES.
- Chapter 6: Starting a game—Next, we start creating our sample game, *Mega Blast*, and display tile graphics for both the title and main game screens.
- Chapter 7: Move and shoot—We display and move the player's ship using input from the joystick and then make the player's ship shoot up the screen.
- Chapter 8: Enemy movement—In this chapter, we make enemies appear and move onscreen.
- Chapter 9: Collision detection—Here we look at how to determine when our various game objects have collided with each other.
- Chapter 10: Keeping score—We look at how you keep track of the player's score, display it on screen, and update it.
- Chapter 11: Player collisions and lives—Next, we check for collisions between the enemy objects and the player, keeping track of the number of remaining player lives.
- Chapter 12: More enemies—We enhance the number and type of enemies being displayed with different visuals and behaviors.
- Chapter 13: Animations and more—We add object and background animations.
- Chapter 14: Sound effects—We learn how to create sound effects and use them in our game.
- Chapter 15: Music—We learn how music is created and how to use it during gameplay.
- Chapter 16: Where to from here?—In our last chapter, we look at further enhancements to our sample game, extending the NES's capabilities, publishing, and other types of games.
- Appendix A: Installation and setup—This appendix covers getting your environment set up with the tools needed to follow the examples provided in the book.
- Appendix B: Memory mappers—The NES can be extended via the game cartridge; this appendix covers the various types and their capabilities.
- Appendix C: Memory and IO map—This appendix provides a detailed memory and IO map for the NES platform.

The book is designed for the reader to work their way through the chapters in order, but if you are already familiar with and understand 6502 Assembler, then you can skip chapters 3 and 4 and get straight into making a code to run on an NES in chapter 5. If you are unfamiliar with 6502 Assembler, then I strongly recommend that you work your way through both chapters 3 and 4, completing the exercises using the provided online assembler.

About the code

The code from chapters 5 to 16 is provided in a GitHub repository located here: https://github.com/tony-cruise/ProgrammingGamesForTheNES.

The example source code assumes the reader is using the CC65 compiler/assembler mentioned in chapter 2. Instructions on setting this up in your environment are located in appendix A.

This book contains many examples of source code both in numbered listings and in line with normal text. In both cases, source code is formatted in a `fixed-width font like this` to separate it from ordinary text. Sometimes code is also in **bold** to highlight code that has changed from previous steps in the chapter, such as when a new feature adds to an existing line of code.

In many cases, the original source code has been reformatted; we've added line breaks and reworked indentation to accommodate the available page space in the book. In rare cases, even this was not enough, and listings include line-continuation markers (➡). Additionally, comments in the source code have often been removed from the listings when the code is described in the text. Code annotations accompany many of the listings, highlighting important concepts.

You can get executable snippets of code from the liveBook (online) version of this book at https://livebook.manning.com/book/classic-game-programming-on-the -nes. The complete code for the examples in the book is available for download from the Manning website at https://www.manning.com/books/classic-game -programming-on-the-nes and from GitHub at https://github.com/tony-cruise/ ProgrammingGamesForTheNES.

liveBook discussion forum

Purchase of *Classic Game Programming on the NES* includes free access to liveBook, Manning's online reading platform. Using liveBook's exclusive discussion features, you can attach comments to the book globally or to specific sections or paragraphs. It's a snap to make notes for yourself, ask and answer technical questions, and receive help from the author and other users. To access the forum, go to https://livebook .manning.com/book/classic-game-programming-on-the-nes/discussion. You can also learn more about Manning's forums and the rules of conduct at https://livebook .manning.com/discussion.

Manning's commitment to our readers is to provide a venue where a meaningful dialogue between individual readers and between readers and the author can take place. It is not a commitment to any specific amount of participation on the part of the author, whose contribution to the forum remains voluntary (and unpaid). We suggest you try asking the author some challenging questions lest his interest stray! The forum and the archives of previous discussions will be accessible from the publisher's website as long as the book is in print.

about the author

TONY CRUISE has worked in IT and application development for more than 40 years, starting with programming and releasing games for multiple 8-bit systems in the 1980s. Author of more than 100 released titles, books, and magazine articles, today he is actively writing new games and utilities and creating resources for other developers working with 8- and 16-bit systems.

about the cover illustration

The figure on the cover of *Classic Game Programming on the NES*, "Anne de Bretagne, Reine de France," or "Anne of Brittany, Queen of France," is taken from a book "Costumes Historiques de la France" by Paul Lacroix, published in 1852.

In those days, it was easy to identify where people lived and what their trade or station in life was just by their dress. Manning celebrates the inventiveness and initiative of the computer business with book covers based on the rich diversity of regional culture centuries ago, brought back to life by pictures from collections such as this one.

Let's program games! 1

Starting from the late 1970s with the release of the groundbreaking game *Space Invaders*, video games gained widespread popularity, and whole arcades were dedicated to just offering *Space Invaders* for patrons to enjoy. Soon a host of other arcade games followed, bringing us classics such as *Donkey Kong, Pac-Man, Galaga*, and many, many more.

Riding on this wave of popularity, home consoles such as the Atari 2600 and Intellivision entered people's homes, bringing simplified versions of arcade games to consumers. These early consoles (and many home computers) started the process of people gaming at home. Meanwhile, in Japan, Nintendo, a toy company that had been creating small handheld video game units, entered the market in 1983 with the Famicom (Family Computer). This small but quite powerful 8-bit system burst onto the local market and introduced gamers to *Super Mario Bros*, using the Mario character from the arcade game *Donkey Kong*, along with a fast horizontal scrolling array of platforms and quirky characters.

Two years later, the Famicom was repackaged and rebranded for its release in the U.S. and Canadian markets as the Nintendo Entertainment System (NES; see figure 1.1). In addition to introducing *Super Mario Bros*, it introduced the world to new game genres with *The Legend of Zelda* and *Metroid* and became one of the best-selling consoles of its time. The NES continues today to be a very popular "retro" console, with a wide range of games that define what a retro game is in a lot of gamers' minds.

Figure 1.1   Nintendo Entertainment System

Back when the console was released, developing a game for the NES required specialized hardware and a substantial financial commitment. However, with today's modern computers able to accurately emulate the hardware, it is now possible for anyone to create new and exciting games for this popular system to either share or sell to fellow retro enthusiasts (see figure 1.2).

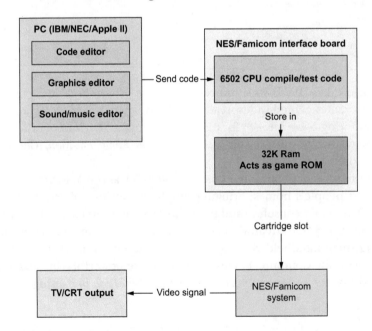

Figure 1.2   Legacy game development

The secrets of the official NES developer's kit are hidden away in the Nintendo archives, but we can glean some details from the non-Nintendo-produced development kits that were produced by third-party companies writing games back when the console was released. Even back then, some form of IBM PC-like computer, expensive mini-computer terminals, or another computer with a 6502 processor like the Apple II was required, along with a hardware board that interfaced the computer directly with a NES (or Famicom) console.

The attraction of developing a new game for a retro system such as the NES is due to its simplicity; it also means most, if not all, the game components (such as graphics, sound, and game code) can be created by either a single author or a small team, rather than the massive teams required to make today's modern games.

The only blockage remaining for most people is working out how to get started. There is a lot of information available on the internet about the NES console, but there is no clear guide on how to get started, what tools you need, and how a game works. In this book, we are going to work through all the things you need to get started and will, step by step, develop a simple but fun game to illustrate how you can bring your game ideas to life.

TIP Find other NES developers on the https://www.nesdev.org/ website.

1.1 Our goal

Our end goal with this guide will be to produce a simple, playable game that demonstrates several game concepts and introduces a lot of the features of the NES platform. The game genre we will be focusing on is a simple space-based shoot-em-up, based on a popular home console game called *Astrosmash* (see figure 1.3).

Figure 1.3 *Astrosmash* **running on the Intellivision**

This is a very simple but fun game and will allow us to go through a lot of important game concepts. We will start with learning about the structure of a game and about programming in the 6502 Assembly language that the console uses. Then we will look at how to create graphics for both background and moving objects, reading input from the game controllers, collision detection, keeping track of the player's score, and bringing the game to life with sound effects and music.

From this start, these same concepts can be used to make other genres of games, such as platformers, adventure games, and games that scroll the screen. We will cover some of the techniques needed to take the next steps later in this book.

1.2   NES architecture

The NES console has quite a unique set of components that make it a very powerful (for when it was released) and flexible gaming system. It is based around a variant of the 6502 processor (a Ricoh 2A03 CPU) along with a custom picture processing unit (PPU) that handles displaying the game output on a TV or monitor and a custom audio processing unit (APU) that can play quite distinctive music and sound effects and even includes the ability to play basic digital audio samples (think of very low-quality digitally recorded sounds).

The console is also quite expandable with the cartridge interface having direct access to the CPU and internal memory, one of the reasons the console enjoyed such a long life, as developers worked out more ways to augment the system with cartridge hardware. Figure 1.4 shows the complexity of the NES architecture.

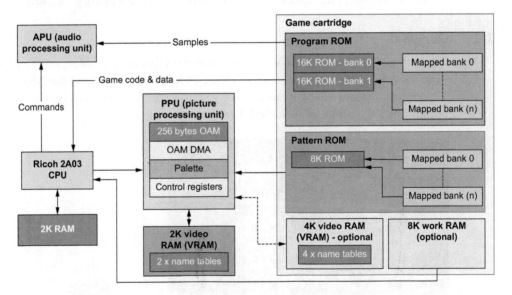

Figure 1.4   NES architecture

We will cover this architecture in more detail as we work through the various parts of our game, but it is broken down into the following areas:

- Ricoh 2A03 CPU (mostly 6502 compatible) with 2K of RAM
- A PPU that handles displaying all images on screen:

- – It has its own 2K of Video RAM (VRAM), which can optionally be added to with RAM from the game cartridge, with the patterns used for the tiles and sprites coming from an 8K section of the game cartridge.
- – This can be supplied by the game cartridge as a single fixed 8K ROM area, as a bank switchable 8K area, or even as 8K of RAM that can be written to by the CPU.
- An APU that handles all sound output and is programmed via commands from the CPU.
- The game cartridge, which not only contains program and data space that is either fixed or bank switched banks with a maximum of 32K available at any one time but also contains an 8K section for the Pattern tables and can optionally add more VRAM, work RAM, or even battery-backed RAM for saving game progress.

1.3 6502 Assembler

The NES console uses a slightly modified version of the popular 8-bit 6502 microprocessor, which was used in many computers and consoles from the late 1970s through most of the 1980s. We will focus on how to write games using 6502 Assembler, just like the developers of the original NES games used back in the day.

It is possible to use higher-level languages (such as C) to make NES games, but due to the limited processing power of the system, use of assembly is required to achieve some features. By learning and using 6502 Assembler, you will be able to take control and make the most of the hardware.

The words "assembly language" make a lot of people, whether they are experienced programmers or starting programming for the first time, think that they will not be able to learn how to use it. The good news is that 6502 Assembler has a relatively short list of instructions to learn, and once you have mastered the basics, you can get something up and running with minimal effort.

1.4 Calling all retro developers

Why would you, the reader, want to create games for a game console released back in the 1980s?

- Retro game consoles like the NES have become very popular to collect, play, and talk about. There is a large variety of games for the system, but there is a compelling challenge to see what the platform can be made to do with the wisdom of the games that have been created for newer generations of systems.
- Modern game development and what goes on "under the hood" are completely obscured by the complexity of whatever 2D/3D development platform is being used. Who will develop the game engines of the future if some of the underlying concepts are forever hidden from view? Sometimes going back to a retro system and being limited by a platform's capabilities can improve the way games are developed for modern platforms.

- Due to the limitations/simplicity of the system, a single developer or small team can create a polished and professional title, compared to the cast of thousands required to create a game for a modern platform.
- Working on a system with strict limits to its capabilities, both in processing power and memory, is similar to and good training for being able to work on modern limited systems such as mobile phones and tablets.
- Showing that you can create a game for a retro system may be the way to demonstrate to a modern development team that making games is what you want to do as a career and may give you an advantage over other applicants when seeking a position in the game industry.

1.5 *The structure of a game*

Throughout this guide, we will be working through the concepts of creating a complete game; to do that, we break a game down into various components and go into detail on each section (see figure 1.5).

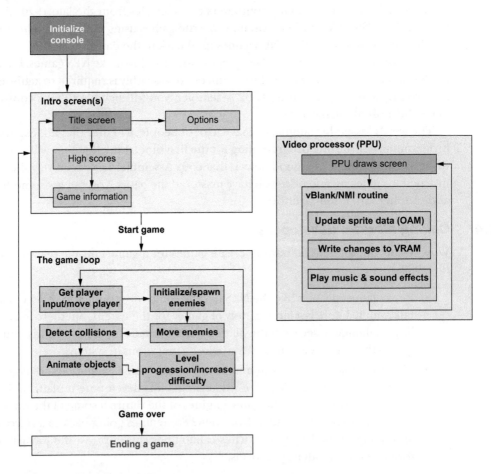

Figure 1.5   The structure of a game

1.5.1 Initialize console

At the start of your game code, you need to set up the console to be ready for your game to run. The NES console has a complex set of custom components, but it has no built-in operating system, so as the developer, we need to start with some important steps as follows:

- Wait for the video hardware and the rest of the NES components to be ready.
- Clear memory so we have a known starting set of values.
- Initialize sound hardware, and ensure any existing sounds are turned off.
- Detect which game controllers are connected depending on which ones our game will support; for example, if your game needs the light gun controller, check that it is connected, and if not, display a message.
- We are going to be displaying graphics, and depending on how the tile and sprite patterns are stored in our game ROM, they may need to be transferred to graphics chip (PPU) video memory.

1.5.2 Intro screen(s)

The next section of a game is the entry point for the players of the game. This is where you tell them what the game is about, its title, what enemies they will be facing, and maybe some high scores to beat. This could be

- A single screen with a title image, waiting for the player to press Fire on the control pad
- A collection of screens showing more information
- Maybe even a demo mode showing the game in action

If the game has some settings that could be adjusted by the player, such as starting lives or player configuration, then an Options screen where they can be selected could be included.

LOAD GRAPHICS AND PATTERNS AND DRAW SCREEN(S)

Before displaying any screens, we first need to set up the graphical patterns that will be used to create our title screen(s). The NES does not have a classical bitmapped display, for example, where every pixel can be individually controlled (at least without cartridge add-ons). It uses a matrix made up of fixed 8×8 pixel tile patterns. These tile patterns need to be loaded from the game ROM into the NES's video memory before they can be used. We will cover this in more detail a bit later.

In addition to the tile patterns that make up the background objects, the NES also has smaller objects, called sprites, that can appear in front of (or behind) the background tiles. These sprites are also defined by 8×8 pixel patterns, and the patterns for these also need to be loaded from the game ROM into the NES's video memory.

INTRO SCREEN LOOP

Once the title screen has been displayed, we need to introduce a simple logic loop that will wait for input from the player controller. The input from the controller could just be waiting for the player to press the Start button, or there might be several menu items to take the player to an Options screen, load a saved game, or enter a code to start the game at a specific level. While we are waiting for player input, we also may want to animate objects on screen, play a catchy music track, or, after a period of time, change to a different screen showing the best high scores or more information about the enemies/characters we are going to encounter.

1.5.3   *The game loop*

Next is the most important part of a game: the main loop that controls the game logic. This is the game engine that drives all the logic of your game; it will vary depending on what type of game you are creating, but it can be split up roughly into the following sections:

- Get player input, move player
- Initialize/spawn enemies
- Move enemies
- Detect collisions
- Animate moving and stationary objects
- Level progression/increase difficulty

GET PLAYER INPUT, MOVE PLAYER

Most games allow the player to control one or more characters (or ships), so we need to get the player's input from the controller, which may move the player's character around the screen or, when detecting a button press, shoot a bullet, drop a bomb, summon magic, or bring up an Options screen.

   If we move the player, then quite often we also want to check where the player is located so that the player character interacts with the background (i.e., stops before going through a wall or lands on a platform). If we are going to shoot a bullet or drop a bomb, we might need to check whether we have a bullet or bomb available to shoot. Some early shoot-em-up games only allowed one bullet! We cover this further in chapter 7.

INITIALIZE/SPAWN ENEMIES

A shoot-em-up would not be much fun without some enemies to shoot at, so next, we need to decide whether new enemies should appear on the screen. This may be a fixed type of enemy for the level of the game or may be selected from several enemy types based on a random event or the player's actions. Once we decide to create a new enemy, we then set up appropriate information for controlling the enemy—for example, place initial sprite(s), and set values in a RAM table. We cover this in more depth in section 8.2.

MOVE ENEMIES

Once we have one or more enemies on screen, we need to move them. In section 8.2, we move any existing enemies based on their current position and their state, using the information in the RAM table we set up when creating the enemy. An enemy might continue to move until it hits a background boundary or might react based on the player's position or actions. We cover this in more depth in section 8.3.

DETECT COLLISIONS

A very important part of our game logic is collision detection; this is where we want to check whether enemies, their bullets, and other objects have hit the player or fixed objects on the screen. Depending on the game, collision detection can be handled within the movement logic of the player and enemies but can also be a separate step. We cover this in more depth in chapter 9.

ANIMATE OBJECTS

We also may want to animate the player's ship, enemies, or background details regularly. Animation can make a game come alive, so it is well worth including. This is usually handled in both the player and enemy movement sections but can also include changes to the background.

INCREASING DIFFICULTY/GAME PROGRESSION

Most types of games can benefit from changes as the player works their way through the game; this can be achieved via the game having things such as

- Multiple screens with different layouts
- Levels to progress through, perhaps with a change in the enemy and/or background graphics, along with an increase in difficulty

Difficulty can also be matched to how well the player is doing. Some shoot-em-up games do this to ensure a less experienced player can still make some advancement in the game. In our example game, we will change the frequency and type of enemies that appear, as well as increase their speed as a player progresses through the game.

1.5.4 Graphics chip draws changes to the screen

The NES has a powerful graphics chip, called the PPU, that handles the drawing of the contents of the screen multiple times per second. What it draws to the screen is contained in special RAM areas known collectively as video RAM or VRAM. This VRAM is not directly accessible from the 6502 CPU, and changes to VRAM need to be sent from ROM or RAM to the PPU via a set of control ports.

Changes to VRAM can only be made when the PPU chip is not busy drawing the screen. The screen is drawn, one row at a time, from left to right, until it reaches the bottom of the screen, as shown in figure 1.6.

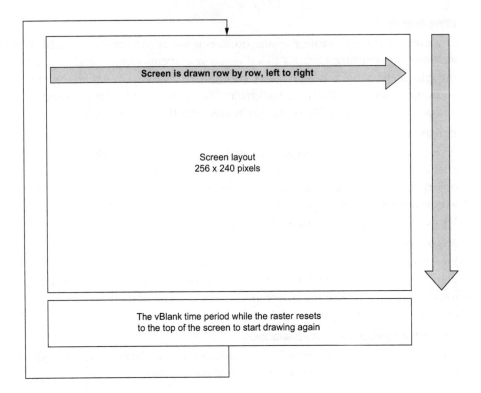

Figure 1.6   NES PPU chip: What is a vBlank?

Once the bottom of the screen has been reached, the PPU chip raises a signal (the vBlank Interrupt) and then needs to wait for the raster, which is drawing the screen, to return to the top in order for it to start drawing again.

This vBlank period is the time to change things in VRAM while the PPU chip is not using it. Trying to change VRAM at the wrong time can lead to incorrect output on the screen. It can be done, just with great care. Note that the time to both read and write VRAM is longer while the screen is being drawn (as the PPU is busy).

The vBlank signal from the PPU graphics chip causes a non-maskable interrupt (NMI) to be generated for the 6502 CPU. The 6502 CPU will stop what it was doing and continue executing from the NMI interrupt routine specified in the Vectors table (see section 5.5). It is the responsibility of the programmer to save any 6502 registers used inside the NMI routine and restore them before exiting.

1.5.5   *Ending a game*

Several early arcade games just keep going, slowly getting harder until the player loses all their lives; the developers never programmed in an ending. In fact, some of these games keep going until a "kill screen" occurs, usually caused by a number, such as the player's score or a level counter running out of memory and causing the game to crash. Well-known examples of these include *Donkey Kong*, where its level timer on level

22 reaches zero, thus killing the player immediately, and *Pac-Man*, which glitches when the player reaches level 256.

Later games allowed the player to work toward a goal or have a fixed number of levels to work through. Working toward a goal gives the player something else to achieve other than just a high score. Also, having a goal allows the development of a background story that can complement the details in the game, either in the game or in the instruction material.

It is a good idea to work out an ending for your game, even if it is just a score summary screen or a nice graphic of your hero sitting down for a well-deserved rest. It gives the player closure and a chance to review how well they have done.

Summary

- By learning and using 6502 Assembler, you will be able to take control and make the most of the hardware.
- Developing games for a retro console can provide a way to demonstrate your skills and passion in the game industry without having to involve a team of people.
- Your game code needs to wait for the NES console hardware to be ready.
- The "game loop" is the most important part of a game.
- Most games have a way to make progress with different levels, enemies, and increased difficulty.
- Player satisfaction is improved if a game has a background story and a defined ending.

Getting set up

2

To start creating games that will run on the Nintendo Entertainment System (NES), you will need a development environment. Back when games for the system were first created, specialized computers hooked up to a hardware-based development system were required, which was quite an expensive undertaking at the time, and these were only handed out to selected parties by Nintendo. Now, due to the availability of modern personal computers, we can not only simulate this development environment completely in software, but we can have far more advanced tools. An easy-to-use development environment with a modern text editor with syntax coloring, along with additional tools to compile and debug your programs, will allow you to focus on developing the functionality of your game.

We will cover getting a development environment set up on Windows-, Linux-, or macOS-based systems, and you will be able to choose the tools that suit your preferences. The selection of tools is far more limited on Linux and macOS systems, but a usable setup can still be achieved.

2.1 Emulation

It is not practical to have a physical NES game console wired up to your personal computer so that you can build, deploy, and debug your game code. Software-based emulators, which emulate all the functionality of the NES hardware but run on your personal computer, are a much better option.

The NES is a very popular 8-bit system, so many emulators do a decent job of emulating the system. Note, however, that they are not perfect at emulating the NES hardware (especially the sound), so any games should be tested on real hardware before releasing to other users.

> **NOTE** To be able to test a game on real NES hardware, several SD-based cartridge adapters can be used; personally, I use the EverDrive N8 cartridge manufactured by Krikzz (see https://krikzz.com/our-products/legacy/edn8-72pin.html).

Quite a few of the emulator solutions are primarily focused on the Windows platform, but there are still a few choices that will run on Linux or macOS systems. Most of the emulators are available as both downloadable binaries, which you can just run on your system, and source code that you can compile on your system.

Some of the emulators also have a built-in or complimentary debugger. A debugger is especially important as it allows you to see your game code running one step (line/statement) at a time. Being able to step through your code and see what registers, flags, and memory are changed can help you find out why your code is not performing how you expect. The term "debug" implies it is a tool to help remove the bugs in your code.

2.1.1 Mesen

Mesen is quite a good choice for emulating the NES hardware (see figure 2.1). It has a high level of emulation accuracy and several handy add-on tools (such as a built-in debugger), plus, most importantly for readers of this book, it can be controlled from other applications. It is also, at the time of writing, actively being updated and supported.

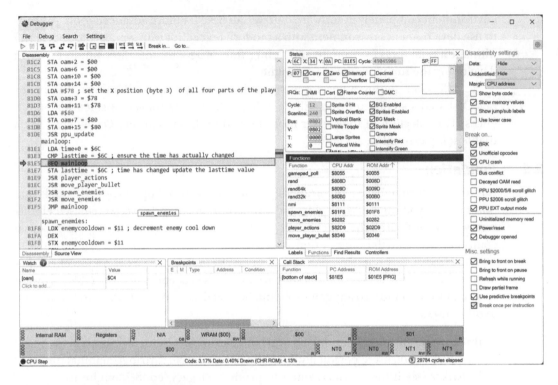

Figure 2.1   Mesen debugger in action

In addition, Mesen supports both Windows and Linux as platforms. For macOS users who want to use Mesen, one of the virtualization apps such as UTM, VMWare Fusion, or Parallels Desktop will allow the Windows version to run in a window on a Mac system and still be able to access the filesystem. The main support website for Mesen is https://www.mesen.ca/docs/index.html.

> **TIP** I have found the Mesen emulator to be the best option for developing titles for the NES, especially since, at the time of writing, it is being actively supported, and the additional tools, such as the debugger, work very well.

2.1.2   *FCEUX*

FCCEUX has been in development since 2008, starting on Windows and later made cross-platform. Its emulation is considered very accurate, and it has several tools built in, such as a debugger and various viewers for all the graphical objects (see figure 2.2).

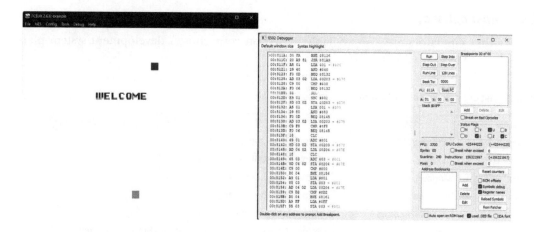

Figure 2.2 FCEUX running on Windows

It is the best choice for those developing on the macOS platform unless you run Mesen using a Windows virtual session. You can download FCEUX for your operating system here: https://fceux.com/web/download.html.

2.1.3 *iNES*

iNES has been in development since 1996, and as of this writing, is currently at version 6.1 (see figure 2.3). iNES's emulation is considered very close to running a game on real hardware and supports many homebrew memory mappers. There are builds for Windows and many Linux distributions including Android devices, but there are, unfortunately, no builds for macOS at the time of writing. It also has a simple debugger built in, which makes it a more attractive option for NES development. You can download a version for your operating system here: http://fms.komkon.org/iNES/#Downloads.

Figure 2.3
iNES emulator
Windows version

Once you have iNES downloaded, installation is very simple. Basically, you select a folder and then unzip the download file contents into the folder.

2.1.4   Other options

Other emulators are also available, based on your chosen development system platform. These are listed in table 2.1.

Table 2.1   **List of other available emulators**

Name	Platforms	Site	Debugger
Mesen	Windows/Linux	https://www.mesen.ca/docs/index.html	Yes
Nestopia UE	Windows/Linux	http://0ldsk00l.ca/nestopia/	
FCEUX	Windows/Linux/macOS	https://fceux.com/web/home.html	Yes
iNES	Multiplatform	http://fms.komkon.org/iNES/	Yes
JNES	Windows/Android	http://jabosoft.com/categories/1	
BizHawk	Windows/macOS	https://github.com/TASEmulators/BizHawk	Yes
VirtualNES	Windows	http://virtuanes.s1.xrea.com/	
RetroArch	Multiplatform	https://www.retroarch.com/index.php	
Higan	Windows	https://higan.readthedocs.io/en/stable/	

2.2   Editor

One of the most important tools needed to write assembly language is an application to edit the source files. This can be something as simple as Windows Notepad or Linux's VIM (or even ED for old-timers like me), but it is a lot better if the assembly text is formatted and colored in such a way as to improve readability and highlight any potential syntax errors (see figure 2.4). It is even better if you can compile your current project and see any errors or warnings from the assembler.

```
34    .segment "HEADER"
35    INES_MAPPER = 0 ; 0 = NROM
36    INES_MIRROR = 1 ; 0 = horizontal mirroring, 1 = vertical mirroring
37    INES_SRAM   = 0 ; 1 = battery backed SRAM at $6000-7FFF
38
39    .byte 'N', 'E', 'S', $1A ; ID
40    .byte $02 ; 16k PRG bank count
41    .byte $01 ; 8k CHR bank count
42    .byte INES_MIRROR | (INES_SRAM << 1) | ((INES_MAPPER & $f) << 4)
43    .byte (INES_MAPPER & %11110000)
44    .byte $0, $0, $0, $0, $0, $0, $0, $0 ; padding
45
46    .segment "ZEROPAGE"
47    nmi_lock:          .res 1 ; prevents NMI re-entry
48    nmi_count:         .res 1 ; is incremented every NMI
49    nmi_ready:         .res 1 ; set to 1 to push a PPU frame update, 2 to turn rendering off next NMI
50    scroll_x:          .res 1 ; x scroll position
51    scroll_y:          .res 1 ; y scroll position
52    scroll_nmt:        .res 1 ; nametable select (0-3 = $2000,$2400,$2800,$2C00)
53    gamepad:           .res 1
54    gamepad_previous:  .res 1
55    gamepad_pressed:   .res 1
56    song_index:        .res 1
57    pause_flag:        .res 1
58    nmt_update_mode:   .res 1   ; update "mode", 0 = nothing to do, 1 = column mode, 2 = row mode + p
59    nmt_update_data:   .res 128 ; nametable update entry buffer for PPU update
60    nmt_update_len:    .res 1 ; number of bytes in nmt_update_data buffer
61    palette:           .res 32  ; palette buffer for PPU update
```

Figure 2.4   **Source text formatting**

There are quite a few powerful and flexible text/code editors available. For this book, we will focus on two: Visual Studio Code and Sublime Text. which are both available on Windows, Linux, and macOS. Some other well-supported text and code editors you could consider are

- Notepad++
- Context
- UltraEdit
- Atom
- TextEdit
- Brackets
- CodePen

2.2.1 Visual Studio Code

Visual Studio Code is a powerful code editor that supports many different programming languages; has an extension framework; runs on Windows, macOS, and Linux; and is free to use (see figure 2.5). To download and install Visual Studio Code, use the official site here: https://code.visualstudio.com/.

Figure 2.5 Visual Studio Code

There are several plugins available that support syntax highlighting and build command mapping for 6502 Assembler. One of the extensions to try is the one from Cole Campbell:ca65 Macro Assembler Language Support (6502/65816) (http://mng .bz/vP2J). To find this in Visual Studio Code, go to the Extensions tab on the left-hand side and type "ca65." The extension should be near the top of the list of items returned. Click it, and click the Install button; you will need to accept and trust the publisher for the extension to be enabled. This extension not only adds syntax highlighting to Visual Studio Code but will also enable the build command to use the CC65 compiler/ assembler to compile your code from within the editor.

NOTE   For Visual Studio Code to be able to find the CC65 compiler, the path of the bin directory will need to be added to your path in your environment.

2.2.2   *Sublime Text*

Sublime Text is a powerful code editor that supports many different programming languages; has an extension framework; and runs on Windows, macOS, and Linux, but requires a paid license to use (see figure 2.6). To download and install Sublime Text, use the official site here: https://www.sublimetext.com/. I have put together a 6502 plugin/extension for Sublime. You can download it from http://mng.bz/46ya.

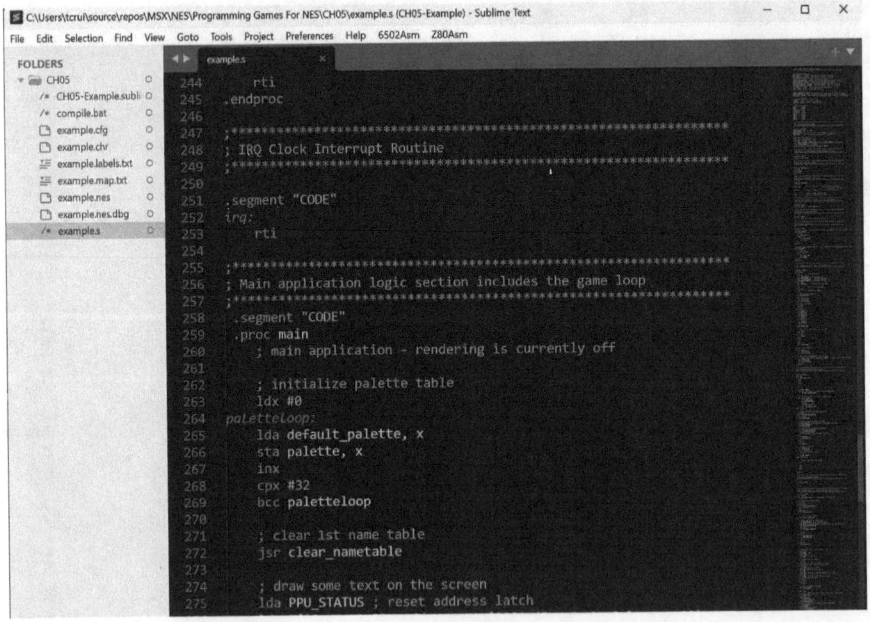

Figure 2.6   Sublime Text editor

2.3 *Assembler*

When writing your game code for the NES console, you need to turn the text instructions that you type into actual machine code that the NES console will be able to understand. To do that, you need a program called an assembler.

The main assembler in the homebrew development community for the 6502 processor is called cc65. It is a C language compiler, but it also supports 6502 assembly language files. It supports many old 6502 machines, one of which, luckily, is the NES console. The home page for the assembler is https://cc65.github.io/. There are two other popular options:

- NESASM (https://github.com/camsaul/nesasm)
- ASM6 (https://github.com/parasyte/asm6)

TIP The code in this book has been tested with the syntax used by the cc65 compiler/assembler, so I strongly recommend it.

2.4 *Graphics creation*

The NES console is known for its colorful game characters and graphics, so a way to create the graphics you will use in your games is a very important part of game creation. The NES graphics hardware (picture processing unit) displays graphics using 8×8 tiles and 8×8 sprites, the patterns of which come from sets of tiles (also called CHR sets). Depending on the cartridge mapper your games use (see APPB Memory Mappers), your game can have one or more sets of tiles, palettes, and tile layouts.

There are quite a few published tools (one of the more popular tools is called Tile Editor Pro) that allow you to hack/edit existing NES ROMs, changing the stored tile and sprite patterns. These types of programs are fine for file hacking but are not very useful when developing modern titles for the NES, especially as some of the more complicated cartridge mappers do not have their tile and sprite data in a fixed position in the cartridge.

2.4.1 *NES Tileset Editor*

During the development of my titles for the NES console, I found the available graphic creation tools that were available did not match what I needed at the time, so I created a tool called the NES Tileset Editor (see figure 2.7). It is written in .Net but currently only targets the Windows platform. I am working on an upgraded version that will use the new MAUI cross-platform targeting capabilities of .Net. You can download the most recent version of my tool here: https://www.electricadventures.net/Pages/Category/34.

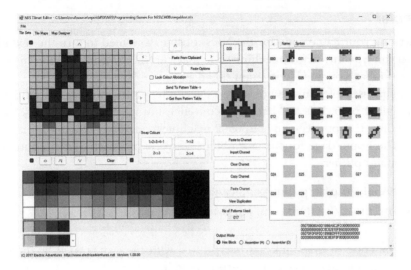

Figure 2.7   NES Tileset Editor

2.4.2   *NEXXT*

NEXXT is a comprehensive tool for making character tiles, sprites, and tile layouts. It is based on Shiru's classic NES Screen Tool but with some extra features to help developers manage the graphics for more complicated titles (see figure 2.8). You can download it from the author's site here: https://frankengraphics.itch.io/nexxt. It is only available for Windows but can be run on macOS using Wine.

Figure 2.8   NEXXT Tile Editor in action

2.4.3 NES Assets Workshop

The NES Assets Workshop (NAW) is designed for artists to be able to use a modern tool but create graphics for the NES, imposing all the limitations without blocking creativity (see figure 2.9). You can download it from the author's site here: https://nesrocks .itch.io/naw. It is only available for Windows but can be run on macOS using Wine.

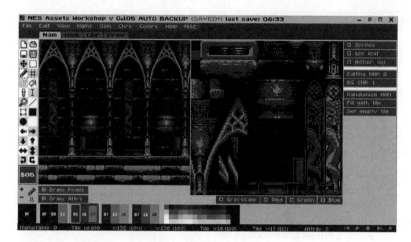

Figure 2.9   NES Assets Workshop in action

2.4.4 NES CHR Editor

NES CHR Editor is a NES-focused tool that allows you to edit the CHR banks in existing ROMS and (since the latest version) edit CHR dumps, which makes it a bit more suitable as a developer tool (see figure 2.10). It is only available for the macOS platform, and you can download it from https://www.ninjasftw.com/squirrel/nes_chr/.

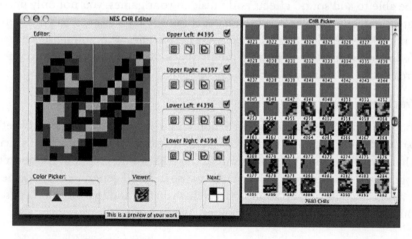

Figure 2.10   NES CHR Editor

2.4.5   *Other options*

Several tools allow you to edit/create graphics for the NES, but they are largely focused on editing existing NES Rom images (see table 2.2).

Table 2.2   Other tools to edit NES graphics

Name	Description	Link
YY-CHR	YY-CHR is a Japanese pixel editing tool for Windows. It is focused on editing/hacking existing ROMs, so it is not that useful for developers, but it can export a CHR set as a single bitmap, so it could be useful for sourcing starting graphics from existing ROMs to modify and use in your projects.	https://w.atwiki.jp/yychr/
Tile Layer Pro	Tile Layer Pro is a popular pixel/tile editor for Windows that supports several platforms, including the NES. It is focused on ROM hacking, so it cannot output a CHR table separately.	http://mng.bz/QR1w
Nestile	NESTile is a simple tile editor built using Python, so it will run on Windows, Linux, and macOS.	https://github.com/jmcmahan/nestile

2.5   *Sound effects and music creation*

The NES console has a very powerful (for its time) sound generator that can even use (simple) sound samples and has multiple channels and different waveforms that can be selected. This gave the NES its very distinctive sound and makes it very popular to use in the modern homebrew music demo scene.

To be able to add sound effects and music to your games, you not only need a tool to create them, but you also need some code, known as an engine, to play them. Each of the music creation/editing tools covered here comes with an engine that you can include in your game title to handle the playback of the music and sound effects you have created.

2.5.1   *FamiTracker*

The tool that has dominated the NES homebrew mod/demo scene is called FamiTracker (see figure 2.11). It is a very comprehensive tracker (multitrack music creation tool) that allows you to get the most out of the NES sound chip, but it does require a fairly significant commitment to learn how to use it. It will generate the code necessary to play any created music and sound effects that you can add to your title. It deserves to be included in any NES developer's tool set.

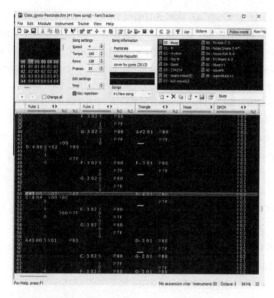

Figure 2.11   FamiTracker

The main limitation of FamiTracker is that it is only available for the Windows platform, so we will use another tool to cover music and sound effects for this guide. You can find FamiTracker for Windows at the supporting website here: https://famitracker.org.

2.5.2   *FamiStudio*

Another option that provides a solution for Windows, Linux, and macOS users is called FamiStudio (see figure 2.12). It is not as powerful as FamiTracker but is a little easier to use (especially for beginners) and comes with a good, but lightweight, playback engine that you can use in your games.

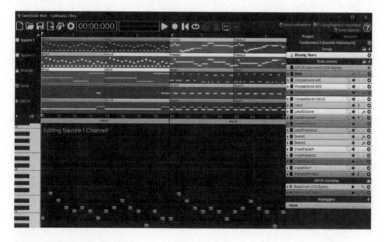

Figure 2.12   FamiStudio

You can find FamiStudio for your system at the supporting website here: https://famistudio.org/. You will need to download both the application itself for your platform of choice and the NES Sound Engine. Make sure you choose the CA65 engine (there are separate downloads supporting NESASM and ASM6). Set that download aside; we will cover adding this to our game code in chapters 14 and 15.

In this chapter, we have gone through the assemblers, text/code editors, graphic creation, and music creation tools that will enable you to get your modern development computer ready to start making games for the NES. In later chapters, we will expand on each one of the tools and use them to put together our first game.

Summary

- To be able to develop your own NES games on a modern desktop system, you will need
  - A text editor to edit the code
  - An assembler to turn that code into a final ROM image
  - A tool to create and edit tile and sprite graphics
  - A tool to create and edit the sound effects and music your game will use
- There are several tools you can choose depending on your desktop platform.
- More of the tools are available for Windows than Linux or macOS platforms.

Starting 6502 Assembler

3

This chapter covers

- Memory and registers
- Moving things around

This will not be a full tutorial on 6502 Assembler, as that would require an entire book, but it should give you a start so you can follow the rest of this book. The 6502 microprocessor was very popular and used for many home computer systems and consoles starting from the late 1970s. Its main appeal at the time was its simplicity and its ability to execute each instruction very quickly. It had a very small set of instructions and was the forefather of the current generation of reduced instruction set (RISC) processors that you would find in the mobile phones we all love to use today.

As the NES console has a 6502 processor with limited memory and registers, it can be difficult for higher-level languages (like C and Basic) to produce assembly code that runs fast enough to be useful for game development. Games require precise timing to ensure objects are drawn to the screen on time and that music and sound effects are played without slowing down. For our first chapter on 6502 Assembler, we will look at how the processor stores and processes information, with examples for each instruction and the different memory modes that can be used.

Recommended reading

While we are on suggested resources, and if you have the budget, then for learning 6502, there is no better book than *Programming the 6502* by Rodney Zaks (SYBEX, 1983). For those with a smaller budget and/or who want to learn about more of the chips that followed the original 6502, I would recommend the book *Programming the 65816: Including the 6502, 65C02, and 65802* by David Eyes and Ron Lichty (Prentice Hall, 1986).

This chapter contains quite a lot of information, which, depending on the reader, can be worked through in full now or by reading each topic's introductory information and referring to the specific instructions as we use them by writing actual code that will run on an NES console.

3.1   *Online Assembler Simulator*

To assist those who want to work through this chapter, I have set up an Online 6502 Assembler Simulator on my GitHub page here: https://tony-cruise.github.io/ (see figures 3.1 and 3.2).

Learning 6502 Assembler

To support readers learning 6502 Assembly Language I have put together an online 6502 Simulator/Assembler (based on the code of Stian Søreng's and Nick Morgan) so that readers can see 6502 commands in action before we get to the part where we setup the NES hardware and get something displaying on screen.

Run the 6502 simulator.

Figure 3.1   Access the Online 6502 Assembler Simulator.

**Figure 3.2
Online Assembler
Simulator in
action**

Once you have clicked on the link to the 6502 Simulator, the simulator will load, and you will have a screen with four key areas:

- *Assembly code area*—This is where you type or paste your code.
- *Debugger*—See changed register values here.
- *Screen output*—Not used for our examples.
- *Output windows*—This is where you will see any messages from the assembler.

To use, click the Reset button, either type in or paste your lines of code into the Assembly Code Area, and click the Assemble button. If you don't get any errors, then you can click the Run button, and the code will be executed. The final value of any of the registers will be shown on the right in the debugger. To see any changes to memory, click the Monitor checkbox, and an additional area will display the contents of memory (in 256-byte sections).

3.2 Memory and registers

Using a computer microprocessor (CPU) and learning assembler is all about getting the CPU to move information from one location to another in the computer's memory or to change information stored in computer memory. A computer only understands things in single bits, either On (1) or Off (0), which in isolation is not very useful, so at least 8 bits are commonly grouped together to form a byte. The different possible combinations of bits in an 8-bit byte allow the numbers from 0 to 255 to be expressed. Computer memory is commonly supplied as a certain number of available bytes. The NES has 2,048 (2K) bytes of random access memory available in the console itself.

Each value stored in a computer's memory can represent many aspects of the game we are creating, for example, the location of the player's ship, how many points have been scored, or what part of our music track is currently playing. Other programming languages use variables to store information. You can think of both the registers and memory locations as the variables you use in your programs (see figure 3.3).

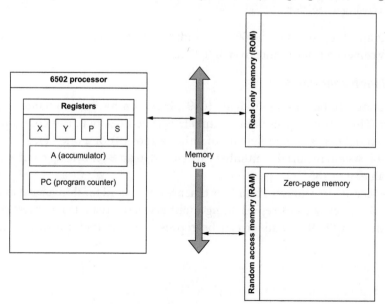

Figure 3.3
6502 processor
difference
between
registers and
memory

The 6502 processor, like most processors, has different ways to store information:

- *Registers*—These are the processor's internal memory locations used for doing calculations like addition and subtraction. They are located inside the processor itself, so they are the quickest place to access information, but they are very limited in number, so they are only suitable for executing parts of a calculation, with the results being stored elsewhere. The 6502 has a particularly small number of registers compared to other 8-bit processors, which is why it can use a special area of random access memory called zero page (discussed later).

- *Read only memory (ROM)*—This is the external ROM that is provided in the game cartridge. Read only memory, as per its name, can only be read from and cannot be changed by the CPU. This is where both the game code and the graphical patterns used for rendering the screen are stored.

- *Random access memory (RAM)*—This is the external RAM that the computer or console has that can be both read and written to. For the NES console, 2K (2,048 bytes) is available to use (unless added to the game cartridge hardware). This is a lot more space than can be stored in the processor registers, but it is located outside the processor, so more time is required to read and write to a memory location.

- *Zero-page memory*—This is a special section of RAM (the first 256 bytes) that the processor can access faster than normal RAM. The 6502 processor can address 64K of memory (ROM or RAM) at any one point in time, so when specifying an address to read or write to, 2 bytes are needed to form the address. For zero-page memory, only 1 byte needs to be specified to say which address the processor should use. Because the CPU only needs to read the instruction and the single byte to execute the instruction, access is faster than normal memory but not as fast as using a register.

Because it is an 8-bit processor, the 6502's standard registers store 8 bits of information; that is, they can each hold a value from 0 to 255.

3.2.1   Numerical representations

Humans count numbers using 10 digits (0–9), based on having two hands each with five fingers. This way of representing numbers is called decimal. But computers only really know numbers as being made up of either a zero (0) or a one (1), and the NES being an 8-bit system means that numbers are stored in an 8-bit byte, each of which can store the values 0 to 255.

To make it easier to represent numbers that are being used for things such as graphic patterns, several new ways of representing numbers were created. The most common number values in 6502 Assembler can be represented in several forms, as listed in table 3.1.

Table 3.1   Common number formats in 6502 Assembler

Number format	Syntax	Decimal value
Binary	%01010101	85
Hexadecimal	$55	85
Decimal	85	85

BINARY NUMBERS

Binary numbers are only either a one (1) or a zero (0), and they represent the underlying bits in the console's memory. As the 6502 is an 8-bit processor, a binary number is normally 8 digits long—that is, an 8-bit byte (or 4 digits long if you are dealing with half a byte) (see table 3.2). The bits are numbered from the right, starting at 0.

Table 3.2   How the bits in an 8-bit byte are numbered

7	6	5	4	3	2	1	0

In 6502 Assembler, we indicate a number value is a binary number using the % symbol, followed by the 0 and 1 characters making up the required number. They can be any length, but any more than 8 digits (i.e., more than 8 bits) will limit which commands they can be used with. For example, %10101010 in binary equals 170 in decimal. To calculate a decimal number from this binary number, you can use a table like table 3.3, where you multiply each bit that is turned on by the power of 2.

Table 3.3   How to calculate a decimal number from a binary number

Bit (n)	7	6	5	4	3	2	1	0
Binary	1	0	1	0	1	0	1	0
Multiple (2n)	X 128	X 64	X 32	X 16	X 8	X 4	X 2	X 1
Line total	128	0	32	0	8	0	2	0
Total	128 + 0 + 32 + 0 + 8 + 0 + 2 + 0 = 170							

HEXADECIMAL NUMBERS

Binary numbers can be quite long, so a shorthand way of representing 4 bits (often called a nibble) at a time was created called hexadecimal. The digits of hexadecimal numbers are made up of the values 0 to 15, but values starting from 10 to 15 are represented by the letters A to F (see table 3.4).

Table 3.4   Hexadecimal numbers to decimal comparison

Hex	0	1	2	3	4	5	6	7	8	9	A	B	C	D	E	F
Decimal	0	1	2	3	4	5	6	7	8	9	10	11	12	13	14	15

This allows 16 values to be represented by a single digit in the number, but combining two hexadecimal numbers together is all that is needed to represent an 8-bit number— for example, $AF = (A)10 \times 16 + (F)15 = 175$ decimal.

In 6502 Assembler, we indicate a number is a hexadecimal number using the $ symbol, followed by one or more hexadecimal digits (0–9, A–F). One digit represents 4 bits, so you need two digits for an 8-bit number and four digits for a 16-bit number.

3.2.2   Registers

Registers are inside the core of the microprocessor and are used for performing calculations and moving information around from one place to another (see figure 3.4).

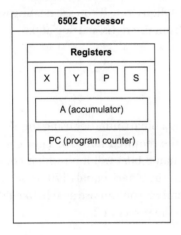

Figure 3.4   The 6502 available registers

The 6502 only has a very limited number of registers compared with other 8-bit CPUs, so a lot of code is devoted to moving information between the registers and the main memory. Each of the available registers has a specific function, as depicted in table 3.5.

Table 3.5   The registers available in a 6502 processor

Register	Size (bits)	Description
A	8	Also called the accumulator. It is the primary register for arithmetic operations and accessing memory.
X	8	Used as an index in some addressing modes.
Y	8	Used as an index in some addressing modes.
PC	16	Also called the program counter. It points to the address of the next instruction to be executed.
S	8	Also called the stack index. It indicates where the next element will be written to the stack.
P	8	Also called the status flag. It contains the current state of the CPU or information about the result of the previous instruction.

3.2.3   Status flags

The 6502 microprocessor has several status flags, which give the programmer access to the results of previous operations or the current state of some conditions (see table 3.6). The 8-bit P register contains the CPU and instruction result flags (we will go through these in more detail as we use them later).

Table 3.6   The available status flags in a 6502 processor

Bit	Symbol	Name	Description
7	N	Negative	After a comparison instruction, this flag will be set if the register's value is less than the input value (and the values are no more than 127 apart).
			Otherwise, this flag will be set if the result value of an instruction is negative (i.e., bit 7 of the result was set).
6	V	Overflow	After an arithmetic operation (Add or Subtract), if the sign of the result differs from the sign of both the input and the accumulator, this flag will be set.
			After a BIT operation, set to bit 6 of the input
5	-	Unused	This flag is unused and will always be set.
4	B	Break	This flag will be set if an interrupt request has been triggered by a BRK instruction.
3	D	Decimal	The NES's implementation of the 6502 does not include the binary decimal instructions, so this flag has no effect on the arithmetic instructions but can be used by the developer for their purposes.
2	I	Interrupt Disable	When set, interrupt requests are disabled.
1	Z	Zero	After doing a Compare instruction, set if the register's value is equal to the input value
			After doing a BIT operation, set if the result of logically ANDing the accumulator with the input results in 0
0	C	Carry	Carry flag used in math and rotate operations
			After an arithmetic operation, set if an overflow occurred during addition or cleared if an overflow occurred during subtraction
			After a compare operation, set if the register's value is greater than or equal to the input value
			After a shifting operation, set to the value of the eliminated bit of the input

3.2.4   Zero-page memory

The 6502 microprocessor has a very limited number of internal registers compared to other microprocessors; its way of getting around this for the programmer is by treating the first 256 bytes of memory using a special mode called *zero page*. Accessing this first part of memory is much faster than accessing the rest of the available memory space, as only 1 byte is required to specify the location to read or write. Each byte the microprocessor needs to load to execute an instruction increases the time taken to execute the instruction.

3.2.5   Stack

A stack is a last-in, first-out data structure. Think of a numbered stack of plates: you can only access the current plate on top of the stack by taking it off or adding a new plate to the stack. You add a value to the stack by "pushing" it onto the stack and remove a value by popping it off the stack (see figure 3.5).

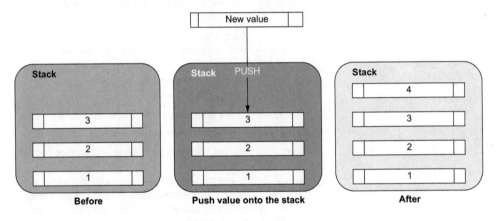

Figure 3.5   Adding (pushing) an item onto a stack of items

Just like a stack of plates, the last value (plate) added to the stack is the first value that will be removed from the stack (see figure 3.6).

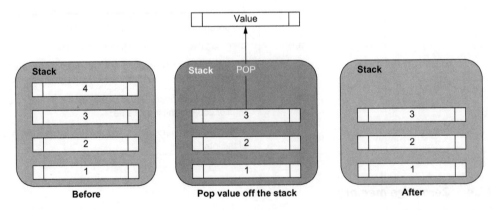

Figure 3.6   Removing (popping) an item off a stack of items

The 6502 has a fixed area of memory $0100 to $01FF that is dedicated as a stack (i.e., 256 bytes). This dedicated area of memory directly follows the zero-page memory area. The stack is used to save the address to return to after a call to a subroutine and can be used by the developer to store register values. The stack-related instructions only take a single byte and thus take a shorter time to execute than instructions that use more bytes. The instructions for using the stack are covered in section 4.4.

3.3 Moving things around

Hopefully, your head is not spinning too fast after studying the previous section. Next, we need to learn how to get data from a memory location and load it into a CPU register so that we can perform some calculations such as adjusting the coordinates of a player object or adding the player's score.

3.3.1 Loading data into a register

We can either move data from memory into a register (loading data) or move data from a register to memory (storing data) (see figure 3.7).

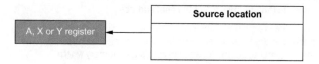

Figure 3.7 Loading data into a register

To load data from memory into a register, there is one set of instructions that starts with the letters LD followed by the letter of the target register:

```
LD<target register> <source>
```

- `<target register>`—This is the register the source information will end up stored in and can be one of A, X, or Y, so the instruction would be LDA, LDX, or LDY.
- `<source>`—This is where the information comes from.

The source location can either be a memory location (either zero-page or normal memory) or an actual direct value entered in the assembly listing. Each of these ways of referring to an immediate value of parts of memory is called an *addressing mode*. The different addressing modes available are shown in table 3.7 (we expand each of these with an example later).

Table 3.7 The available addressing modes

Mode	Description
Immediate	The actual numerical value is specified immediately after the statement.
Zero-page memory	The value is obtained from a location in zero-page memory using an 8-bit offset.
Absolute memory	The value is obtained from anywhere in memory using a 16-bit memory address.
Zero-page index with X or Y	The value is obtained from a location in zero-page memory by adding an 8-bit offset address to the value in either the X or Y index registers to get the final 8-bit offset.
Absolute memory indexed with X or Y	The value is obtained from a location anywhere in memory starting at a specified 16-bit memory address and adding the value in either the X or Y index to determine the final memory address to get the value from.
Zero-page indirect indexed with Y	The value is obtained from a location anywhere in memory starting at the base address stored in the specified 2 bytes of zero-page memory, and then the value in the Y register is added to that address to get the final address.
Zero-page Indexed indirect with X	The value is obtained from a location anywhere in memory starting at the base zero-page offset and adding the value in the X register to get the location in zero-page memory where the final address is specified in 2 bytes of memory.

Each of these addressing modes is quite different, so we will go through them again but with some specific examples and diagrams.

IMMEDIATE VALUE

An immediate value is an actual numerical value specified in the source code. The # symbol is used in front of the value to indicate to the assembler that the actual value specified should be used instead of a memory location (see figure 3.8).

Figure 3.8 Loading an immediate value into a register

Here is an example of loading the actual value $05 into the A, X, and Y registers:

```
lda #$05                          Immediate
ldx #$05                          value load
ldy #$05
```

After executing these instructions, the A, X, and Y registers will contain the value 5.

Exercise 3.1

Try pasting the previous three commands into the Online Assembler Simulator. Click the Assemble button and then the Run button. The Debug window should now contain the following information:

```
A=$05 X=$05 Y=$05
SP=$ff PC=$0607
NV-BDIZC
00110000
```

ZERO-PAGE MEMORY

Now if the # symbol is omitted and the value is between 0 and 255, the assembler will use the value to determine which part of zero-page memory to read and place in the specified register (see figure 3.9).

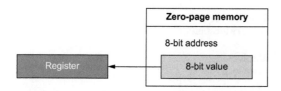

Figure 3.9   Loading a value stored in zero-page memory into a register

For this example, we will load the value stored in the zero-page memory location 05 into the A, X, and Y registers. For this example to be complete, we need to use a command (sta) that is covered in section 3.3.2:

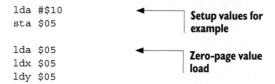

```
lda #$10                         Setup values for
sta $05                          example

lda $05                          Zero-page value
ldx $05                          load
ldy $05
```

So if the zero-page memory location contained the value 10, then each of the A, X, and Y registers would now be set to the value 10.

Exercise 3.2

Try pasting the previous commands into the Online Assembler Simulator. Click the Assemble button and then the Run button. The Debug window should now contain the following information:

```
A=$10 X=$10 Y=$10
SP=$ff PC=$060b
NV-BDIZC
00110000
```

ABSOLUTE MEMORY

To copy a value from any address in memory, you just specify the full address as a 16-bit value (see figure 3.10).

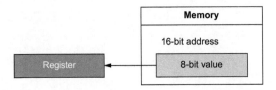

Figure 3.10   Load a value stored anywhere in memory into a register.

For this example, we will load the value stored in the memory location $0300 into the A, X, and Y registers. For this example to be complete, we need to use a command (sta) that is covered in section 3.3.2:

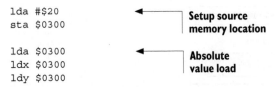

```
lda #$20            ◄─────┐ Setup source
sta $0300                 │ memory location

lda $0300           ◄─────┐ Absolute
ldx $0300                 │ value load
ldy $0300
```

So if the memory location $0300 contained the value 20, then each of the A, X, and Y registers would now be set to the value $20.

Exercise 3.3

Try pasting the previous commands into the Online Assembler Simulator. Click the Assemble button and then the Run button. The Debug window should now contain the following information:

```
A=$20 X=$20 Y=$20
SP=$ff PC=$060f
NV-BDIZC
00110000
```

ZERO-PAGE INDEX WITH X OR Y

The first three modes are straightforward, but the next three start getting a bit more complicated by using the X and Y registers to calculate an offset. The first of these modes is called *zero-page memory with index* where the location the value is loaded from is calculated from a starting zero-page location, adding the value in either the X or Y registers to the address and then getting the value from there (see figure 3.11).

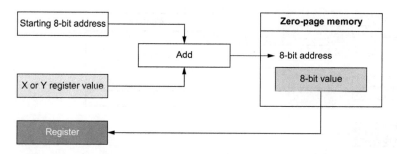

Figure 3.11 **Loading a value from zero-page memory using an index register**

In this example, we will start with a base address of $01 in zero-page memory and then add the current contents of the X register ($02) to end up with a zero-page memory address of $01 + $02 = $03. We will then load the value located there into the A register. For this example to be complete, we need to use a command (sta) that is covered in section 3.3.2:

```
lda #$20
sta $03
```
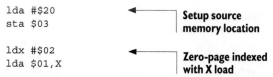

Setup source memory location

```
ldx #$02
lda $01,X
```

Zero-page indexed with X load

So if the zero-page memory location $03 contained the value $20, then the A register would be set to $20. This instruction can use either the X or Y registers for the index value.

Exercise 3.4

Try pasting the previous commands into the Online Assembler Simulator. Click the Assemble button and then the Run button. The Debug window should now contain the following information:

```
A=$20 X=$02 Y=$00
SP=$ff PC=$0609
NV-BDIZC
00110000
```

ABSOLUTE MEMORY INDEXED WITH X OR Y

The next addressing mode works similarly to the previous one, but instead of specifying a zero-page address, you are specifying any location in memory. You start with a base memory address, add the value in either the X or Y registers to that address, and then load the value from there (see figure 3.12).

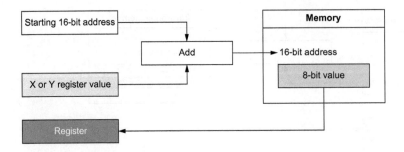

Figure 3.12   Loading a value from memory using an index register

In this example, we will start with a base address of `$0300` in memory and then add the current contents of the X register (`$02`) to end up with the memory address of `$0300 + $02 = $0302`. We will then load the value located there into the A register. For this example to be complete, we need to use a command (`sta`) that is covered in section 3.3.2:

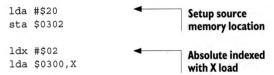

```
lda #$20
sta $0302
```
Setup source memory location

```
ldx #$02
lda $0300,X
```
Absolute indexed with X load

So if the memory location `$0302` contained the value `$20`, then the A register would be set to $20.

Exercise 3.5

Try pasting the previous commands into the Online Assembler Simulator. Click the Assemble button and then the Run button. The Debug window should now contain the following information:

```
A=$20 X=$02 Y=$00
SP=$ff PC=$060C
NV-BDIZC
00110000
```

ZERO-PAGE INDIRECT INDEXED WITH Y

The next way to load a value from a memory location uses the Y index register, but the Y value is added to the address stored at the original address specified (see figure 3.13).

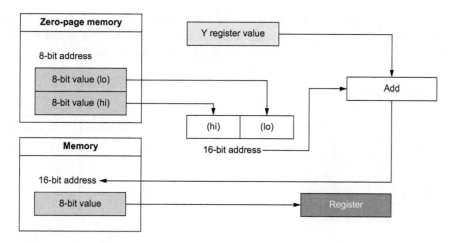

Figure 3.13 Loading a value from memory using a calculated location

This addressing mode is specified using round brackets around the zero-page memory address and the Y register after a trailing comma (,):

```
LDA (<zero-page address>),Y
```

Let's have a look at this using an example. To set up, we will have to use 2 bytes of zero-page memory to specify the address $0300. We split that address into 2 bytes called hi = $30 and lo = $00. The lo byte is placed in the zero-page memory first, directly followed by the hi byte as follows:

Zero-page memory location	Value
$05	$00
$06	$03

In this example, the Y register is loaded with the value $06, which is added to the 16-bit address located at zero-page memory location $05 ending with a final address of $0300 + $06 = $0306. The A register is then loaded with the value stored at that address. For this example to be complete, we need to use a command (sta) that is covered in section 3.3.2:

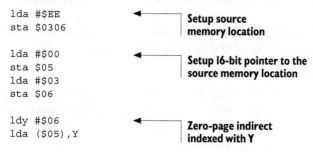

```
lda #$EE            ◄─── Setup source
sta $0306               memory location

lda #$00            ◄─── Setup 16-bit pointer to the
sta $05                 source memory location
lda #$03
sta $06

ldy #$06            ◄─── Zero-page indirect
lda ($05),Y             indexed with Y
```

So if the memory address $0306 contained the value $EE, then after this code had executed, the A register would also contain the value $EE. We will cover this statement in more detail when we use it in some of our game code later in the book.

Exercise 3.6

Try pasting the previous commands into the Online Assembler Simulator. Click the Assemble button and then the Run button. The Debug window should now contain the following information:

```
A=$ee X=$00 Y=$06
SP=$ff PC=$0612
NV-BDIZC
10110000
```

ZERO-PAGE INDEXED INDIRECT WITH X

There is one more way to load a value from any memory location specified using an address stored in a zero-page memory location, with the zero-page memory location being specified with the starting 8-bit offset plus the current value of the X register (see figure 3.14).

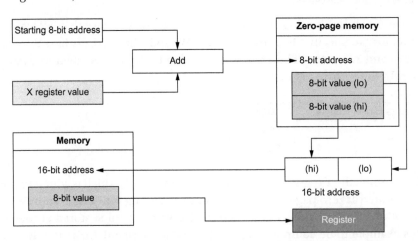

Figure 3.14   Loading a value from a memory address specified by an indexed zero-page address

This addressing mode is specified with the zero-page memory address, followed by a comma (,) and the X register surrounded by rounded brackets:

```
LDA (<zero-page address>, X)
```

Let's have a look at this using an example. Before our code, we will have to use 2 bytes of zero-page memory to specify the address $0300. We split that address into 2 bytes called hi = $30 and lo = $00. The lo byte is placed in the zero-page memory first, directly followed by the hi byte, as in table 3.8.

Table 3.8 Starting memory values

Zero-page memory location	Value
$05	$00
$06	$03

In this example, the X register is loaded with the value $03, which is added to the 8-bit offset address $02 to end up with the zero-page memory location $02 + $03 = $05. Located at zero-page memory location $05 is the 2-byte $0300. The A register is then loaded with the value stored at that address. For this example to be complete, we need to use a command (sta) that is covered in section 3.3.2:

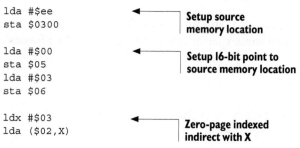

```
lda #$ee          ◄──────── Setup source
sta $0300                   memory location

lda #$00          ◄──────── Setup 16-bit point to
sta $05                     source memory location
lda #$03
sta $06

ldx #$03          ◄──────── Zero-page indexed
lda ($02,X)                 indirect with X
```

This would

- Add the value in X, $03, to the base zero-page address of $02, giving the zero-page memory address $05
- Then retrieve the two-byte pair, stored starting in the zero-page address $05 and $06 making up the absolute memory address $0300 (addresses are stored in reverse order, referred to as *least significant byte first*)
- Then copy the value stored in that address into the A register; for example, if the value $EE was stored at the memory address $0300, then the A register would also then contain the value $EE

We will cover this statement in more depth when we use it in some of our game code later in the book.

Exercise 3.7

Try pasting the previous commands into the Online Assembler Simulator. Click the Assemble button and then the Run button. The Debug window should now contain the following information:

```
A=$ee X=$03 Y=$00
SP=$ff PC=$0612
NV-BDIZC
10110000
```

3.3.2   *Storing register data in memory*

Just like loading data, for storing data there is also one set of instructions starting with the letters ST followed by the name of the source register and the destination memory address (see figure 3.15).

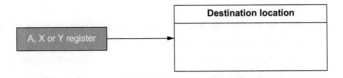

Figure 3.15   Storing a register value in a memory location

The source register can be A, X, or Y, and the destination can be either a zero-page or normal memory address, with some special modes using indexed addresses via the X and Y index registers:

ST<source register> <destination>

- <source register>—This is the register supplying the value that will be stored in the destination memory location.
- <destination>—This is the destination memory location.

The destination memory location is specified using one of five different addressing modes (see table 3.9).

Table 3.9   The available addressing modes

Mode	Description
Zero-page memory	The destination location is in zero-page memory using an 8-bit offset.
Absolute memory	The destination location is anywhere in memory using a 16-bit memory address.
Zero-page indexed with X or Y	The destination location in zero-page memory is specified by adding an 8-bit offset address to the value in either the X or Y index registers.
Absolute memory indexed with X or Y	The value is obtained from a location anywhere in memory starting at a specified 16-bit memory address and adding the value in either the X or Y index to determine the final memory address from which to get the value.
Zero-page indirect indexed with Y	The value is obtained from a location anywhere in memory starting at the base address stored in the specified 2 bytes of zero-page memory, and then the value in the Y register is added to that address to get the final address.
Zero-page index indirect with X	The value is obtained from a location anywhere in memory starting at the base zero-page offset, then adding the value in the X register to get the location in zero-page memory where the final address is specified in 2 bytes of memory.

ZERO-PAGE MEMORY

The first method is to store the value of the A, X, or Y registers in a specified zero-page memory location—that is, in the first 256 bytes of memory (see figure 3.16):

```
lda #$10
sta $06
ldx #$11
stx $07
ldy #$12
sty $08
```

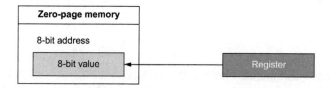

Figure 3.16   Storing a registers value in a zero-page memory location

This example loads each of the registers A, X, and Y with the values $10, $11, and $12, respectively, and then stores the values they contain in the zero-page memory locations $06, $07, and $08.

Exercise 3.8

Try pasting the previous commands into the Online Assembler Simulator. Click the Assemble button; then click the Monitor checkbox followed by the Run button. The Debug window should now contain the following information:

```
A=$10 X=$11 Y=$12
SP=$ff PC=$060d
NV-BDIZC
00110000
```

The first part of zero-page memory will contain

```
0000: 00 00 00 00 00 00 10 11 12 00 00 00 00 00 00 00
```

ABSOLUTE MEMORY

The next method is to store the value of one of the registers in a specified absolute memory location—that is, specify a full 16-bit memory address (see figure 3.17):

```
lda #$10
sta $0300
ldx #$11
sta $0301
ldy #$12
sty $0302
```

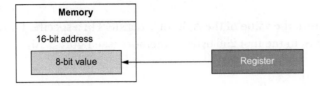

Figure 3.17   **Storing a register's value in an absolute memory location**

This example loads each of the registers A, X, and Y with the values $10, $11, and $12, respectively, and then stores the values they contain in the memory locations $0300, $0301, and $0302.

Exercise 3.9

Try pasting the previous commands into the Online Assembler Simulator. Click the Assemble button, and change the Start box to 0300 and the End box to 03ff; then click the Monitor checkbox followed by the Run button. The Debug window should now contain the following information:

```
A=$10 X=$11 Y=$12
SP=$ff PC=$0610
NV-BDIZC
00110000
```

The memory starting at $0300 will contain

```
0300: 10 10 12 00 00 00 00 00 00 00 00 00 00 00 00 00
```

ZERO-PAGE INDEXED WITH X OR Y

In addition, and only with the A register, you can also store a value based on a starting zero-page memory address and add either of the index registers, that is, X or Y (see figure 3.18).

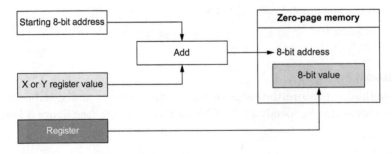

Figure 3.18   **Storing a register's value in a zero-page memory location and an index**

```
ldx #$01              ◄──────┐  Stores zero-page
lda #$ee                     │  indexed with X
sta $01,x
```

This would take the base zero-page address of $01 and add the value in X ($01), giving the final zero-page address of $01 + $01 = $02, where it would then store the value in the A register ($ee).

Exercise 3.10

Try pasting the previous commands into the Online Assembler Simulator. Click the Assemble button; then click the Monitor checkbox followed by the Run button. The Debug window should now contain the following information:

```
A=$ee X=$01 Y=$00
SP=$ff PC=$0607
NV-BDIZC
10110000
```

The first part of zero-page memory will contain

```
0000: 00 00 ee 00 00 00 00 00 00 00 00 00 00 00 00 00
```

ABSOLUTE MEMORY INDEXED WITH X OR Y

In addition, and only with the A register, you can also store a value based on a starting absolute memory address and add either of the index registers, that is, X or Y (see figure 3.19):

```
ldx #$01
lda #$ee
sta $0300,x
```

Stores absolute indexed with X

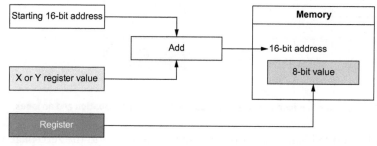

Figure 3.19 Storing a register's value in a memory location and an index

This would take the base absolute address $0300 and add the value in X ($01), making the destination address $0300 + $01 = $0301, where it would store the value in the A register ($ee).

Exercise 3.11

Try pasting the previous commands into the Online Assembler Simulator. Click the Assemble button, and change the Start box to 0300 and the End box to 03ff; then click the Monitor checkbox followed by the Run button. The Debug window should now contain the following information:

```
A=$ee X=$01 Y=$00
SP=$ff PC=$0607
NV-BDIZC
10110000
```

The memory starting at $0300 will contain

```
0300: 00 ee 00 00 00 00 00 00 00 00 00 00 00 00 00 00
```

ZERO-PAGE INDIRECT INDEXED WITH Y

The next way to store a value to a memory location uses the Y index register, but the Y value is added to the address stored at the original address specified (see figure 3.20).

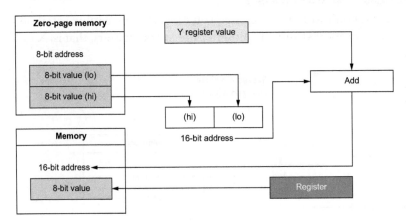

Figure 3.20   Storing value in a memory location specified by zero-page location and an index

This addressing mode is specified using round brackets around the zero-page memory address and the Y register after a trailing comma (,):

```
STA (<zero-page address>),Y
```

Let's have a look at this using an example. To set up, we will have to use 2 bytes of zero-page memory to specify the address $0300. We split that address into 2 bytes called hi = $30 and lo = $00. The lo byte is placed in the zero-page memory first, directly followed by the hi byte as follows:

Zero-page memory location	Value
$05	$00
$06	$03

In this example, the Y register is loaded with the value $06, which is added to the 16-bit address located at the zero-page memory location $05 ending with a final address of $0300 + $06 = $0306. The value in the A register ($EE) is then stored at that address:

```
ldy #$06
lda #$ee
sta ($05),y
```

Zero-page indirect indexed with Y

So after this code, the memory address $0306 will contain the value $EE. We will cover this statement in more detail when we use it in some of our game code later in the book.

Exercise 3.12

Try pasting the previous commands into the Online Assembler Simulator. Click the Assemble button, and change the Start box to 0300 and the End box to 03ff; then click the Monitor checkbox followed by the Run button. The Debug window should now contain the following information:

```
A=$ee X=$00 Y=$06
SP=$ff PC=$0607
NV-BDIZC
10110000
```

The first part of zero-page memory will contain

```
0000: 00 00 00 00 00 00 ee 00 00 00 00 00 00 00 00 00
```

ZERO-PAGE INDEXED INDIRECT WITH X

There is one more way to store a value to any memory location specified using an address stored in zero-page memory location, with the zero-page memory location being specified with the starting 8-bit offset plus the current value of the X register (see figure 3.21).

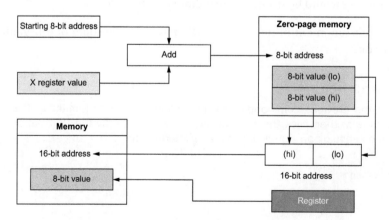

Figure 3.21 Storing a value to a memory address specified by an indexed zero-page address

This addressing mode is specified with the zero-page memory address, followed by a comma (,) and the X register surrounded by rounded brackets:

```
STA (<zero-page address>, X)
```

Let's have a look at this using an example. To set up, we will use 2 bytes of zero-page memory to specify the address $0300. We split that address into 2 bytes called hi = $30 and lo = $00. The lo byte is placed in the zero-page memory first, directly followed by the hi byte as follows:

Zero-page memory location	Value
$05	$00
$06	$03

In this example, the X register is loaded with the value $03, which is added to the 8-bit offset address $02 to end up with the zero-page memory location $02 + $03 = $05. Located at the zero-page memory location $05 is the 2-byte address $0300. The value in the A register ($EE) is then stored at that address:

```
ldx #$03
lda #$ee            ◄─────────── Zero-page indexed
sta ($02,x)                      indirect with X
```

This would

- Add the value in X, $03, to the base zero-page address of $02, giving the zero-page memory address $03 + $02 = $05
- Then retrieve the two bytes pair, stored starting in the zero-page address $05 and $06 making up the absolute memory address $0300 (addresses are stored in reverse order, referred to as least significant byte first)
- Then copy the value stored in the A register to that address; so in this example, the value $EE would be stored at the memory address $0300

We will cover this statement in more depth when we use it in some of our game code later in the book.

Exercise 3.13

Try pasting the previous commands into the Online Assembler Simulator. Click the Assemble button; then click the Monitor checkbox followed by the Run button. The Debug window should now contain the following information:

```
A=$ee X=$03 Y=$00
SP=$ff PC=$0607
NV-BDIZC
10110000
```

The first part of zero-page memory will contain

```
0000: ee 00 00 00 00 00 00 00 00 00 00 00 00 00 00 00
```

In the next chapter, we will extend this knowledge, learning how to do some math, change the flow of our code, and manipulate individual bits.

Summary

- The main command to load data from memory into a register starts with the letters LD followed by the register name and either a direct value or a memory address.

- The main command to save data from a register into memory starts with the letters ST followed by the register name and the destination memory address.

- There are a lot of different ways to specify the memory location to either get data from or store data to. Refer to this chapter and the results from the examples to help work out which will work best for your code.

Math, loops, conditions, and bits

4

This chapter covers

- Doing some math
- Conditions
- Jumps, branches, and calls
- Bytes, bits, and nibbles
- Using the stack

In the last chapter, we covered loading and storing values between the registers in the CPU and memory. In this chapter, we will look at performing some simple math, making decisions (conditions), jumping to other places in your code, and then finally instructions that help us look at and change individual bits and use the special area of memory used for the stack.

4.1 Let's do some math

Let's do something with some numbers and some basic math operations. Math operations with computer processors are based on addition, subtraction, and manipulation of bits. Adding, subtracting, and changing bits are vital in game development, from changing object positions to working out what color or shape to make an enemy next. For this quick look, we will do some simple addition and subtraction to get you started.

4.1.1   Addition

To add two 8-bit numbers together, we must use the A register and the command ADC (ADd with Carry) as follows.

> **Listing 4.1   Adding with carry**

```
clc                    ◄——————— Clear carry flag
adc <source>
```

This takes the current value of register A, adds the value from the source plus the value of the carry flag, and stores the result in A (see figure 4.1).

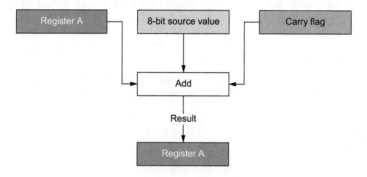

Figure 4.1   Adding an 8-bit value to the A register

For the start of an addition calculation to ensure the carry flag is reset and will not affect your calculation, an additional instruction CLear Carry (CLC) flag is used.

DIRECT VALUE

Add a direct value, specified by using the # symbol, to the A register.

> **Listing 4.2   Adding a direct value**

```
clc                    ◄——————— Clear the carry flag
lda #$01
adc #$05
```

This example adds the value $05 to the value already in the A register ($01), making the A register equal to $06.

Exercise 4.1

Try pasting the previous commands into the Online Assembler Simulator. Click the Assemble button and then the Run button. The Debug window should now contain the following information:

```
A=$06 X=$00 Y=$00
SP=$ff PC=$0606
NV-BDIZC
00110000
```

ABSOLUTE MEMORY ADDRESS

Add the value stored in the specified memory location to the A register. For this example, the memory location $0300 contains the value $10.

> **Listing 4.3   Adding value from an absolute memory address**

```
Lda #$10
sta $0300
clc                    ◄──────── Clear the carry flag
lda #$20
adc $0300
```

This example adds the value stored in the memory address $0300 ($10) to the value already in the A register, and then the A register contains $20 + $10 = $30.

> ### Exercise 4.2
>
> Try pasting the previous commands into the Online Assembler Simulator. Click the Assemble button and then the Run button. The Debug window should now contain the following information:
>
> ```
> A=$30 X=$00 Y=$00
> SP=$ff PC=$060c
> NV-BDIZC
> 00110000
> ```

ZERO-PAGE MEMORY ADDRESS

Add the value stored in the specified zero-page memory location to the value currently in the A register. For this example, the memory location $06 contains the value $10.

> **Listing 4.4   Adding a value from a zero-page address**

```
Lda #$10
sta $06
clc
lda #$04
adc $06
```

This example adds the value stored in the zero-page memory location $06 ($10) to the value already in the A register $04, and then the A register contains $04 + $10 = $14.

> ### Exercise 4.3
>
> Try pasting the previous commands into the Online Assembler Simulator. Click the Assemble button and then the Run button. The Debug window should now contain the following information:

```
A=$14 X=$00 Y=$00
SP=$ff PC=$060a
NV-BDIZC
00110000
```

ZERO-PAGE ADDRESS INDEXED WITH X OR Y

Add the X or Y register to the specified zero-page address, and then add the value stored in that memory address to the A register. For this example, the memory location $08 contains the value $12.

> **Listing 4.5   Adding a value from a zero-page address indexed with X**

```
lda #$12
sta $08
clc
lda #$10
ldx #$02
adc $06,x
```

This example adds the value in the X register ($02) to the zero-page address $06, giving the zero-page address $06 + $02 = $08. Then it adds the value stored in that memory address ($12) to the value already in the A register ($10), and then the A register contains $10 + $12 = $22.

> ## Exercise 4.4
>
> Try pasting the previous commands into the Online Assembler Simulator. Click the Assemble button and then the Run button. The Debug window should now contain the following information:
>
> ```
> A=$22 X=$02 Y=$00
> SP=$ff PC=$060c
> NV-BDIZC
> 00110000
> ```

ABSOLUTE ADDRESS INDEXED WITH X OR Y

Add the X or Y register to the specified absolute address, and then add the value stored in that memory address to the A register. For this example, the memory address $0302 contains the value $05.

> **Listing 4.6   Adding a value from an absolute address indexed with X**

```
lda #$05
sta $0302
clc
lda #$10
ldx #$02
adc $0300,x
```

This example adds the value in the X register ($02) to the absolute address $0300, giving the absolute address $0302. Then it adds the value stored in that memory address ($05) to the value already in the A register ($10), making the A register equal to $10 + $05 = $15.

Exercise 4.5

Try pasting the previous commands into the Online Assembler Simulator. Click the Assemble button and then the Run button. The Debug window should now contain the following information:

```
A=$15 X=$02 Y=$00
SP=$ff PC=$060e
NV-BDIZC
00110000
```

ZERO-PAGE INDIRECT ADDRESS INDEXED BY Y

Get the 2-byte pair stored in the address store in the specified zero-page memory location; then add the value in the Y register to the address. Get the value stored in that address, and add it to the value already in the A register. For this example, zero-page memory locations $02 and $03 contain values that specify the address $0300, and address $0302 contains the value $14.

Location	Value
$02	$00
$03	$03

Listing 4.7   Adding a value from an indirect address indexed by Y

```
lda #$00        ◄──────  Sets up a 16-bit pointer to
sta $02                  the source location
lda #$03
sta $03

lda #$14        ◄──────  Sets up the source
sta $0302                memory location

clc             ◄──────  Zero-page indirect
lda #$10                 address indexed by Y
ldy #$02
adc ($02),y
```

This example gets the 2-byte pair stored in the zero-page address starting at $02 to specify the absolute memory address $0300. The value of Y is then added to this address, giving the address $0300 + $02 = $0302. The contents of that address ($14) are then added to the value already in the A register ($10), making the A register equal to $14 + $10 = $24.

Exercise 4.6

Try pasting the previous commands into the Online Assembler Simulator. Click the Assemble button and then the Run button. The Debug window should now contain the following information:

```
A=$24 X=$00 Y=$02
SP=$ff PC=$0615
NV-BDIZC
00110000
```

ZERO-PAGE INDIRECT ADDRESS INDEXED BY X

Add the X register to the zero-page memory location, and then get the 2-byte pair stored in that address to specify an absolute address. Get the value stored in that address, and add it to the value already in the A register. For this example, zero-page memory locations $02 and $03 contain values that specify the address $0300, and address $0300 contains the value $12.

Location	Value
$02	$00
$03	$03

Listing 4.8   Adding a value from an indirect address index by X

```
lda #$00          ◄─────── Sets up the 16-bit pointer
sta $02                    to the source location
lda #$03
sta $03

lda #$12          ◄─────── Sets up the source
sta $0300                  memory location

clc               ◄─────── Zero-page indirect
lda #$10                   address indexed by X
ldx #$01
adc ($01,x)
```

This example adds the value in the X register ($01) to the specified zero-page address ($01) to specify the zero-page address $01 + $01 = $02. Then the 2-byte pair stored starting at that address gives the absolute address $0300. The contents of that address ($12) are then added to the value already in the A register ($10), making the A register equal to $12 + $10 = $22.

4.1.2 *Subtraction*

In addition to adding to numbers such as the score in our game, we also will need to subtract numbers, such as when we want an object to move up the screen. To subtract two 8-bit numbers together, we must use the A register in the following listing.

Listing 4.9   Subtracting a value from the A register

```
sec          ◀─────── Sets the carry flag
sbc <source>
```

This takes the current value of register A, subtracts the value from the source, and then subtracts an extra 1 if the carry flag is clear and stores the result in A (see figure 4.2).

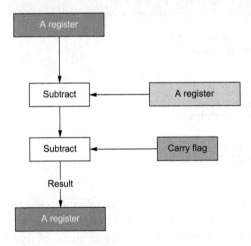

Figure 4.2   Subtracting an 8-bit value from the A register

To ensure the carry flag is set before a subtraction operation, there is a special instruction called SEt Carry (sec) flag.

DIRECT VALUE

Subtract a direct value from the A register.

Listing 4.10   Subtracting a direct value from the A register

```
sec
lda #$06
sbc #$05
```

This example subtracts the value $05 from the value already in the A register ($06), making the A register equal to $06 - $05 = $01.

Exercise 4.8

Try pasting the previous commands into the Online Assembler Simulator. Click the Assemble button and then the Run button. The Debug window should now contain the following information:

```
A=$01 X=$00 Y=$00
SP=$ff PC=$0606
NV-BDIZC
00110001
```

DIRECT ADDRESS

Subtract the value stored in the specified memory location from the A register.

Listing 4.11   Subtracting a value stored in a memory location

```
lda #$02
sta $0300
sec
lda #$08
sbc $0300
```

This example subtracts the value stored in the memory address $0300 ($02) from the value already in the A register ($08), making the A register equal to $08 - $02 = $06.

Exercise 4.9

Try pasting the previous commands into the Online Assembler Simulator. Click the Assemble button and then the Run button. The Debug window should now contain the following information:

```
A=$06 X=$00 Y=$00
SP=$ff PC=$0606
NV-BDIZC
00110001
```

ZERO-PAGE ADDRESS

Subtract the value stored in the specified zero-page memory location from the A register.

Listing 4.12   Subtracting a value stored in a zero-page memory location

```
lda #$04
sta $06
sec
lda #$10
sbc $06
```

This example subtracts the value stored in the zero-page memory location $06 ($04) from the value already in the A register ($10), making the A register equal to $10 – $04 = $0c.

Exercise 4.10

Try pasting the previous commands into the Online Assembler Simulator. Click the Assemble button and then the Run button. The Debug window should now contain the following information:

```
A=$0c X=$00 Y=$00
SP=$ff PC=$060a
NV-BDIZC
00110001
```

ZERO-PAGE ADDRESS INDEXED WITH X OR Y

Add the X or Y register to the specified zero-page address, and then subtract the value stored in that memory address from the A register.

Listing 4.13   Subtracting a value stored in a zero-page memory location indexed by X

```
lda #$02
sta $08
ldx #$02
sec
lda #$10
sbc $06,x
```

This example adds the value in the X register ($02) to the zero-page address $06, giving the zero-page address $08. Then it subtracts the value stored in that memory address ($02) from the value already in the A register ($10), making the A register equal to $10 – $02 = $0e.

Exercise 4.11

Try pasting the previous commands into the Online Assembler Simulator. Click the Assemble button and then the Run button. The Debug window should now contain the following information:

```
A=$0e X=$02 Y=$00
SP=$ff PC=$060c
NV-BDIZC
00110001
```

ABSOLUTE ADDRESS INDEXED WITH X OR Y

Add the X or Y register to the specified absolute address, and then subtract the value stored in that memory address from the A register.

> **Listing 4.14** **Subtracting a value stored in an absolute memory location indexed by X**

```
lda #$04
sta $0302
ldx #$02
sec
lda #$16
sbc $0300,x
```

This example adds the value in the X register ($02) to the absolute address $0300, giving the absolute address $0302. Then it subtracts the value stored in that memory address ($04) from the value already in the A register ($16), making the A register equal to $16 - $04 = $12.

Exercise 4.12

Try pasting the previous commands into the Online Assembler Simulator. Click the Assemble button and then the Run button. The Debug window should now contain the following information:

```
A=$12 X=$02 Y=$00
SP=$ff PC=$060e
NV-BDIZC
00110001
```

ZERO-PAGE INDIRECT ADDRESS INDEXED BY Y

Get the 2-byte pair stored in the address store in the specified zero-page memory location; then add the value in the Y register to the address. Get the value stored in that address, and subtract it from the value already in the A register. For this example, zero-page memory locations $02 and $03 specify the address $0300, and the memory address $0302 contains the value $04.

Location	Value
$02	$00
$03	$03

> **Listing 4.15** **Subtracting a value stored in an indirect memory location indexed by Y**

```
lda #$00
sta $02
lda #$03
sta $03

lda #$04          ◄────────   Sets up the data in the
                              source memory address
```

```
sta $0302
```

```
ldy #$02
sec
lda #$14
sbc ($02),y
```

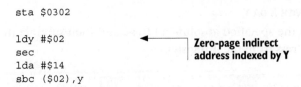

Zero-page indirect
address indexed by **Y**

This example gets the 2-byte pair stored in the zero-page address starting at $02 to spec-ify the absolute memory address $0300. The value of Y is then added to this address, giving the address $0300 + $02 = $0302. The contents of that address ($04) are then subtracted from the value already in the A register ($14), making the A register equal to $14 - $04 = $10.

Exercise 4.13

Try pasting the previous commands into the Online Assembler Simulator. Click the Assemble button and then the Run button. The Debug window should now contain the following information.

```
A=$14 X=$00 Y=$02
SP=$ff PC=$0615
NV-BDIZC
00110001
```

ZERO-PAGE INDIRECT ADDRESS INDEXED BY **X**

Add the X register to the zero-page memory location, and then get the 2-byte pair stored in that address to specify an absolute address. Get the value stored in that address and subtract it from the value already in the A register. For this example, zero-page memory locations $02 and $03 specify the address $0302, which contains the value $06.

Location	Value
$02	$00
$03	$03

Listing 4.16   Subtracting a value from an indirect memory location indexed by X

```
lda #$00
sta $02
lda #$03
sta $03
```
Sets up the 16-bit pointer
to the source address

```
lda #$12
sta $0300
```
Sets up the
source value

```
sec
lda #$20
ldx #$01
sbc ($01,x)
```
Zero-page indirect
address indexed by **X**

This example adds the value in the X register ($02) to the specified zero-page address ($00) to specify the zero-page address $02. Then the 2-byte pair is stored starting at $02 to specify the absolute address $0300. The contents of that address ($06) are then subtracted from the value already in the A register ($12), making the A register equal to $20 – $12 = $0e.

Exercise 4.14

Try pasting the previous commands into the Online Assembler Simulator. Click the Assemble button and then the Run button. The Debug window should now contain the following information:

```
A=$0c X=$01 Y=$00
SP=$ff PC=$0615
NV-BDIZC
00110001
```

4.2   *Increasing and decreasing*

One more type of adding and subtracting is to increase (increment) or decrease (decrement) a value by 1. This could be done by just adding or subtracting the direct value 1 using the statements we looked at earlier, but to save both instruction space and increase speed, most processors have instructions to do this directly. The 6502 versions work as follows.

INCREMENT ZERO-PAGE ADDRESS

Increment the value stored at the specified zero-page memory location.

Listing 4.17   Incrementing the value stored at a zero-page memory location

```
lda #$10
sta $05
inc $05
```

This example increments the value stored in the memory location $05 ($10) by 1, making it equal $10 + $01 = $11.

INCREMENT ABSOLUTE ADDRESS

Increment the value stored at the specified absolute memory location.

Listing 4.18   Incrementing the value stored at an absolute memory location

```
lda #$10
sta $0300
inc $0300
```

This example increments the value stored in the memory location $0300 ($10) by 1, making it equal $10 + $01 = $11.

INCREMENT ZERO-PAGE ADDRESS INDEXED BY X OR Y

Add the value in the X register to the specified zero-page memory location; then increment the value stored in that location.

Listing 4.19   Incrementing the value stored at a zero-page memory location indexed by X

```
lda #$05
sta $07
ldx #$02
inc $05,x
```

This example adds the value in the X register ($02) to the specified zero-page memory address ($05), giving the address $07. Then the value stored in that address ($05) is incremented by 1, making it equal $05 + $01 = $10.

INCREMENT ABSOLUTE ADDRESS INDEXED BY X OR Y

Add the value in the X register to the specified absolute memory location; then increment the value stored in that location.

Listing 4.20   Incrementing a value stored at an absolute memory location indexed by X

```
lda #$05
sta $07
ldx #$02
inc $0300,x
```

This example adds the value in the X register ($02) to the specified absolute memory address ($0300), giving the address $0300 + $02 = $0302. Then the value stored in that address ($05) is incremented by 1, making it equal $05 + $01 = $10.

INCREMENT X REGISTER

Increment the value stored in the X register by 1:

```
Inx
```

INCREMENT Y REGISTER

Increment the value stored in the Y register by 1:

```
Iny
```

DECREMENT ZERO-PAGE ADDRESS

Decrement the value stored at the specified zero-page memory location:

```
Dec $05
```

This example decrements the value stored in the memory location $05.

DECREMENT ABSOLUTE ADDRESS

Decrement the value stored at the specified absolute memory location:

```
Dec $0300
```

This example decrements the value stored in the memory location $0300.

DECREMENT ZERO-PAGE ADDRESS INDEXED BY X OR Y

Add the value in the X register to the specified zero-page memory location; then decrement the value stored in that location:

```
lda #$02
dec $05,X
```

This example adds the value in the X register ($02) to the specified zero-page memory address ($05), giving the address $07. Then the value stored in that address is decremented by 1.

DECREMENT ABSOLUTE ADDRESS INDEXED BY X OR Y

Add the value in the X register to the specified absolute memory location; then decrement the value stored in that location:

```
ldx $02
dec $0300,X
```

This example adds the value in the X register ($02) to the specified absolute memory address ($0300), giving the address $0302. Then the value stored in that address is decremented by 1.

DECREMENT X REGISTER

Decrement the value stored in the X register by 1:

```
dex
```

DECREMENT Y REGISTER

Decrement the value stored in the Y register by 1:

```
dey
```

4.3 Conditions

Any programming language needs a way for different code to be executed depending on conditions being met or as the result of executing instructions. Most processors have flags that signal a particular event has occurred after executing an instruction. In the game we will be creating in this book, we will need to jump to different parts of our code based on whether certain conditions have been met, such as whether the player pressed a direction on the gamepad.

The 6502 gives us eight flags that can be used to check whether a required condition has been met (see table 4.1).

Table 4.1   6502 status flags

Bit	Symbol	Name	Description
7	N	Negative	After a comparison instruction, this flag will be set if the register's value is less than the input value (and the values are no more than 127 apart).
			Otherwise, this flag will be set if the result value of an instruction was negative (i.e., bit 7 of the result was set).
6	V	Overflow	After an arithmetic operation (Add or Subtract), if the sign of the result differs from the sign of both the input and the accumulator, this flag will be set.
			After a BIT operation, set to bit 6 of the input
5	-	Unused	This flag is unused and will always be set.
4	B	Break	This flag will be set if an interrupt request has been triggered by a BRK instruction.
3	D	Decimal	The NES's implementation of the 6502 does not include the binary decimal instructions, so this flag is not set by any operations but can be used by the developer for their purposes.
2	I	Interrupt Disable	When set, interrupt requests are disabled.
1	Z	Zero	After doing a compare instruction, set if the register's value is equal to the input value
			After doing a BIT operation, set if the result of logically ANDing the accumulator with the input results in 0
0	C	Carry	Carry flag used in math and rotate operations
			After an arithmetic operation, set if an overflow occurred during addition or subtraction
			After a compare operation, set if the register's value is greater than or equal to the input value
			After a shifting operation, set to the value of the eliminated bit of the input

These flags are stored in a special register called P that you do not access directly. The flags are set automatically after you execute most of the other commands. To check a value against what is stored in the A register, we use the CoMPare (CMP) instruction. The CMP instruction takes the value specified (or in the specified register) and subtracts it from the value currently in the A register. The contents of the A register are not harmed, but the flags are set as if you had performed a subtraction operation:

```
Lda #$79
cmp #$80
```

Executing this code would result in the CPU taking the original value in the A register ($79) and subtracting the supplied value ($80), which would end up with a result of $f9. The result amount is discarded, but as bit 7 of the result is set, the negative flag would be set.

4.4   Jumps, branches, and calls

Now we will have a look at how you can jump/move to another section of your code: by always jumping, by branching based on a condition, or by calling a subroutine. This allows you to jump to another section of your game or call a subroutine that might check whether an enemy needs to fire a bullet.

4.4.1   Jumps

Jumps in 6502 change the program counter (PC), with the next instruction being executed at the new location. This is similar to how a GOTO statement in BASIC would operate. You can jump anywhere in memory, either in your game's ROM code or to a place in the console's RAM (see figure 4.3).

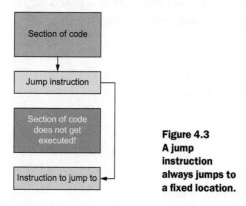

**Figure 4.3
A jump
instruction
always jumps to
a fixed location.**

There are no checks, so it is up to the programmer to make sure they are jumping to a place where there is valid code to execute. For example, 6502 instructions are just numbers, so data for your graphic objects will be treated as code instructions if you jumped into the middle of it:

```
Jmp $8100
```

This would jump to the code located at the address $8100 and continue execution. It is best to use labels (see section 4.3.4) and allow the assembler to work out the actual address when your code is compiled into machine code. We will start using the jmp instruction in the next chapter as we build an example NES program.

4.4.2   *Branches*

You can also jump to a new location but only when a condition has occurred based on a flag; this is known as branching. Most of the flags are set after each instruction the 6502 processor executes, and there is a branch instruction for each of the flags being set or cleared (see figure 4.4).

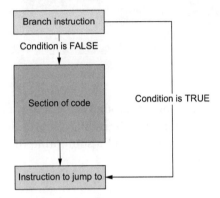

Figure 4.4   A branch instruction jumps over a section of code when a condition is true.

If you are used to other programming languages, another way to think of a branch is as an IF THEN ELSE type of statement where if a specified condition is met, a section of code will be executed; otherwise, it will be skipped over. The flag tested for the jump is indicated by the name of the branch instruction, as shown in table 4.2.

Table 4.2   The different branch instructions

Instruction	Description
BPL	Branch on plus
BMI	Branch on minus
BVC	Branch on overflow clear
BVS	Branch on overflow set
BCC	Branch on carry clear (unsigned lower)
BCS	Branch on carry set (unsigned higher or same)
BNE	Branch on not equal
BEQ	Branch on equal

Let's go through these one by one with a bit more detail:

- *Branch on plus (BPL)*—When the negative flag (bit 7 of the status register and known as "N") is not set (0), this instruction will execute the jump.
- *Branch on minus (BMI)*—When the negative flag (bit 7 of the status register and known as "N") is set (1), this instruction will execute the jump.

- *Branch on overflow clear (BVC)*—When the overflow flag (bit 6 of the status register and known as "V") is not set (0), this instruction will execute the jump.
- *Branch on overflow set (BVS)*—When the overflow flag (bit 6 of the status register and known as "V") is set (1), this instruction will execute the jump.
- *Branch on carry clear (BCC)*—When the carry flag (bit 0 of the status register and known as "C") is clear (0), this instruction will execute the jump.
- *Branch on carry set (BCS)*—When the carry flag (bit 0 of the status register and known as "C") is set (1), this instruction will execute the jump.
- *Branch on not equal (BNE)*—When the zero flag (bit 1 of the status register and known as "Z") is clear (0), this instruction will execute the jump.
- *Branch on equal (BEQ)*—When the zero flag (bit 1 of the status register and known as "Z") is set (1), this instruction will execute the jump.

Branch instructions do have a limitation, as they only have a single byte that determines where the code will branch to. This single byte is either added to the program counter if bit 7 is 0, or the byte is subtracted from the program counter. This allows you to jump a maximum of 129 bytes forward or 126 bytes backward (counting from the position of the branch instruction).

It is best to use labels (see section 4.2.4) and allow the assembler to work out the actual address when your code is compiled into machine code. The assembler will warn you if a jump is further than the allowed number of bytes.

Listing 4.21 Example branch instruction

```
    lda #05
    cmp #05
    beq SKIPCODE        ◄──────   This code would be skipped
    lda #06                       over as A = #05.
SKIPCODE:
```

In this example, as register A contains 05, the code jumps to the label `SKIPCODE`. If you have too many statements between your branch instruction and the destination label, the assembler will warn you with an Out of Range error.

4.4.3 Calling a subroutine

Rather than having to repeat the same sequence of code multiple times in your program, it is often better to turn that code into a subroutine or function that can be called from multiple sections of your program (see figure 4.5). This has the advantage of saving space in your program and making the code easier to read, but it does increase execution time, as the CPU needs to spend time remembering where the subroutine was called from so it can return when the subroutine is finished. I generally favor readability first when programming, only optimizing for speed where it is necessary.

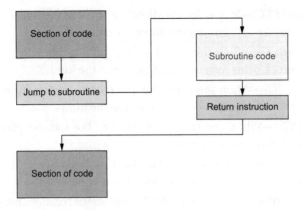

Figure 4.5   Calling a subroutine

To call a subroutine, we have three new instructions: JSR to jump into a subroutine and either RTS to return from a normal subroutine or RTI to return from a subroutine called by an interrupt. Both of these return statements return to the statement after the original JSR instruction.

When the JSR command is executed, the address of the next instruction is pushed onto the stack, and then the program counter is changed so that execution will continue at the start of the address of the subroutine until the RTS or RTI command is reached. This will cause the address to be popped off the stack and the program counter set so that execution will continue at the instruction directly after the JSR instruction.

You can fall into a common trap if you use any of the stack instructions inside a subroutine—that is, push some items on the stack. You need to make sure the stack is back to the same position (i.e., all the items you pushed on the stack need to be popped off) by the time the RTS or RTI command is reached, or else the address that is popped off the stack won't be the original return location and could cause your program to crash. The following example calls a subroutine twice to perform a set calculation.

Listing 4.22   Jumping to a subroutine example

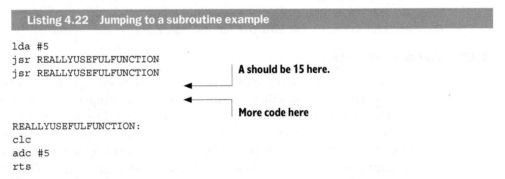

```
lda #5
jsr REALLYUSEFULFUNCTION
jsr REALLYUSEFULFUNCTION                    A should be 15 here.


                                            More code here
REALLYUSEFULFUNCTION:
clc
adc #5
rts
```

This section of code sets the A register to the value 5, and then the REALLYUSEFULFUNCTION subroutine is called twice, which adds another 10 to the A register, making it equal to 15.

4.4.4 Labels

You would normally not specify an actual memory address for a jump, branch, or subroutine call; it is better to use a label and allow the assembler to work out the actual address when your code is compiled into machine code. A label in 6502 Assembler is specified by a sequence of alphanumeric characters (not starting with a number) without any spaces and ending with a colon (:) symbol. It doesn't matter whether you use upper or lower case for the label. To reference a label, you use the same sequence of alphanumeric characters but without the trailing colon (:).

Listing 4.23 Example of using a label

```
jmp NEWCODE

NEWCODE:                          Next section of code here
```

This example makes code execution jump to the code directly after the place where the label NEWCODE: is positioned. The trouble with having to label every spot in code that you want to jump to is coming up with a suitable name for the label. This can end up with programmers needing to use numbered labels (e.g., LOOP1, LOOP2, etc.). Especially for jumps that are only a short distance and where you have functions that you use across many projects, it would be nice if you didn't end up having to deal with label name clashes. To assist the programmer, most of the assemblers allow three more types of labels: local references, cheap local labels, and unnamed labels.

LOCAL LABELS

Local references introduce the concept of having separate sections of code where any labels created inside them will not clash with any other labels in your code. This is useful when you have a library of functions that you want to reuse across multiple programs. To define a function/procedure, you use the .proc statement followed by the name that you will call the function/procedure with; that is, it defines the label you will call the function/procedure with. You end the function/procedure with the .endproc statement.

Listing 4.24 Example function/procedure definition

```
.proc    ClearMemory
lda #$00
ldy #20
L1:    dey
sta Mem,y
bne L1
rts
.endproc
```

CHEAP LOCAL LABELS

Another option for local labels, especially for short loops, is called *cheap local labels*. They are defined like a normal label but start with an @ symbol. They only stay in scope and are valid until another label is encountered.

Listing 4.25   Example cheap local label

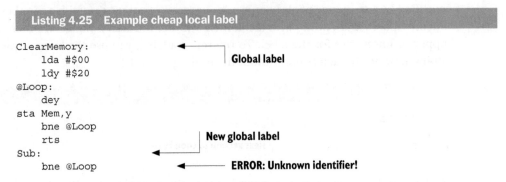

```
ClearMemory:
    lda #$00                          Global label
    ldy #$20
@Loop:
    dey
sta Mem,y
    bne @Loop
    rts                               New global label
Sub:
    bne @Loop                         ERROR: Unknown identifier!
```

In this example, the label @Loop goes out of scope as soon as the next label is defined (i.e., at the Sub: label definition), so this would cause an error to be generated when the next reference to @Loop is encountered. Due to these types of labels going out of scope when any other label is defined, they cannot be nested, so they can only be used for a section of code where they are the only label present.

UNNAMED LABELS

The third option for labels is called *unnamed labels*, and they are exactly that—each label does not have a name, only a position marked with the colon (:) symbol and called by one or more + or − symbols after a colon (:) symbol. Each + or − symbol included indicates the number of unnamed labels to move to after the statement; for example, :+ would skip forward to the next unnamed label, whereas :++ would skip forward to the second unnamed label it encountered in the code.

Listing 4.26   Example unnamed label

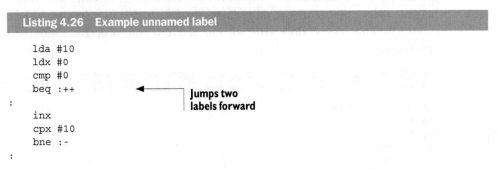

```
    lda #10
    ldx #0
    cmp #0
    beq :++                           Jumps two
:                                     labels forward
    inx
    cpx #10
    bne :-
:
```

With this method of labeling, you can jump any number of labels in either direction, but if overused, it can lead to code that is hard to understand, and it makes it quite easy to make a mistake and have a branch/jump end up in the wrong place. A named label adds information to your code listing, so unnamed labels should be used sparingly, perhaps in nested loops inside of portable code where you can't use a cheap local label.

4.5   Bytes, bits, and nibbles

We are almost done covering the basics of 6502 programming, but before we move on to our game code, it's a good idea to cover bits, as our game will use pixels, which are represented by one or more bits stored in our system's memory. A byte could represent which pixels are turned on or off in a tile pattern or the X or Y coordinate of a sprite, or it could contain flags in each of the separate bits.

Computers are made up of electronic circuits, and computer memory is made up of many single locations that can either be On (1) or Off (0) and are each known as a bit. In an 8-bit computer, these bits are grouped to form an addressable memory location called a byte. Each bit in a byte is numbered from 0 to 7 starting from the right-hand side, as shown in table 4.3.

Table 4.3   A single memory location or byte

7	6	5	4	3	2	1	0

The number of combinations you can place the 8 bits in allows each byte to contain numbers from 0 to 255. We make larger numbers by combining bytes (a topic for another time). One more thing to know is that the two halves of a byte (bits 0–3 and 4–7) are known as *nibbles*, and each nibble represents a number from 0 to 15 or 0 to F in hexadecimal. Several instructions allow you to set bits, check that a bit is set, and move bits around.

4.5.1   Bit test

There is a single dedicated instruction for checking whether a particular bit (or bits) has been set in either a zero-page or absolute memory location. The current value and the bits set in the A register are used to indicate which bits should be tested. The functionality of this instruction can also be covered by the AND operation, but it does aid in the readability of code and is nondestructive; that is, it does not affect either of the values stored in the A register or the memory location being tested:

```
lda #%00000001
bit $05
```

This example would reset the zero flag if bit 0 was set in the value stored in the zero-page memory location $05.

4.5.2   Logical operations

There are three logical operations available that allow you to modify a value based on the bits set in both the A register and either a direct value or memory location-based comparison value.

AND OPERATION

The AND operator will look at each of the bits of the A register with the same bits in a specified memory location or direct value, and where both corresponding bits are 1, the same bit will be set to 1 in the result, which will be stored in the A register (see table 4.4).

Table 4.4   Single-bit AND

Source	Destination	Result
0	0	0
1	0	0
0	1	0
1	1	1

This is probably easier to explain with an example, as shown in table 4.5.

Table 4.5   Example of the effect of an AND operation

Bit number	7	6	5	4	3	2	1	0		Hex
Source byte	0	1	0	1	0	1	0	1		$55
Destination byte	1	0	1	1	0	0	1	1		$B3
Result after AND operation	0	0	0	1	0	0	0	1		$11

EOR OPERATION

The exclusive OR (EOR or XOR) operation will look at each of the bits of the accumulator with the same bits in a specified memory location or direct value, and where either corresponding bit is set to 1, but they are not both set to 1, then the same bit will be set to 1 in the result, which then gets stored in the A register (see table 4.6). This operation is often referred to as *bit toggling*, flipping the bits where there is a 1 and leaving them alone when there is a 0. Table 4.7 shows an example using EOR on 2 bytes.

Table 4.6   Single-bit EOR

Source	Destination	Result
0	0	0
1	0	1
0	1	1
1	1	0

Table 4.7 **Example of the effect of an EOR operation**

Bit number	7	6	5	4	3	2	1	0		Hex
Source byte	0	1	0	1	0	1	0	1		$55
Destination byte	1	0	1	1	0	0	1	1		$B3
Result after EOR operation	1	1	1	0	0	1	1	0		$E6

ORA OPERATION

The ORA operation (more commonly known as OR) will compare the bits of the accumulator with a specified memory location or direct value, and where either of the corresponding bits is 1, then the same bit will be set to 1 in the result, which then gets stored in the A register (see table 4.8). The OR operation is often used to ensure particular bits in a byte are set. Table 4.9 shows an example using OR on 2 bytes.

Table 4.8 **Single-bit OR**

Source	Destination	Result
0	0	0
1	0	1
0	1	1
1	1	1

Table 4.9 **Example of the effect of an OR operation**

Bit number	7	6	5	4	3	2	1	0		Hex
Source byte	0	1	0	1	0	1	0	1		$55
Destination byte	1	0	1	1	0	0	1	1		$B3
Result after OR operation	1	1	1	1	0	1	1	1		$F7

4.5.3 *Shifting and rotating operations*

Four operations allow you to either shift or rotate bits in a value either left or right. These operations can be used for fast x2 multiplication or division, as well as for manipulating values that represent graphic patterns.

ARITHMETIC SHIFT LEFT (ASL)

This instruction will shift the bits of either the accumulator or a memory location to the left; that is, the value in bit 0 is moved to bit 1, bit 1 is moved to bit 2, etc. A zero is moved into bit 0, and the value in bit 7 is moved into the carry flag (see table 4.10). This is called arithmetic shift left (ASL), as doing this to a value is a very quick way of multiplying the value by a factor of 2.

Table 4.10   Example of the effect of an ASL operation

Bit number/carry flag	C		7	6	5	4	3	2	1	0
Byte and carry flag before ASL	0		1	1	0	1	0	1	0	1
Byte and carry flag after ASL	1		1	0	1	0	1	0	1	0

LOGICAL SHIFT RIGHT(LSR)

This instruction will shift the bits of either the accumulator or a memory location to the right; that is, the value in bit 7 is moved to bit 6, bit 6 to bit 5, etc. A zero is moved into bit 7, and the value in bit 0 is moved into the carry flag.

This instruction is very useful for dividing a value by 2. Any remainder will be discarded; that is, 5 after a logical shift right (LSR) instruction will be 2 (see table 4.11).

Table 4.11   Example of the effect of an LSR operation

Bit number/carry flag	7	6	5	4	3	2	1	0		C
Byte and carry flag before LSR	1	1	0	1	0	1	0	1		0
Byte and carry flag after LSR	0	1	1	0	1	0	1	0		1

ROTATE LEFT (ROL)

The rotate left (ROL) instruction will also shift the bits of either the accumulator or a memory location to the left (like ASL), but instead of a 0 being moved into bit 0, the current value of the carry flag is moved into bit 0, and the value in bit 7 is moved into the carry flag (see table 4.12). If this instruction is repeated eight times, the value will be back to where we started.

Table 4.12   Example of the effect of a ROL operation

Bit number/carry flag	7	6	5	4	3	2	1	0		C
Byte and carry flag before ROL	1	1	0	1	0	1	0	1		1
Byte and carry flag after ROL	1	0	1	0	1	0	1	1		1

ROTATE RIGHT (ROR)

The rotate right (ROR) instruction will also shift the bits of either the accumulator or a memory location to the right (like LSR), but instead of a 0 being moved into bit 7, the current value of the carry flag is moved into bit 7, and the value in bit 0 is moved into the carry flag (see table 4.13). If this instruction is repeated eight times, the value will be back where we started.

Table 4.13   Example of the effect of a ROR operation

Bit number/carry flag	7	6	5	4	3	2	1	0		C
Byte and carry flag before ROR	1	1	0	1	0	1	0	1		0
Byte and carry flag after ROR	0	1	1	0	1	0	1	0		1

4.6   Using the stack

A stack is a last-in, first-out data structure. Think of a stack of plates: you can only access the current plate on top of the stack by taking it off or adding a new plate to the stack. You add a value to the stack by "pushing" it onto the stack and remove a value by popping it off the stack (see figure 4.6). Just like a stack of plates, the last value (plate) added to the stack is the first value that will be removed from the stack (see figure 4.7).

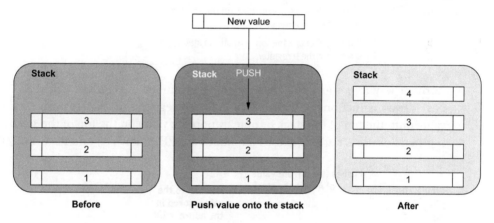

Figure 4.6   Adding (pushing) an item onto a stack of items

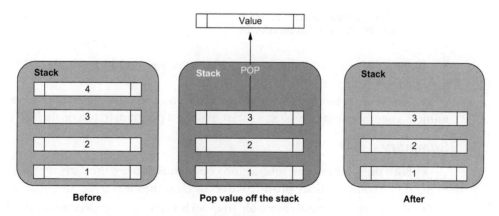

Figure 4.7   Removing (popping) an item off a stack of items

The 6502 has a fixed area of memory $0100 to $01FF that is dedicated as a stack (i.e., 256 bytes). This dedicated area of memory directly follows the zero-page memory area. The stack is used to save the address to return to after a call to a subroutine and can be used by the developer to store register values. The stack-related instructions only take a single byte and thus take a shorter time to execute than instructions that use more bytes. There are four commands available, as shown in table 4.14.

Table 4.14   Commands for using the stack

Command	Name
pha	Push A—Pushes the contents of the A register onto the stack
php	Push P—Pushes the contents of the P register onto the stack
pla	Pull/Pop A—Pops the top item off the stack and stores it in the A register
plp	Pull/Pop P—Pops the top item off the stack and stores it in the P register

Another way to get around the very limited number of registers that the 6502 CPU has is two instructions for each of the A and P registers to quickly push their current value onto the top of the stack or quickly pop the value on the top of the stack into the register. For the A register, these commands are PHA (Push A) and PLA (Pull/Pop A):

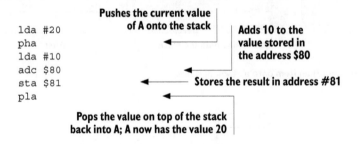

For the P register, these commands are PHP (Push P) and PLP (Pull/Pop P). We will see examples of this being used in chapter 5.

Hopefully, these last two chapters have given you a start on understanding programming in assembly language. Next we start making a program to run on an NES console.

Summary

- Both the addition and subtraction commands also use the carry register, so additional commands are provided to set or clear the carry flag.
- There are commands available to quickly increment or decrement the X and Y registers.

- Branches can only jump 127 bytes either forward or backward.
- To return from a normal subroutine, use the RTS statement, but to return from a subroutine called by an interrupt, use an RTI statement.
- There are eight different branch instructions. Each one branches when its corresponding flag is either On (1) or Off (0).
- Bytes can be shifted to the left or right.
- Bytes can also be rotated to the left or right.

Starting somewhere 5

This chapter covers

- NES code structure and memory configuration
- Initializing the NES hardware
- Loading tile and sprite shape data
- Displaying some text on the screen
- Displaying a bat and a ball using sprites
- Moving the ball and bat around the screen

We are going to create a simple space shooting game throughout the rest of this book, but before we get too carried away, we should start with a simpler demo NES project that provides the basic template for making a game. This demo does all the required setup to get the console up and running, placing some text on the screen along with two objects, a ball that bounces around the screen and a bat that is moved via the game controller.

We will work our way through this sample template code step by step, explaining each section of code as we go. You can type each section of code we will cover or follow the complete sample code from the supporting download site. The files for this chapter can be downloaded from the following GIT repository: https://github .com/tony-cruise/ProgrammingGamesForTheNES/tree/main/CH05.

In this chapter, we will put together the following physical files:

- *example.cfg*—NES configuration
- *example.s*—Contains the 6502 source code
- *example.bat (or example.sh)*—The script to compile the source code into an NES ROM
- *example.chr*—The patterns to use for the characters and sprites (download the sample from the previously cited repository for this chapter)

5.1 *NES cartridge code structure*

The NES loads game software from game cartridges, which contain ROM (i.e., memory that does not go away when the power is turned off). Any programs that you make need to follow a specific structure so that the NES console will recognize it as a valid title (see figure 5.1).

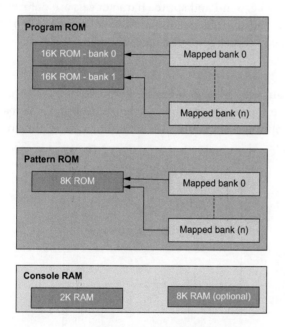

Figure 5.1 The various memory areas in the NES console

Sections of your game code will either be in the game cartridge itself (ROM) or refer to the Random Access Memory (RAM) that is inside the NES console (or optionally provided in the cartridge as well). RAM memory can be written to and hold values but will forget the values when the console is turned off. The NES has 2,048 (2K) bytes of RAM available, with a couple of areas dedicated to specific functions (we will cover these in more detail later in this chapter).

There are some configuration sections that need to be added to your game code so that it will be considered a valid cartridge. Each of these is indicated in your source code using a special assembler command as follows:

```
.segment "<name of segment>".
```

You can start any section of code with a .segment command, and the assembler will place the code or data under that segment into the corresponding section in the ROM or RAM. They can be in any order, and you can change segments as often as you like. Next we will define all of the sections and segments that we will use in our example.

5.2   NES memory configuration

To produce our final NES ROM image, we need a configuration file that maps the segment names we specify to actual memory locations in the NES's memory space. For our example, we are using the default NES memory mapper, so we only have two continuous banks of ROM starting from $8000 and ending at $FFFF (i.e., $2 \times 16K = 32K$ of ROM space), and both the background and sprite character sets are defined in the ROM itself as raw data. The configuration file is split into two sections, labeled MEMORY and SEGMENTS. For our example in this chapter, the file is called example.cfg.

5.2.1   Memory

In the first section of the configuration file, we define six key areas of the NES memory space. Each line specifies where the area starts, how long it is, whether it is read-only (RO) or read/write (RW), an optional file name, and whether to prefill the area for a particular value (see figure 5.2).

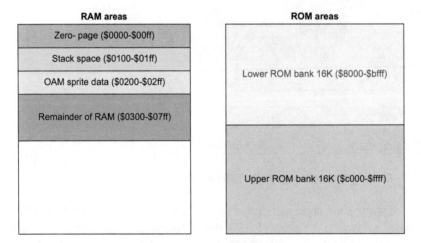

Figure 5.2   Relative position of the RAM and ROM areas

For our example in this chapter, we use the following configuration for our areas.

Listing 5.1 NES memory configuration (example.cfg)

```
MEMORY {
    ZP:      start = $00,     size = $0100, type = rw, file = "";
    OAM:     start = $0200,   size = $0100, type = rw, file = "";
    RAM:     start = $0300,   size = $0500, type = rw, file = "";
    HDR:     start = $0000,   size = $0010, type = ro, file = %O, fill = yes,
➥ fillval = $00;
    PRG:     start = $8000,   size = $8000, type = ro, file = %O, fill = yes,
➥ fillval = $00;
    CHR:     start = $0000,   size = $2000, type = ro, file = %O, fill = yes,
➥ fillval = $00;
}
```

The six key areas are as listed in table 5.1.

Table 5.1 NES memory key areas

Section	Description	Type	Size (bytes)
ZP	This is the special section of RAM that the 6502 CPU uses as zero-page memory.	Read/write	256
OAM	This is the special section of RAM set aside for the local copy of the sprite definition table (object attribute memory [OAM]). This table contains the position, shape, and attributes of each of the sprites displayed on the screen.	Read/write	256
RAM	This is the remainder of the 2K of RAM where we can store more variables and set aside space for object tables. We might use this space to keep track of our enemies in our game or larger blocks of space for tracking changes to the background layout.	Read/write	1280
HDR	This is a special section of our ROM that is used to indicate to NES console emulators that the cartridge is an NES cartridge and that allows some details of the features that the cartridge uses. It is added as a header on the NES ROM file.	Read only	16
PRG	This is our main ROM area where the code and data for our program are stored. For now, we will only have 2 × 16K = 32K of ROM, which will be more than enough for our purposes, but later in the book, we will look at how you can have much larger cartridges.	Read only	32k
CHR	This area of our ROM contains the patterns for our tiles and sprites. In an NES cartridge, depending on the cartridge type, we can have multiple of these pattern tables or even, in some cases, none. The advantage of having set pattern (CHR) tables is that we don't have to copy them into the graphic processor's video memory; we can simply specify which section to use, and the NES console will do the rest. The disadvantage of this approach is that the pattern tables, especially when you need a few different sets, take up a lot of room. By taking over this process, you can use compression to store even more data. The memory in this area is not directly accessible by the 6502 CPU; only the picturing processing unit can access it.	Read only	8k

5.2.2 *Segments*

In the second section of the configuration file, we map the labels we are going to use in our code (e.g., ZEROPAGE, CODE, etc.) to the actual areas of memory we defined in the first section. You can have multiple labeled sections that end up being stored in the same memory space by default. If you have more than one section going into an area of memory, they will be positioned one after another. We will use the following segments for our example in this chapter.

Listing 5.2   NES segment configuration (example.cfg)

```
SEGMENTS {
    ZEROPAGE: load = ZP,  type = zp;
    OAM:      load = OAM, type = bss, align = $100;
    BSS:      load = RAM, type = bss;
    HEADER:   load = HDR, type = ro;
    CODE:     load = PRG, type = ro,  start = $8000;
    RODATA:   load = PRG, type = ro;
    VECTORS:  load = PRG, type = ro,  start = $FFFA;
    TILES:    load = CHR, type = ro;
}
```

The commands in this section of the file are

- load—The section this label points to
- type—The type of memory: zp (zero page), bss (RAM), or ro (read only)
- align—Ensures this segment starts on the boundary specified
- start—Ensures this segment starts at the location specified

We will expand on why we have defined these segments and fill out their contents throughout the rest of this chapter. Save the two sections of configuration code in their own source file called example.cfg in the directory where you save your other code files.

5.3 *Defined values*

Rather than repeat various system values throughout your code, it is a much better practice (and makes code much easier to understand) to define these values once and allocate a meaningful label. That way, in the code, you see a readable label that describes the value, and the assembler will replace the label with the actual value for you.

For the example in this chapter, we will define some of the NES system values that give us access to various aspects of the graphics processor (picture processing unit [PPU]), the sound processor (audio processing unit [APU]), and the player controllers. These definitions don't change, so they can be used in other NES projects. Add this code as the first part of a new file called example.s, which will be our main assembly source code file.

Listing 5.3   Defining register values (example.s)

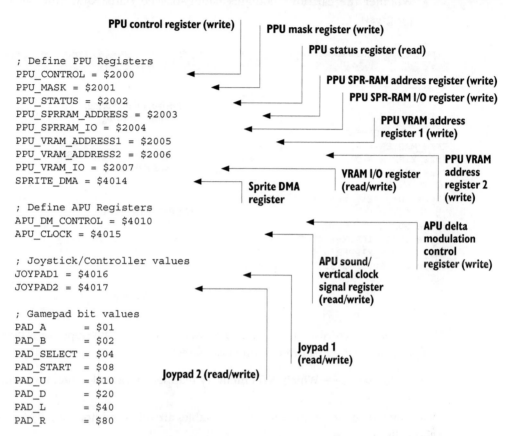

```
; Define PPU Registers
PPU_CONTROL = $2000
PPU_MASK = $2001
PPU_STATUS = $2002
PPU_SPRRAM_ADDRESS = $2003
PPU_SPRRAM_IO = $2004
PPU_VRAM_ADDRESS1 = $2005
PPU_VRAM_ADDRESS2 = $2006
PPU_VRAM_IO = $2007
SPRITE_DMA = $4014

; Define APU Registers
APU_DM_CONTROL = $4010
APU_CLOCK = $4015

; Joystick/Controller values
JOYPAD1 = $4016
JOYPAD2 = $4017

; Gamepad bit values
PAD_A      = $01
PAD_B      = $02
PAD_SELECT = $04
PAD_START  = $08
PAD_U      = $10
PAD_D      = $20
PAD_L      = $40
PAD_R      = $80
```

PPU control register (write)

PPU mask register (write)

PPU status register (read)

PPU SPR-RAM address register (write)

PPU SPR-RAM I/O register (write)

PPU VRAM address register 1 (write)

PPU VRAM address register 2 (write)

VRAM I/O register (read/write)

Sprite DMA register

APU delta modulation control register (write)

APU sound/ vertical clock signal register (read/write)

Joypad 1 (read/write)

Joypad 2 (read/write)

We will investigate what each of these is used for in more detail later in this book and will also add to these settings as we progress, but these settings will cover what we need to get our initial demo/example program going.

5.4   NES header

This part of your source code must always be included, as it lets the NES emulator or flash cartridge know how your cartridge will provide it with the information it needs to run your game. This is where the NES console is extremely powerful and flexible, as many options exist for improving on the hardware available in the NES console itself. The header indicates not only that the cartridge is a valid NES title but also the following:

- Which mapper you are using (see appendix B)
- How many banks of ROM are available
- How many tile pattern (CHR) banks are available

- Which way the name tables are mirrored (see section 6.5.1)
- Whether the cartridge contains battery-backed static RAM (for saving game progress)

Listing 5.4   Example NES header (example.s)

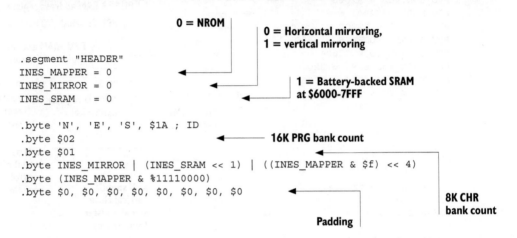

```
0 = NROM

0 = Horizontal mirroring,
1 = vertical mirroring

.segment "HEADER"
INES_MAPPER = 0
INES_MIRROR = 0              1 = Battery-backed SRAM
INES_SRAM   = 0              at $6000-7FFF

.byte 'N', 'E', 'S', $1A ; ID
.byte $02                    16K PRG bank count
.byte $01
.byte INES_MIRROR | (INES_SRAM << 1) | ((INES_MAPPER & $f) << 4)
.byte (INES_MAPPER & %11110000)
.byte $0, $0, $0, $0, $0, $0, $0, $0
                                                           8K CHR
                                                           bank count
                                        Padding
```

This header stays consistent between NES projects, with the developer only needing to change values to the first three defined as follows:

- `INES_MAPPER`—Which NES memory mapper or cartridge memory model the game uses
- `INES_MIRROR`—Whether the name tables are mirrored horizontally (0) or vertically (1)
- `INES_SRAM`—Set to 1 if the cartridge contains battery-backed RAM at `$6000-$7fff`

The only other values that need to be changed are the second and third byte statements, indicating how many 16K program ROM banks and how many 8K character ROM banks the cartridge contains. In our example, we have two 16K program ROM banks and a single 8K character ROM bank, so we use the values 2 and 1, respectively.

5.5   *Vectors*

This part of your source code must always be included and lets the NES console know where to find the three key interrupt or starting point vectors. An interrupt is when the CPU stops what it is currently doing when it receives a signal from an external device:

- *NMI*—The non-maskable interrupt (NMI) handler, called when the screen has been drawn and the raster is moving to the top of the screen (also known as a vBlank).

- *RESET*—The starting point (or reset point) of your game title.
- *IRQ*—The interrupt indicating a clock tick has occurred. The NES console and most NES cartridge mappers do not have a built-in clock, so this interrupt is not used very often, and developers need to use the NMI interrupt, along with a counter, to create timers. The IRQ interrupt can also be triggered using the BRK instruction, so it can also be used as a single subroutine, called with a single byte instruction.

The assembler, based on our configuration file, will place this segment of code in the game ROM at the address $FFFA to $FFFF. This is where the CPU will expect to find the three vectors.

Add the following listing to our example.s source file.

> **Listing 5.5 Example vector table (example.s)**

```
.segment "VECTORS"
.word nmi
.word reset
.word irq
```

5.6   Zero page

Any segments marked as zero page (ZEROPAGE) will be placed in the first 256 bytes of memory and are accessible in code using single-byte (zero-page) instructions. This is where you declare any variables you will be using in your code.

Note that you cannot define any code to be in zero page, as it is RAM and not part of your ROM. All you can do is set aside 1 or more bytes of RAM, assigned to a label. We do this using the .res assembly statement that reserves the number of bytes you specify. Here we set up the zero-page values we will use in the example in the rest of the chapter. They include

- [nmi_ready] —A flag for determining whether we want to allow the display to be rendered. This will allow us to make changes to video memory without causing graphics corruption.
- [gamepad] —Stores the results of reading the game controller.
- [d_x] —The X velocity of the ball.
- [d_y] —The Y velocity of the ball.

Add the following listing to our example.s source file.

Listing 5.6   Our zero-page memory allocations (example.s)

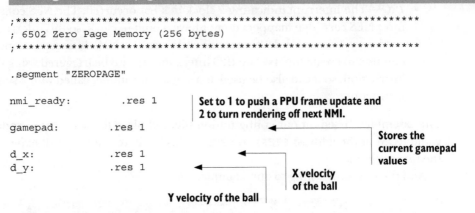

```
;***************************************************************
; 6502 Zero Page Memory (256 bytes)
;***************************************************************

.segment "ZEROPAGE"

nmi_ready:         .res 1
gamepad:           .res 1
d_x:               .res 1
d_y:               .res 1
```

Set to 1 to push a PPU frame update and 2 to turn rendering off next NMI.

Stores the current gamepad values

X velocity of the ball

Y velocity of the ball

5.7   Sprite data

This is the section of RAM memory dedicated to the sprite OAM table. This table holds the position (X and Y) and attributes (color and pattern) of each of the 64 8 × 8 sprites, 4 bytes per sprite. As it is in CPU memory, you can update the values whenever you want, but the changed values will only affect the actual sprites once the details are copied to the PPU, usually in your NMI routine (see section 5.13). We will cover the details of the sprite OAM table in chapter 7.

Add the following listing to our example.s source file.

Listing 5.7   Sprite OAM data (example.s)

```
;***************************************************************
; Sprite OAM Data area - copied to VRAM in NMI routine
;***************************************************************

.segment "OAM"
oam: .res 256              ◄────────  Sprite OAM data
```

5.8   Code

Any section of your code marked as CODE will be placed in the ROM first, followed by sections of code marked as RODATA. The default mapper has 2 × 16K sections of ROM in a row making up a single 32K section. Other mappers add more ROM sections, which need to be swapped in and out, as you can only have 32K of ROM available at any time.

For our simple example in this chapter, we will use the RODATA segment to store our default palette and the text that will appear on the screen. As these are actually set values that will be stored in our ROM cartridge, we use the .byte assembly command to specify 1 or more individual bytes of data.

The NES has two palette tables: one for the background tiles and one for the sprites. Each table contains four sets of four colors. We will cover how these are used for tiles in chapter 6 and sprites in chapter 7.

Add the following listing to our example.s source file.

Listing 5.8   `RODATA` **code segment (example.s)**

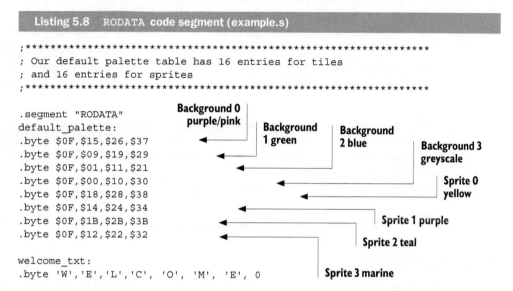

```
;*******************************************************************
; Our default palette table has 16 entries for tiles
; and 16 entries for sprites
;*******************************************************************

.segment "RODATA"
default_palette:
.byte $0F,$15,$26,$37
.byte $0F,$09,$19,$29
.byte $0F,$01,$11,$21
.byte $0F,$00,$10,$30
.byte $0F,$18,$28,$38
.byte $0F,$14,$24,$34
.byte $0F,$1B,$2B,$3B
.byte $0F,$12,$22,$32

welcome_txt:
.byte 'W','E','L','C', 'O', 'M', 'E', 0
```

5.9   *Chars*

Any section of your code marked as (TILES) will be placed in the ROM but marked as tile patterns used for background and sprites. Each set of tile patterns is 8K long and consists of two sets of 256 patterns.

For our example, we will include an external file example.chr that contains our two sets of 256 patterns. We only need a set of alphabetical characters in positions 65 to 90 in the tile pattern table and two shapes for the ball and bat in the first two positions of the sprite pattern table. We also have a blank pattern in position 0 of the table for the areas of the screen where you don't want to see any pattern. You can create one using the tools shown in chapter 2, grab one from an existing NES ROM, or use the one provided in the files for this chapter. We use the .incbin assembly command, which includes a binary file that will be copied as is into our final NES ROM image.

Add the following listing to our example.s source file.

Listing 5.9   **Importing character sets (example.s)**

```
;*******************************************************************
; Import both the background and sprite character sets
;*******************************************************************

.segment "TILES"
.incbin "example.chr"
```

5.10   RAM

Any segments marked as BSS will be placed in the remaining RAM memory of the NES after the memory is set aside for the zero-page and OAM areas. Access to these addresses requires 2 bytes to specify the address, so any commands will be slower than when accessing zero-page addresses.

As it is a RAM area, you cannot define any code or values to set; you can only reserve 1 or more bytes of RAM, assigned to a label. We use the same .res command we used for the zero-page variables earlier. For our simple example, we have a small buffer allocated to save the current color palette we are using. Add the following listing to our example.s source file.

Listing 5.10   Normal RAM (BSS) (example.s)

```
;********************************************************************
; Remainder of normal RAM area
;********************************************************************

.segment "BSS"
palette: .res 32          ◀────────── The current palette buffer
```

5.11   IRQ interrupt

Even if our cartridge does not add hardware to generate IRQ interrupts, we will need to add a handler for the vector we defined earlier to jump to.

Listing 5.11   IRQ clock interrupt (example.s)

```
;********************************************************************
; IRQ Clock Interrupt Routine
;********************************************************************

.segment "CODE"
irq:
    rti
```

5.12   Initializing the NES hardware

Before we can start controlling the NES console with our code, we need to initialize the NES hardware by turning off sound, clearing RAM, and making sure there are no sprites on screen. Upon powering up, the NES PPU takes a while (29,658 cycles) before it is ready to receive commands, so it is good practice to use a pair of loops while waiting for a change in the vBlank flag.

Our first section code is called by the NES at startup, so starting with the reset label that indicates this is the startup/reset section of code, we immediately turn off all normal interrupts and ensure that we disable NMI signals, stop the PPU from rendering the screen, disable the direct memory transfers, and finally disable the sound processor

(APU). This ensures that we won't see any random artifacts on the screen or hear random sounds.

We use the assembly command `.proc`, followed by a label name to indicate the start of a section of code. You could just use a label and start the code, but the `.proc` command and its matching `.endproc` are very good visual aids as to what lines make a section of code.

We use a 6502 command we did not cover in chapters 3 and 4, called `sei`, which clears the interrupt flag (i.e., disables interrupts). We then load the value zero (0) into the A register using LDA (see section 3.3.1) and use STA (see section 3.3.2) to then store the value in A in three of the control registers, two for the PPU and APU.

We then load the value $40 into the A register and store that in the control register for the second control pad. The circuitry for reading the control pad is part of the APU. APU interrupts can also be controlled through this port. Add the following listing to our example.s source file.

Listing 5.12   Initializing the NES (example.s)

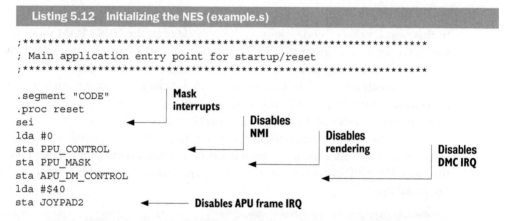

After that, disable decimal mode, as the NES's version of the 6502 does not support it. The next command sets the X register to the value $ff and then sets the current stack pointer offset value. Here we use a 6502 command we did not cover in chapters 3 and 4, called `txs`, which transfers the value in the X register to the S register. The stack starts at the location specified, and for each item that is pushed onto the stack, the stack pointer offset value will decrease by 1:

TIP   When in Binary-Coded Decimal (BCD) mode, the 6502 processor treats each byte (8 bits) as a set of two decimal numbers (0–9) located in each of the low and high 4 bits (also known as nibbles). The CLD command clears the use decimal flag so that normal math operations are performed, whereas the SED command sets the use decimal flag so that any math operations will work in decimal mode.

Our next section of code is designed to wait until the first vBlank has been signaled (the screen has been drawn for the first time). We start by reading the PPU status register, using the BIT instruction. We are just seeing if bit 7 of the PPU status register has been cleared, so it doesn't matter what the A register is set to. The BIT command will set the negative (N) flag if the value we are testing has the negative bit (bit 7) set.

The first read of the status register will clear the "vBlank has happened" flag, ensuring that we will wait until a full frame has been rendered. Then, inside our loop, we continually check the PPU status register, only exiting once bit 7 has been set. The BPL instruction will execute its jump if the negative flag (bit 7) is clear.

Listing 5.13   Waiting for the first vBlank (example.s)

```
bit PPU_STATUS
wait_vblank:
    bit PPU_STATUS
    bpl wait_vblank
```
Waits for the first vBlank

In this next section of code, we use a loop to clear all the NES's RAM memory (2K in total). We set the A register to 0, which will be the value we write to each RAM location. Then we set the X register to 0 to act as our loop counter. As the 6502 only has 8-bit registers, which have a maximum value of 255, we can only count from 0 to 255 before introducing more logic, so in this case, we reuse the current value of X and write to eight different blocks of memory each loop (8 × 256 = 2048 = 2K).

To finish our loop, we increment the X register, and if is not equal to 0 (the zero flag will be set if X is 0 after the increment instruction), then it will jump back to the start of the loop. The BNE instruction will execute its jump if the Z register is clear (i.e., X does not equal 0).

Listing 5.14   Clearing all RAM (example.s)

```
    lda #0
    ldx #0
clear_ram:
    sta $0000,x
    sta $0100,x
    sta $0200,x
    sta $0300,x
    sta $0400,x
    sta $0500,x
    sta $0600,x
    sta $0700,x
    inx
    bne clear_ram
```
Clears all RAM to 0

In the next section of code, we set the Y position (stored in the 256-byte section of RAM marked with the oam label) of each of the sprites to equal 255, which will ensure the sprite is off the bottom of the displayed screen and that none of the sprites are visible.

The Y position of a sprite is controlled by the first byte (of 4 bytes), so after setting a sprite's Y position, we increment the X register four times to skip to the next Y value. See table 5.2 to learn how the four bytes are used to control the sprites.

Listing 5.15   Placing sprites offscreen (example.s)

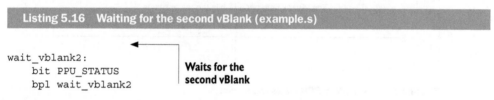

```
    lda #255
    ldx #0
clear_oam:
    sta oam,x
    inx
    inx
    inx
    inx
    bne clear_oam
```

Places all sprites offscreen at Y = 255

Next we have another loop to wait for the second vBlank to occur; this should ensure the NES has had enough time to properly initialize. This is the same as the loop we did earlier.

Listing 5.16   Waiting for the second vBlank (example.s)

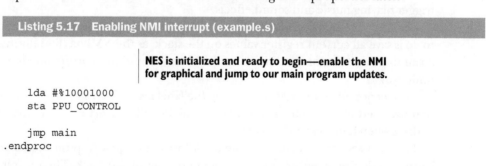

```
wait_vblank2:
    bit PPU_STATUS
    bpl wait_vblank2
```

Waits for the second vBlank

Next we enable NMI interrupts and jump to our main program where we can start adding the actual logic of our example. We are setting bits 3 and 7 of the PPU control register. This indicates that our sprites will use the second of the pattern tables for its shapes (bit 3 set), and setting bit 7 is what tells the PPU to start generating NMI interrupts. We will cover more of the PPU control register's properties later.

Listing 5.17   Enabling NMI interrupt (example.s)

NES is initialized and ready to begin—enable the NMI for graphical and jump to our main program updates.

```
    lda #%10001000
    sta PPU_CONTROL

    jmp main
.endproc
```

5.13 NMI routine

Every time the NES graphics chip (PPU) has finished drawing to the screen, it generates a Non-Maskable Interrupt (NMI; also called the vBlank). For a short period of time, the NES PPU waits for the output screen raster (the beam that is causing the pixels to appear on the TV) to return to the top of the screen so it can start drawing again (see figure 5.3).

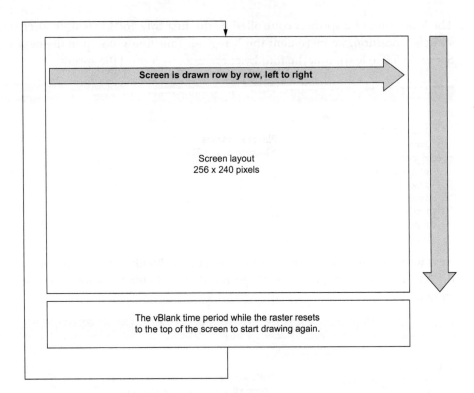

Figure 5.3   How the NES PPU draws the screen

This interrupt happens 60 times per second on NTSC consoles and 50 times per second on PAL consoles. The interrupt then calls the NMI routine defined in the vector table (see section 5.5) and executes the code there. This is where any changes you want to make to the screen should be sent to the PPU's VRAM, and it is also a good time to trigger playing music and sound effects.

Let's put together a simple NMI routine for this chapter. The first thing that we need to do is save all current register values on the stack, as the NMI has literally interrupted a running code section, and we want to make sure we don't corrupt anything that was underway.

This section of code starts by defining the label `nmi`, which should be the same label that was used in the vector table. The assembler will convert this label into an actual address when it makes the NES ROM.

The next section of code uses the stack instruction `pha` to push the current value stored inside the A register onto the next position of the stack. Then it transfers the value in the X register into the A register, using the `txa` command (transfer X into A), and uses the `pha` command (push A) to push that value onto the stack, repeating the same for the Y register using the `tya` command (transfer Y into A). This now means that the current values that were stored in the three registers A, X, and Y have now been saved on the stack.

Listing 5.18 Start of NMI routine (example.s)

```
.segment   "CODE"
.proc nmi
    ; save registers
pha
txa
pha
tya
pha
```

To make it easier to control when changes are rendered to the screen and, most importantly, enable us to turn off rendering so we can write larger amounts of changes to
video memory without running into corruption, we use one of our zero-page values,
nmi_ready, to control when we should skip rendering to the screen. In this example, if
our nmi_ready variable is set to 0, we will jump to ppu_update_end and skip any writes
to the video memory. If our nmi_ready variable is set to 2, we clear the PPU_MASK register, which will disable rendering; that is, the PPU will no longer draw anything to the
screen, and we set our nmi_ready flag back to 0. Finally, if our nmi_ready flag is set to
1, then we will continue to the rest of our NMI routine.

Listing 5.19 Do we need to render? (example.s)

```
    lda nmi_ready
    bne :+

        jmp ppu_update_end
    :
    cmp #2                          ◄——  nmi_ready == 2 turns
    bne cont_render                       rendering off.
        lda #%00000000              ◄————  Disables rendering
        sta PPU_MASK
        ldx #0
        stx nmi_ready
        jmp ppu_update_end
cont_render:
```

We need to transfer the table of values in CPU memory that holds the locations and
current patterns of the sprites (OAM) to PPU video memory. Luckily, the NES hardware has a single operation for performing this, called a direct memory access (DMA)
transfer. This transfers the whole sprite OAM memory block to the PPU's video memory without tying up the CPU. This means we can do it every time an NMI occurs (and
we want to draw to video memory) without worrying about how much time it takes or
whether there have been any changes to the sprite OAM table.

You will notice that we use a special symbol with the LDA instruction. oam is a label
that points to a location in memory, so is itself a 16-bit value (it will be $0200 for our
example). The A register is only 8 bits in size, so the > symbol causes the high byte of the
OAM address ($02) to be assigned to the A register. If we used the < symbol, it would

cause the low byte of the OAM address ($00) to be assigned. We then store the value of A in the sprite DMA register, which will trigger the PPU to transfer all 256 bytes to the PPU's built-in sprite data area.

Listing 5.20   Transferring the sprite table to video memory (example.s)

```
ldx #0
stx PPU_SPRRAM_ADDRESS          Transfers sprite OAM
lda #>oam                       data using DMA
sta SPRITE_DMA
```

We ensure that the NMI interrupt is still enabled by writing to the PPU control register again (see section 5.12). We also need to transfer our current palette values from RAM to video RAM (VRAM); unfortunately, we don't have another DMA transfer available, so we need to first set the starting address in video memory that we want to write to using the PPU_VRAM_ADDRESS2 register. Writing the high part of the address first ($3f) and then the low part of the address second ($00) will set the address to $3f00, which is where the PPU stores the current palette. We then write each of the 32 palette values to VRAM by repeatedly sending values to the PPU_VRAM_IO register. After each write, the VRAM address will automatically increment by 1 (there is another mode, which we will cover later).

We use the bcc branch instruction to keep on looping until the carry flag has been set (i.e., while X is smaller than 32, the CPX #32 instruction will clear the carry flag). Once X equals or is larger than 32, the carry flag will be set, and the loop will exit.

Listing 5.21   Transferring the palette table to video memory (example.s)

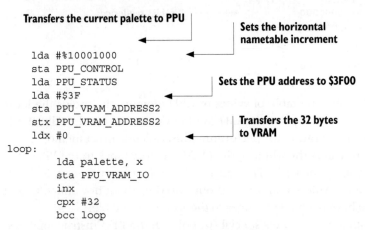

```
          Transfers the current palette to PPU
                                              Sets the horizontal
                                              nametable increment
        lda #%10001000
        sta PPU_CONTROL
        lda PPU_STATUS                Sets the PPU address to $3F00
        lda #$3F
        sta PPU_VRAM_ADDRESS2
        stx PPU_VRAM_ADDRESS2         Transfers the 32 bytes
        ldx #0                        to VRAM
loop:
        lda palette, x
        sta PPU_VRAM_IO
        inx
        cpx #32
        bcc loop
```

Now that we have written all the changes to PPU VRAM, we need to signal the PPU to render the screen and reset our nmi_ready flag.

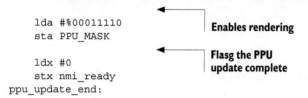

Listing 5.22 Enabling rendering (example.s)

```
    lda #%00011110
    sta PPU_MASK

    ldx #0
    stx nmi_ready
ppu_update_end:
```

Enables rendering

Flasg the PPU
update complete

Lastly, we need to restore all the registers and use the special `rti` instruction to return from an interrupt. We use the `pla` instruction to pull the top value off the stack, and then use the `tay` instruction (transfer A to Y) to transfer the value in A to the Y register. We then repeat for X using the `tax` instruction (transfer A to X), and the last value stays in the A register. So by popping the values off the stack, we will have restored the A, X, and Y registers to the same values that they were at the start of the NMI procedure.

Listing 5.23 Restoring registers and returning (example.s)

```
    pla
    tay
    pla
    tax
    pla
    rti
.endproc
```

Restores registers
and returns

5.14   *Some useful functions*

Before we start putting together the main logic of our example program, we will add some simple, useful functions that we can call from our code.

5.14.1 *PPU update*

This function will turn on rendering and then wait until the next NMI has occurred. This will ensure that rendering has finished.

We first set our nmi_ready variable to 1 and wait until the nmi_ready variable has been set to 0. Setting the nmi_ready variable to 1 will trigger the NMI routine to turn rendering on, and then the nmi_ready variable will only be reset once the next NMI has completed, meaning the screen will have been rendered to the display by the PPU.

Listing 5.24 PPU update function (example.s)

```
.segment "CODE"
; ppu_update: waits until next NMI and turns rendering on (if not already)
.proc ppu_update
    lda #1
    sta nmi_ready
loop:
```

```
        lda nmi_ready
        bne loop
    rts
.endproc
```

5.14.2 *PPU off*

If you need to transfer a large amount of data to the PPU's VRAM, such as manually copying over tile patterns or changing a whole name table, you will need to disable rendering to ensure that your transfer is not interrupted. This function uses our nmi_ ready flag to indicate that rendering should be turned off, waiting until the flag has been cleared. Once the flag has been cleared, you are safe to start transferring your data to video RAM.

> **Listing 5.25   PPU off function (example.s)**

```
.segment "CODE"
; ppu_off: waits until next NMI and turns rendering off
; (now safe to write PPU directly via PPU_VRAM_IO)
.proc ppu_off
    lda #2
    sta nmi_ready
    loop:
        lda nmi_ready
        bne loop
    rts
.endproc
```

5.14.3 *Clearing the name table*

A key thing that needs to be done a lot in most games is to clear the current screen. The NES has at least two (sometimes four) separate screen name tables (see section 6.5.1). These name tables control what tile is used for each 8 × 8 area on a screen.

Directly following each name table are 64 bytes that set the attributes of each 16 × 16 area of the screen. The attributes allow the palette used for each 16 × 16 block to be specified.

As we are putting together a simple example, this code is hardwired to only clear the first name table. So we start by setting the destination VRAM address ($2000), which is the location of the first name table. Then we use two nested loops to send 30 rows of 32 values to the VRAM. As we are sending zeros and our first tile pattern is blank, this has the effect of clearing the screen. We have a final loop to send the last 64 values to clear the attribute table.

> **Listing 5.26   Clearing the name table (example.s)**

```
.segment "CODE"
.proc clear_nametable
    lda PPU_STATUS          ◄────    Resets the
                                     address latch
```

```
        lda #$20              ◄────────    Sets the PPU
        sta PPU_VRAM_ADDRESS2              address to $2000
        lda #$00
        sta PPU_VRAM_ADDRESS2


                    ◄─────    Empty the name table
        lda #0
        ldy #30         ◄────────    Clears 30 rows
        rowloop:
            ldx #32         ◄────────    32 columns
            columnloop:
                sta PPU_VRAM_IO
                dex
                bne columnloop
            dey
            bne rowloop              Empty attribute
                                     table

        ldx #64              ◄────────    The attribute table
        loop:                              is 64 bytes.
            sta PPU_VRAM_IO
            dex
            bne loop
        rts
    .endproc
```

5.14.4 *Poll game pad*

Another important function to have is the ability to read input from the player from the game controller. Each NES gamepad is polled separately, so for our simple example, we will only look at the gamepad in the first controller port.

To read a gamepad, we strobe the port by writing a 1, followed by a 0, before reading the port eight times. Each read gets the status of a single button (the directions are considered individual buttons), and we use a loop to store a bit for each button in a single byte.

We use the AND command and the value %00000011, as we only want the first 2 bits of the current value that was in JOYPAD1. We use the ROR command (see section 4.3.3) here for the first time to rotate the carry flag, set by cmp #%00000001 if the specific button was pressed into the A register.

> **Listing 5.27   Poll game pad (example.s)**

```
;****************************************************************
; gamepad_poll: this reads the gamepad state into the variable
; labeled "gamepad".
; This only reads the first gamepad, and also if DPCM samples
; are played they can conflict with gamepad reading,
; which may give incorrect results.
;****************************************************************

.segment "CODE"
.proc gamepad_poll
```

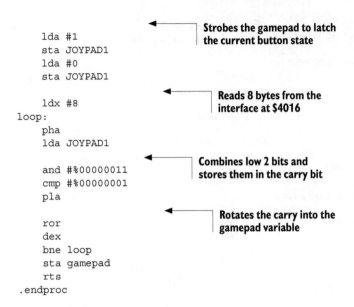

```
    lda #1
    sta JOYPAD1
    lda #0
    sta JOYPAD1

    ldx #8
loop:
    pha
    lda JOYPAD1

    and #%00000011
    cmp #%00000001
    pla

    ror
    dex
    bne loop
    sta gamepad
    rts
.endproc
```

Strobes the gamepad to latch the current button state

Reads 8 bytes from the interface at $4016

Combines low 2 bits and stores them in the carry bit

Rotates the carry into the gamepad variable

5.15 Main application logic

Now we can put together our main application logic. We want to finish setting things up for our example, such as setting the palette, clearing the screen, displaying our text, and putting our two sprites on screen in their initial positions. Starting our main logic, we copy our palette colors from our ROM into the palette RAM area.

Listing 5.28 Copying palette (example.s)

```
;****************************************************************
; Main application logic section includes the game loop
;****************************************************************
.segment "CODE"
.proc main
```

Main application—rendering is currently off

Initializes the palette table

```
    ldx #0
paletteloop:
    lda default_palette, x
    sta palette, x
    inx
    cpx #32
    bcc paletteloop
```

Next we can clear the screen using the useful `clear_nametable` function we defined earlier.

Listing 5.29 Clearing the name table (example.s)

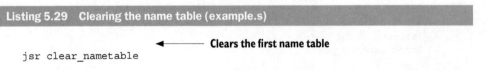

Clears the first name table

```
    jsr clear_nametable
```

Now that we have the screen cleared, we can write our text message to the screen. This first sets the location in the name table where we want to place the text (row 4, column 10, address − base address + 32 × row + column). We then use a loop to copy each byte of the message until we find a 0 in the message. This section of code is something that we will expand on and turn into another useful function in the game we are working on as we progress through this book.

Listing 5.30   Drawing some text (example.s)

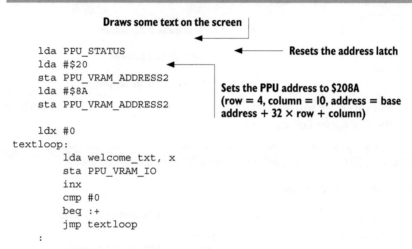

```
                     Draws some text on the screen

        lda PPU_STATUS
        lda #$20                              Resets the address latch
        sta PPU_VRAM_ADDRESS2
        lda #$8A                      Sets the PPU address to $208A
        sta PPU_VRAM_ADDRESS2         (row = 4, column = 10, address = base
                                      address + 32 × row + column)
        ldx #0
textloop:
        lda welcome_txt, x
        sta PPU_VRAM_IO
        inx
        cmp #0
        beq :+
        jmp textloop
    :
```

We are going to use two sprites in our example. The first one will be our bat, positioned near the bottom of the screen, and the player will be able to move left and right using the gamepad. To place our sprite, we need to set four values, as shown in table 5.2.

Table 5.2   NES sprite definition

Byte	Description
0	This is the Y coordinate of the top-left corner of our 8 × 8 pixel sprite. A sprite does not appear until the next scanline, so effectively each sprite is drawn at Y + 1.
	If this is set in the range 239—255, the sprite will not be visible on the screen; we use 255 as a set value to detect that a sprite is not in use.
1	This is the index number of tile patterns to use for the sprite. The pattern is taken from the currently selected sprite tile pattern table.
2	This byte sets the attributes of the sprite as follows:
	Bits 0—1—Set which of the four sprite palettes to use for the sprite
	Bit 5—Indicates whether the sprite is drawn in front of (0) or behind (1) the background
	Bit 6—Indicates whether to flip the sprite pattern horizontally
	Bit 7—Indicates whether to flip the sprite pattern vertically
3	The final value sets the X coordinate of the top-left corner of the sprite.

For our bat sprite, we will set the Y coordinate to 180 and the X coordinate to 120. We will use sprite pattern 1 and use the first sprite color palette.

Listing 5.31   Placing bat sprite on screen (example.s)

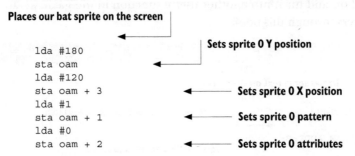

Places our bat sprite on the screen

```
lda #180
sta oam
lda #120
sta oam + 3
lda #1
sta oam + 1
lda #0
sta oam + 2
```

Sets sprite 0 Y position

Sets sprite 0 X position

Sets sprite 0 pattern

Sets sprite 0 attributes

For our ball sprite, we will set both the X and Y coordinates to 124, use sprite pattern 2, and use the first sprite color palette.

Listing 5.32   Placing ball sprite on screen (example.s)

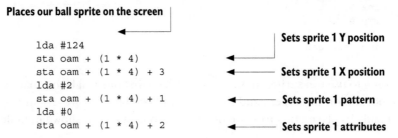

Places our ball sprite on the screen

```
lda #124
sta oam + (1 * 4)
sta oam + (1 * 4) + 3
lda #2
sta oam + (1 * 4) + 1
lda #0
sta oam + (1 * 4) + 2
```

Sets sprite 1 Y position

Sets sprite 1 X position

Sets sprite 1 pattern

Sets sprite 1 attributes

As the ball sprite will move around the screen and bounce off the screen edges, we need to set values for both the X and Y velocity. This will be the value we will add to our X and Y coordinates to make the ball move around the screen.

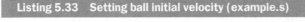
Listing 5.33   Setting ball initial velocity (example.s)

```
lda #1
sta d_x
sta d_y
```

Sets the ball velocity

Now, before we start our game loop, we need to turn on rendering so all our changes are written to the screen and wait for them to be displayed before we move on. To do that, we use our ppu_update function we defined earlier.

Listing 5.34   Getting the screen to render (example.s)

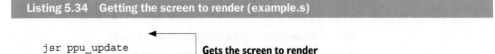

```
jsr ppu_update
```

Gets the screen to render

Now that all our setup is out of the way, we can start our "game loop." In our game loop, we want to poll the game controller, and if the player has pressed left or right, move the bat sprite in the appropriate direction. Also, we want to move the ball sprite based on its current X and Y velocity values, making sure we detect the screen edges and change our ball velocity values so it bounces.

At the start of our game loop, if we are currently rendering the screen, we want to skip making any more changes, so we use our `nmi_ready` flag to skip our further logic if rendering is in progress.

> **Listing 5.35 Start of game loop—checking render status (example.s)**

```
mainloop:

    lda nmi_ready          ◄──────  Skips the reading controls if the
    cmp #0                          change has not been drawn
    bne mainloop
```

Now we can poll the game controller and then move the bat left or right if the player has pressed the corresponding direction on the gamepad. Before moving left or right, we need to make sure the bat is not already as far left or right as it can go before we adjust the X position of the bat sprite.

After getting our current gamepad values, we first test to see if the gamepad is being pressed in the left direction. If it is not pressed, we jump to the next section (NOT_ GAMEPAD_LEFT). Otherwise, we get the current X position of our bat, and if it is not already at the left of the screen, we subtract 1 from its value and store it as our new X value. We repeat the same for the gamepad being pressed to the right, except we test to make sure the bat has not reached the right of the screen before we increase the X value.

> **Listing 5.36 Reading the gamepad and moving the bat (example.s)**

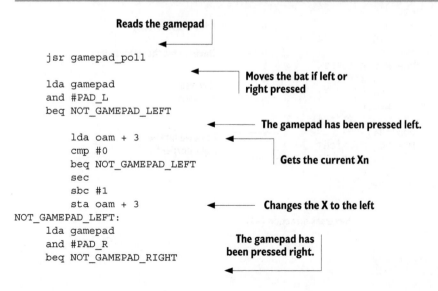

```
                   Reads the gamepad

    jsr gamepad_poll       ◄

    lda gamepad            ◄──────  Moves the bat if left or
    and #PAD_L                      right pressed
    beq NOT_GAMEPAD_LEFT

        lda oam + 3        ◄──────  The gamepad has been pressed left.
        cmp #0             ◄
        beq NOT_GAMEPAD_LEFT        Gets the current Xn
        sec
        sbc #1
        sta oam + 3        ◄──────  Changes the X to the left
NOT_GAMEPAD_LEFT:
    lda gamepad
    and #PAD_R                      The gamepad has
    beq NOT_GAMEPAD_RIGHT           been pressed right.
                           ◄
```

```
        lda oam + 3          ◄─────── Gets the current X
        cmp #248
        beq NOT_GAMEPAD_RIGHT
        clc
        adc #1
        sta oam + 3          ◄─────── Changes the X to the left
NOT_GAMEPAD_RIGHT:
```

Next we can adjust the position of the ball using our X and Y velocity values. Most importantly, we want to change the velocity value when the ball hits any of the sides.

The next listing adjusts the ball's Y position by our current Y velocity and then checks whether the ball has reached either the top or bottom boundaries; if so, it inverts our Y velocity. We repeat the same logic for X but check the left and right boundaries instead.

Listing 5.37   Moving our ball (example.s)

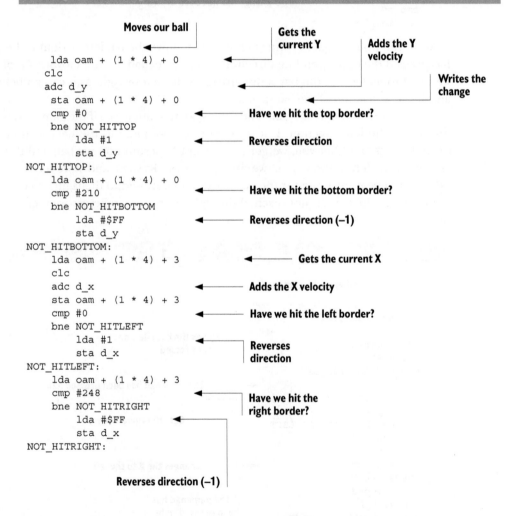

In the last part of our game loop, we are going to both force rendering so our changes are written to the screen and wait until they have been written, which will also have the effect of slowing down our example. If we didn't do this, both the ball and bat would move around the screen so quickly that you would barely be able to see them. This is a crude way of adjusting our timings, but it will suffice for getting our simple example going.

Listing 5.38   Ensuring our changes are rendered (example.s)

```
    lda #1
    sta nmi_ready          ◄─────┐   Ensures our changes are
    jmp mainloop                 │   rendered
.endproc
```

5.16   Compile script

Now that we have some code, along with our memory configuration file, we will need to create a batch/script file to compile and link our source code and produce the final NES ROM image that can be run in an emulator or on a real NES using an SD cartridge.

Listing 5.39   Windows compile script (compile.bat)

```
@del example.o
@del example.nes
@del example.map.txt
@del example.labels.txt
@del example.nes.ram.nl
@del example.nes.0.nl
@del example.nes.1.nl
@del example.nes.dbg
@echo.
@echo Compiling...
\cc65\bin\ca65 example.s -g -o example.o
@IF ERRORLEVEL 1 GOTO failure
@echo.
@echo Linking...
\cc65\bin\ld65 -o example.nes -C example.cfg example.o -m example.map.txt
[CA] Ln example.labels.txt --dbgfile example.nes.dbg
@IF ERRORLEVEL 1 GOTO failure
@echo.
@echo Success!
@GOTO endbuild
:failure
@echo.
@echo Build error!
:endbuild
```

The script needs to first make sure any output files from previous runs are cleared; then we compile our source files and finally link the outputs and produce the NES ROM image as the final output. This script assumes you are using the CC65 compiler and are on a computer running a Windows operating system. After saving your code, run this batch file from a command prompt using the command `.\compile.bat`, and you should see output like the following:

```
Compiling...

\cc65\bin\ca65 example.s -g -o example.o

Linking...

cc65\bin\ld65 -o example.nes -C example.cfg example.o -m example.map.txt
➥ -Ln example.labels.txt --dbgfile example.nes.dbg

Success!
```

Linux and macOS users can use a bash script like the following.

Listing 5.40   Linux and macOS bash compile script

```bash
#! /bin/bash

set -e

rm -f example.o
rm -f example.nes
rm -f example.map.txt
rm -f example.labels.txt
rm -f example.nes.*
rm -f example.dbg

echo Compiling...
ca65 example.s -g -o example.o

echo Linking...
ld65 -o example.nes -C example.cfg example.o -m example.map.txt
➥ -Ln example.labels.txt --dbgfile example.dbg
echo Success!
```

Run this in your Linux or macOS command terminal with `.\compile.sh`. This will produce several output files, but the main one we are interested in is the example.nes file. This is our finished ROM file that we can run either in an emulator or by loading it onto an SD card and an SD cartridge on a real NES console. Running it on an emulator, you should see a screen like that shown in figure 5.4.

Figure 5.4   Our example program running on an emulator

We have covered a lot of ground in this chapter, but most importantly, we have made a set of code that demonstrates how to get the NES setup ready for your main game logic.

Summary

- All NES programs need a memory configuration file and a matching compile script to build the final ROM application.
- You use the segments defined in the memory configuration file to control where each part of your code and data sections ends up in the final ROM cartridge and how it uses the NES's system memory.
- Your code needs to include a segment that identifies the final ROM as being valid for an NES system and indicates what features your cartridge will use.
- The final ROM applications that you build can be run on an emulator or by using an SD cartridge on real NES hardware.

Starting a game

This chapter covers

- Setting up our game project
- Creating a shared library
- Initializing the console
- How the NES displays background graphics
- Displaying the graphics on both our title screen and the main screen of the game

In this chapter, we are going to start making our game, called *Mega Blast*. This game is based on the Intellivision game *Astro Smash*, a simple space shooting game with our "hero" ship down at the bottom of the screen and various "enemies" dropping down toward the bottom of the screen (see figure 6.1).

Figure 6.1 *Astro Smash* **on the Intellivision**

Why a space shooting game, you may ask? This type of game has simple-to-understand gameplay elements. These will allow us to cover several common game mechanics, such as object movement, animation, and collision detection, and then move on to more advanced topics such as sound effects and music.

6.1 Setting up our game project

As we start to put together our game, we need to set up the various support files that will make up our project. This will allow us to build and test our code as we go. This will mostly be the code we have covered in the previous chapter with some modifications to suit our game, but we will go through the differences.

As a first step, create a new directory that will hold all the source files for the game. You are free to place this directory anywhere you like and call it whatever you like, but for the rest of this book, I will refer to a project directory called Megablast. We will create the following files in this chapter:

- *megablast.cfg*—NES memory configuration
- *compile.bat (or compile.sh)*—The script to compile the source code in an NES ROM
- *megablast.s*—The main assembly source code file of our game
- *neslib.s*—The assembly code that we can reuse in other projects
- *megablast.chr*—The patterns to use for the characters and sprites

6.1.1 Memory configuration

We will use the same memory configuration as we used in the previous chapter (see section 5.2), so create a file called megablast.cfg in the project directory Megablast with the following contents.

Listing 6.1 Megablast memory configuration

```
MEMORY {
    ZP:      start = $00,    size = $0100, type = rw, file = "";
    OAM:     start = $0200,  size = $0100, type = rw, file = "";
    RAM:     start = $0300,  size = $0500, type = rw, file = "";
    HDR:     start = $0000,  size = $0010, type = ro, file = %O, fill = yes,
➥ fillval = $00;
    PRG:     start = $8000,  size = $8000, type = ro, file = %O, fill = yes,
➥ fillval = $00;
    CHR:     start = $0000,  size = $2000, type = ro, file = %O, fill = yes,
➥ fillval = $00;
}
SEGMENTS {
    ZEROPAGE: load = ZP,   type = zp;
    OAM:      load = OAM, type = bss, align = $100;
    BSS:      load = RAM, type = bss;
    HEADER:   load = HDR, type = ro;
    CODE:     load = PRG, type = ro,   start = $8000;
    RODATA:   load = PRG, type = ro;
    VECTORS:  load = PRG, type = ro,   start = $FFFA;
    TILES:    load = CHR, type = ro;
}
```

6.1.2 Compiling script

We will use a similar build script (save as compile.bat or compile.sh, depending on your operating system) to what we used in the previous chapter, where we reference the project's new name (i.e., Megablast instead of example).

Listing 6.2 Windows compile script (compile.bat)

```
@del megablast.o
@del megablast.nes
@del megablast.map.txt
@del megablast.labels.txt
@del megablast.nes.ram.nl
@del megablast.nes.0.nl
@del megablast.nes.1.nl
@del *.dbg
@echo.
@echo Compiling...
\cc65\bin\ca65 megablast.s -g -o megablast.o
@IF ERRORLEVEL 1 GOTO failure
@echo.
@echo Linking...
\cc65\bin\ld65 -o megablast.nes -C megablast.cfg megablast.o -m
➥ megablast.map.txt -Ln megablast.labels.txt --dbgfile megablast.dbg
@IF ERRORLEVEL 1 GOTO failure
@echo.
@echo Success!
@GOTO endbuild
:failure
@echo.
```

```
@echo Build error!
:endbuild
```

Linux and macOS users can use a bash script like the following.

Listing 6.3 Linux and macOS bash compile script (compile.sh)

```
#! /bin/bash

set -e

rm -f megablast.o
rm -f megablast.nes
rm -f megablast.map.txt
rm -f megablast.labels.txt
rm -f megablast.nes.*
rm -f megablast.dbg

echo Compiling...
ca65 megablast.s -g -o megablast.o

echo Linking...
ld65 -o megablast.nes -C megablast.cfg megablast.o -m megablast.map.txt
➥-Ln megablast.labels.txt --dbgfile megablast.dbg
echo Success!
```

6.2 *Creating a code library*

Our game code will continue to grow as we work through it, so it is a good idea to start splitting the code into separate files. Separating out generic sections of code will allow you to reuse them across multiple projects and will reduce your development time on future titles.

The first step is to create a new file in the project directory called neslib.s. Then, to get started, let's add our list of NES control registers (see section 5.3) to improve the readability of our code. These don't change, so they are very well suited to being included in our NES function library.

Listing 6.4 Starting NES library by defining register values (neslib.s)

```
;****************************************************************
; neslib.s: NES Function Library
;****************************************************************

; Define PPU Registers
PPU_CONTROL = $2000
PPU_MASK = $2001
PPU_STATUS = $2002
PPU_SPRRAM_ADDRESS = $2003
PPU_SPRRAM_IO = $2004
```

PPU control register 1 (write)

PPU control register 2 (write)

PPU status register (read)

PPU SPR-RAM address register (write)

PPU SPR-RAM I/O register (write)

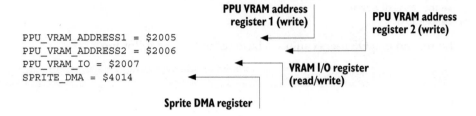

```
PPU_VRAM_ADDRESS1 = $2005
PPU_VRAM_ADDRESS2 = $2006
PPU_VRAM_IO = $2007
SPRITE_DMA = $4014
```

PPU VRAM address register 1 (write)

PPU VRAM address register 2 (write)

VRAM I/O register (read/write)

Sprite DMA register

Define PPU control register masks used for setting the PPU control registers:

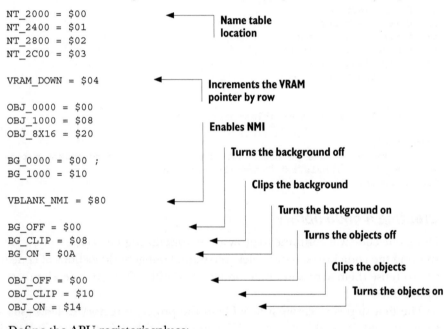

```
NT_2000 = $00
NT_2400 = $01
NT_2800 = $02
NT_2C00 = $03

VRAM_DOWN = $04

OBJ_0000 = $00
OBJ_1000 = $08
OBJ_8X16 = $20

BG_0000 = $00 ;
BG_1000 = $10

VBLANK_NMI = $80

BG_OFF = $00
BG_CLIP = $08
BG_ON = $0A

OBJ_OFF = $00
OBJ_CLIP = $10
OBJ_ON = $14
```

Name table location

Increments the VRAM pointer by row

Enables NMI

Turns the background off

Clips the background

Turns the background on

Turns the objects off

Clips the objects

Turns the objects on

Define the APU register's values:

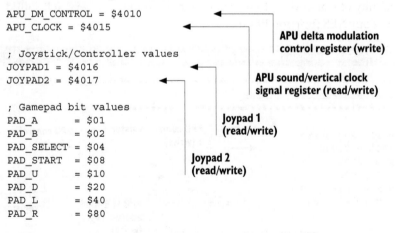

```
APU_DM_CONTROL = $4010
APU_CLOCK = $4015

; Joystick/Controller values
JOYPAD1 = $4016
JOYPAD2 = $4017

; Gamepad bit values
PAD_A       = $01
PAD_B       = $02
PAD_SELECT = $04
PAD_START  = $08
PAD_U       = $10
PAD_D       = $20
PAD_L       = $40
PAD_R       = $80

; Useful PPU memory addresses
```

APU delta modulation control register (write)

APU sound/vertical clock signal register (read/write)

Joypad 1 (read/write)

Joypad 2 (read/write)

```
NAME_TABLE_0_ADDRESS      = $2000
ATTRIBUTE_TABLE_0_ADDRESS     = $23C0
NAME_TABLE_1_ADDRESS      = $2400
ATTRIBUTE_TABLE_1_ADDRESS     = $27C0
```

As part of making a stand-alone library, it's important to also include any memory and references these functions need so the file can truly be used between projects without any local changes needed. This also shows how you can add to any memory segment using the .segment command. The useful functions we covered in the previous chapter would all be good candidates for our separate utility library, so let's start by adding the three PPU functions:

- The wait_frame function sets the nmi_update flag and waits for it to be reset at the end of the NMI routine.
- The ppu_update function waits until the next NMI and turns rendering on (if not already on), which will upload the OAM sprite data, palette settings, and any name table updates to the PPU.
- The ppu_off function waits until the next NMI turns rendering off so that it is now safe to write to the PPU directly via PPU_VRAM_IO.

Listing 6.5   Adding functions to the library (neslib.s)

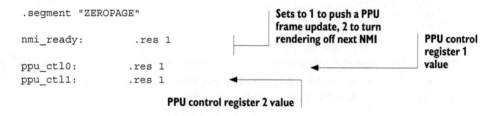

```
.segment "ZEROPAGE"

nmi_ready:          .res 1

ppu_ctl0:           .res 1
ppu_ctl1:           .res 1
```

Sets to 1 to push a PPU frame update, 2 to turn rendering off next NMI

PPU control register 1 value

PPU control register 2 value

The wait_frame function sets the nmi_update flag and waits for it to be reset at the end of the NMI routine:

```
.segment "CODE"

.proc wait_frame
    inc nmi_ready
@loop:
    lda nmi_ready
    bne @loop
    rts
.endproc
```

The ppu_update function waits until the next NMI and turns rendering on (if not already on), which will upload the OAM sprite data, palette settings, and any name table updates to the PPU:

```
.segment "CODE"

.proc ppu_update
    lda ppu_ctl0
    ora #VBLANK_NMI
    sta ppu_ctl0
    sta PPU_CONTROL
    lda ppu_ctl1
    ora #OBJ_ON|BG_ON
    sta ppu_ctl1
    jsr wait_frame
    rts
.endproc
```

The `ppu_off` function waits for the screen to be rendered and then turns rendering off so that it is now safe to write to the PPU directly without causing corruption:

```
.segment "CODE"

.proc ppu_off
    jsr wait_frame
    lda ppu_ctl0
    and #%01111111
    sta ppu_ctl0
    sta PPU_CONTROL
    lda ppu_ctl1
    and #%11100001
    sta ppu_ctl1
    sta PPU_MASK
    rts
.endproc
```

We can also reuse the other two useful functions—the `clear_nametable` and `poll_gamepad` functions—so let's add them to the same file. The `clear_nametable` function will clear the first PPU name table:

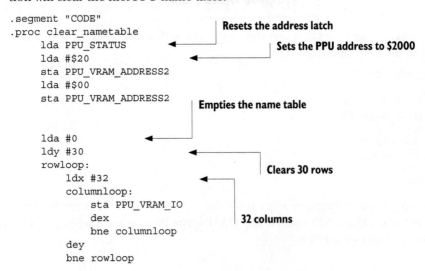

```
.segment "CODE"
.proc clear_nametable
    lda PPU_STATUS              Resets the address latch
    lda #$20                    Sets the PPU address to $2000
    sta PPU_VRAM_ADDRESS2
    lda #$00
    sta PPU_VRAM_ADDRESS2

    lda #0                      Empties the name table
    ldy #30
    rowloop:                    Clears 30 rows
        ldx #32
        columnloop:
            sta PPU_VRAM_IO     32 columns
            dex
            bne columnloop
        dey
        bne rowloop
```

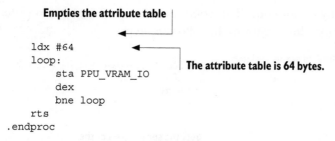

```
        ldx #64
        loop:
            sta PPU_VRAM_IO
            dex
            bne loop
        rts
    .endproc
```

The `gamepad_poll` function reads the gamepad state into the variable labeled gamepad. This only reads the first gamepad, and if DPCM samples are played, they can conflict with gamepad reading, which may give incorrect results:

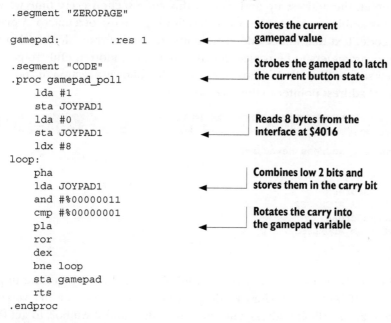

```
.segment "ZEROPAGE"

gamepad:            .res 1

.segment "CODE"
.proc gamepad_poll
    lda #1
    sta JOYPAD1
    lda #0
    sta JOYPAD1
    ldx #8
loop:
    pha
    lda JOYPAD1
    and #%00000011
    cmp #%00000001
    pla
    ror
    dex
    bne loop
    sta gamepad
    rts
.endproc
```

6.3 *Adding some macros*

We have created some functions to define named reusable sections of code that are called from our main code using the `jsr` (jump to subroutine) command. However, using these functions comes with a performance (speed) overhead, as the 6502 needs to

- Push the current program address onto the stack
- Call the location of the function
- Pop the program address off the stack and continue execution when the `rts` (return from subroutine) instruction is reached

There are some other code sequences we will be using again and again but that are not worth adding the overhead of calling a function, but it would be nice if we didn't have to add lines directly to our code. This could be setting the address to write to in the PPU's video memory, which requires the following steps:

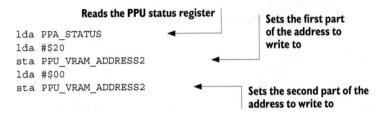

Reads the PPU status register

```
lda PPA_STATUS
lda #$20
sta PPU_VRAM_ADDRESS2
lda #$00
sta PPU_VRAM_ADDRESS2
```

Sets the first part of the address to write to

Sets the second part of the address to write to

This example sets the PPU memory address to $2000. We would like to not have to manually break the address up and type in this code section every time we want to use it. Our assembler comes to the rescue by allowing the use of a macro. A macro is a section of code/text that will be added to your code by the assembler but that smartly allows some parameters to be passed, making them even more useful. To get started, create a new source file called macros.s, and add the following section of code that will set the VRAM address pointer to the specified address.

Listing 6.6   Starting a macros file (macros.s)

```
.macro vram_set_address newaddress

    lda PPU_STATUS
    lda #>newaddress
    sta PPU_VRAM_ADDRESS2
    lda #<newaddress
    sta PPU_VRAM_ADDRESS2

.endmacro
```

This section of the code uses two special symbols (> and <) that get the upper and lower part of a 16-bit address. This uses the parameter newaddress, which you can pass to the macro as the 16-bit address, and then uses the > and < symbols to get the high and low bytes of the address. This allows our original code to be replaced with a single line call to the name of the macro along with the full address we want to set the PPU video address to:

```
vram_set_address $2000
```

When the assembler encounters this line, it will replace the line with the output from the macro, so the end code would end up as follows:

```
lda PPU_STATUS
lda #>$2000
sta PPU_VRAM_ADDRESS2
lda #<$2000
sta PPU_VRAM_ADDRESS2
```

Some of the functions we will be adding will need to work with a 16-bit address, which involves setting up a pair of zero-page memory locations with the address we want to use. Let's turn that into a macro in our macros.s file as follows by adding a macro to set the RAM address pointer to a specified address.

Listing 6.7   Assigning a 16-bit address (macros.s)

```
.macro assign_16i dest, value

    lda #<value
    sta dest+0
    lda #>value
    sta dest+1

.endmacro
```

This macro has two parameters. The first is the location in zero-page memory where we want to write the 16-bit address, and the second is the 16-bit address.

Listing 6.8   Clearing the VRAM address pointer (macros.s)

```
.macro vram_clear_address

    lda #0
    sta PPU_VRAM_ADDRESS2
    sta PPU_VRAM_ADDRESS2

.endmacro
```

This macro will clear the VRAM address pointer. To make the macros available in our code, we need to include the new source file, as it is something we will want to reuse, and add it to the neslib.s file after our existing ZEROPAGE section as follows (changes in bold).

Listing 6.9   Including macros.s in our library (neslib.s)

```
.segment "ZEROPAGE"

nmi_ready:        .res 1
```
◄──── **Set to 1 to push a PPU frame update, 2 to turn rendering off next NMI.**

```
.include "macros.s"
```
◄──── **Add this line.**

6.4   *Initializing the console*

Just as we covered in the previous chapter, we need to start our main application file by defining some standard values; adding the NES header, along with the other segments needed to make it valid as a NES title; and, of course, including the library functions we made earlier. To get started, create a new file in the project directory called mega-blast.s, and add the following sections to set up the standard memory segments we covered in the previous chapter and include our new library code.

Listing 6.10   Setting up NES header and memory segments (megablast.s)

```
.segment "HEADER"       0 = NROM          0 = horizontal
INES_MAPPER = 0                           mirroring, 1 =
INES_MIRROR = 0                           vertical mirroring    1 = battery-backed
INES_SRAM  = 0                                                  SRAM at $6000-7FFF

.byte 'N', 'E', 'S', $1A ; ID            16K PRG bank count
.byte $02
.byte $01
.byte INES_MIRROR | (INES_SRAM << 1) | ((INES_MAPPER & $f) << 4)
.byte (INES_mapper & %11110000)
.byte $0, $0, $0, $0, $0, $0, $0, $0     8K CHR bank count

                                          Padding
```

Import both the background and sprite character sets:

```
.segment "TILES"
.incbin "megablast.chr"
```

Define the NES interrupt vector addresses:

```
.segment "VECTORS"
.word nmi
.word reset
.word irq
```

Place any variable storage for any 6502 zero-page memory variables in this section of code:

```
.segment "ZEROPAGE"
```

Then we define the sprite OAM data area, which will be copied to VRAM in the NMI routine:

```
.segment "OAM"          Sprite OAM data
oam: .res 256
```

Next we make sure to include our library of useful NES functions:

```
.include "neslib.s"
                        Includes the contents of the
                        neslib.s file
```

Memory allocations that are larger segments are best placed in the normal RAM area:

```
.segment "BSS"
palette: .res 32
                        Current palette
                        buffer
```

We need to allow a location for any IRQ Clock Interrupt Routine to call, even if our cartridge configuration does not generate one:

```
.segment "CODE"
irq:
    rti
```

Our default palette table has 16 entries for tiles and 16 entries for sprites. Here we set the initial values we are going to use for each palette:

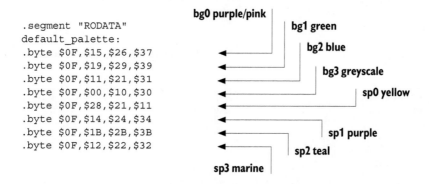

```
.segment "RODATA"
default_palette:
.byte $0F,$15,$26,$37
.byte $0F,$19,$29,$39
.byte $0F,$11,$21,$31
.byte $0F,$00,$10,$30
.byte $0F,$28,$21,$11
.byte $0F,$14,$24,$34
.byte $0F,$1B,$2B,$3B
.byte $0F,$12,$22,$32
```

Following this, we add the same `reset` function as our example in the last chapter, where we clear all memory and hardware control settings; then we patiently wait for the NES to be ready for further action.

Listing 6.11   Main application entry point called at startup or reset (megablast.s)

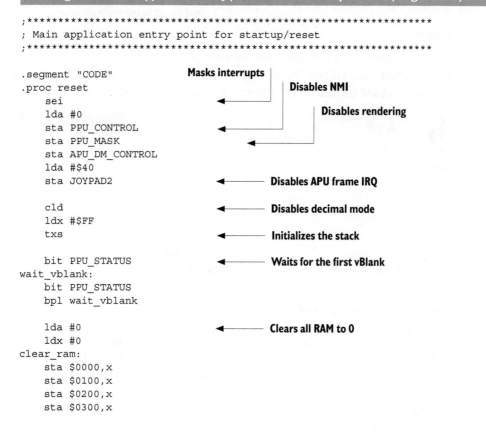

```
;****************************************************************
; Main application entry point for startup/reset
;****************************************************************

.segment "CODE"
.proc reset
    sei
    lda #0
    sta PPU_CONTROL
    sta PPU_MASK
    sta APU_DM_CONTROL
    lda #$40
    sta JOYPAD2

    cld
    ldx #$FF
    txs

    bit PPU_STATUS
wait_vblank:
    bit PPU_STATUS
    bpl wait_vblank

    lda #0
    ldx #0
clear_ram:
    sta $0000,x
    sta $0100,x
    sta $0200,x
    sta $0300,x
```

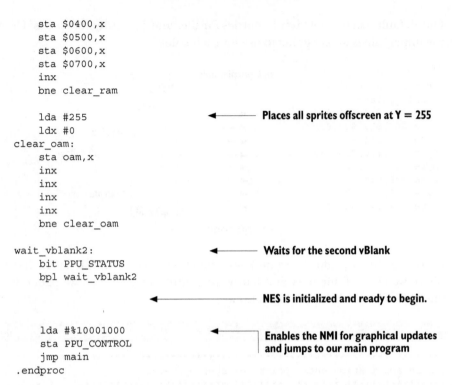

```
    sta $0400,x
    sta $0500,x
    sta $0600,x
    sta $0700,x
    inx
    bne clear_ram

    lda #255                    ◄──────── Places all sprites offscreen at Y = 255
    ldx #0
clear_oam:
    sta oam,x
    inx
    inx
    inx
    inx
    bne clear_oam

wait_vblank2:                   ◄──────── Waits for the second vBlank
    bit PPU_STATUS
    bpl wait_vblank2

                                ◄──────── NES is initialized and ready to begin.

    lda #%10001000              ◄──────── Enables the NMI for graphical updates
    sta PPU_CONTROL                       and jumps to our main program
    jmp main
.endproc
```

The next function we can keep like the example in the last chapter is the NMI routine that is called each vBlank. We will add some more code to this in later chapters. The NMI routine will be called every time a vBlank is generated.

Listing 6.12   NMI routine (megablast.s)

```
.segment "CODE"
.proc nmi
    pha                         ◄──────── Saves registers
    txa
    pha
    tya
    pha

    bit PPU_STATUS              ┐  Transfers sprite OAM
    lda #>oam                   ◄── data using DMA
    sta SPRITE_DMA              ┘
```

Transfer the current palette to the PPU:

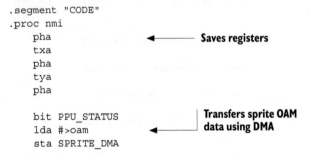

```
    vram_set_address $3F00      ◄──────┐
    ldx #0                      ◄─────┐│  Sets the PPU
@loop:                                └  address to $3F00
    lda palette, x
    sta PPU_VRAM_IO             ┐ Transfers the 32
    inx                         └ bytes to VRAM
    cpx #32
    bcc @loop
```

Write the current scroll and control register settings to the PPU:

```
lda #0
sta PPU_VRAM_ADDRESS1
sta PPU_VRAM_ADDRESS1
lda ppu_ctl0
sta PPU_CONTROL
lda ppu_ctl1
sta PPU_MASK
```

Flag that the PPU update has been completed:

```
ldx #0
stx nmi_ready
pla              ◄──── Restores registers
tay                    and returns
pla
tax
pla
rti
.endproc
```

The final bit of setup code we need to add is our main function that contains the rest of our setup and, most importantly, our game loop. When the main function starts, rendering is currently off, so we set up our initial palette values in the table that will be copied in the NMI routine and then set our game settings in the PPU control registers. For our example game, the background tile patterns will be stored in the first pattern table and the sprite patterns will be in the second pattern table. We set both the background and sprites to be turned on.

Listing 6.13   Main function (megablast.s)

```
.segment "CODE"

.proc main
    ;
    ldx #0              ◄──── Initializes the
paletteloop:                  palette table
    lda default_palette, x
    sta palette, x
    inx
    cpx #32
    bcc paletteloop

    lda #VBLANK_NMI|BG_0000|OBJ_1000   ◄──── Sets our game
        sta ppu_ctl0                         settings
        lda #BG_ON|OBJ_ON
        sta ppu_ctl1

    jsr ppu_update

mainloop:
    jmp mainloop
.endproc
```

6.5   *NES background graphics*

Now that we have the framework set up for our game, we can start creating the actual game itself. Let's look at how the NES displays background graphics, which we will use for both our title screen and the main screen in the game (see figure 6.2).

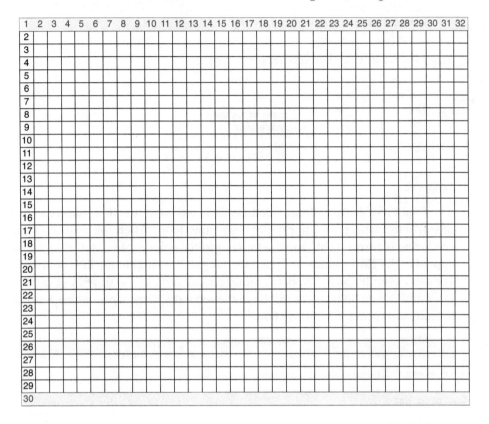

Figure 6.2   NES tile layout (top and bottom rows not visible on NTSC consoles—depending on type of display)

The background graphics displayed by the NES console are made up of 8 × 8 pixel tiles, 32 across the screen and 30 down the screen, and are stored in video memory as a name table. This means a total of 960 tiles make up a screen, at an end resolution of 256 × 240 pixels. An important point to note is there are some differences between NES consoles released in regions that use the NTSC (USA/Canada/Japan) television standard and those released in regions that use the PAL (Europe/Australia) television format. For NTSC NES consoles, the top and bottom rows of tiles will not be visible on the screen (i.e., they will be cut off, and the screen will be refreshed 60 times per second), whereas PAL NES consoles will display all 30 rows, but the screen will only be refreshed 50 times per second. When designing a game, you need to consider the different number of visible screen rows, adjust any timing driven by the screen refresh frequency, and ensure that all screen changes can occur within the vBlank period.

6.5.1 Tile name tables

The NES has enough video memory for two name tables, with each name table mirrored in one of four fixed layouts as shown in figure 6.3.

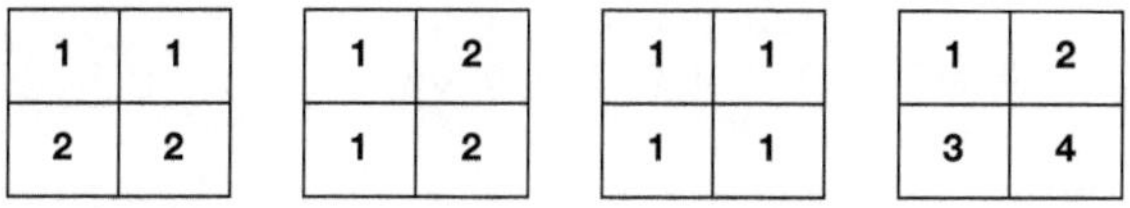

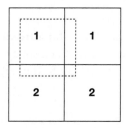

Figure 6.3   The four different name table layouts

The first two layouts mirror the two name tables either horizontally or vertically. The third layout has the first name table in all positions. There is a fourth one that has four separate name tables (i.e., not mirrored), but this does require the game cartridge to provide an additional 2 KB of video RAM. What is displayed on the screen is controlled by two scroll positions, overlayed on one of the previous tile layouts (see figure 6.4).

Figure 6.4   Visible screen area with scroll positions set

For the moment, we won't cover scrolling the screen, but note that with the two name tables (and no scrolling), it's easy to swap very quickly between one table and the other. This is useful for things like quickly showing a status screen without having to wait for it to be drawn.

6.5.2 Tile patterns

The shape of each of the tiles is determined by the data stored in a pattern table. Each row of 8 pixels is defined in this table by 2 bytes (16 bits), which allows four colors per pixel of each tile. For each pixel, the two source bits are combined to make a 2-bit number (i.e., giving the values 0, 1, 2, or 3; see figure 6.5).

Address	Value	Address	Value
$0000	0 0 0 1 0 0 0 0	$0008	0 0 0 0 0 0 0 0
	0 0 0 0 0 0 0 0		0 0 1 0 1 0 0 0
	0 1 0 0 0 1 0 0		0 1 0 0 0 1 0 0
	0 0 0 0 0 0 0 0		1 0 0 0 0 0 1 0
	1 1 1 1 1 1 1 0		0 0 0 0 0 0 0 0
	0 0 0 0 0 0 0 0		1 0 0 0 0 0 1 0
	(1) 0 0 0 0 0 1 0		(1) 0 0 0 0 0 1 0
$0007	0 0 0 0 0 0 0 0	$000F	0 0 0 0 0 0 0 0

Result

```
0 0 0 1 0 0 0 0
0 0 2 0 2 0 0 0
0 3 0 0 0 3 0 0
2 0 0 0 0 0 2 0
1 1 1 1 1 1 1 0
2 0 0 0 0 0 2 0
(3) 0 0 0 0 0 3 0
0 0 0 0 0 0 0 0
```

Figure 6.5   How the two pattern table bytes combine

When a tile is placed on the screen, it is combined with another 2-bit attribute value, which specifies which of the four palettes the tile is displayed with. Each square of four tiles (2 × 2 tiles) shares an attribute value (i.e., they all need to point to the same color palette; see figure 6.6).

Square 0		Square 1	
$0	$1	$4	$5
$2	$3	$6	$7
Square 2		Square 3	
$8	$9	$C	$D
$A	$B	$E	$F

Figure 6.6   An attribute value defines the palette for four 2 × 2 tile areas (i.e., 8 × 8 tiles).

There are four palette tables that are used for the background tiles (the sprites use their own separate palette tables; see figure 6.7). Each palette table has four color values, 0 to 3, with the 0 value being the shared background color; that is, only the first palette table 0 color will be used; the rest will be ignored. This gives you a total of 3 × 4 + 1 background color—13 colors that can be used on-screen at once. Each of the color values can be any of the available 52 colors.

00	01	02	03	04	05	06	07	08	09	0A	0B	0C	0D	0E	0E
10	11	12	13	14	15	16	17	18	19	1A	1B	1C	1D	1E	1F
20	21	22	23	24	25	26	27	28	29	2A	2B	2C	2D	2E	2F
30	31	32	33	34	35	36	37	38	39	3A	3B	3C	3D	3E	3F

Figure 6.7   NES color palette values

6.6   *Defining the tile set*

For our initial title screen, we will utilize a set of tile patterns where we have the letters of the alphabet (A–Z) in uppercase, starting from position 65 through to position 90 (see figure 6.8). This allows us to use normal text values in our code without having to translate between the characters and their positions in the tile pattern table.

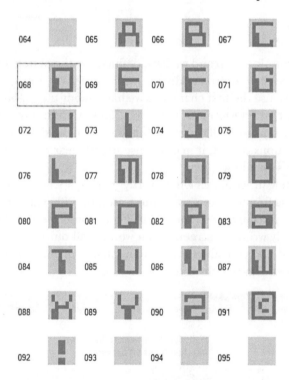

Figure 6.8   Uppercase alphabet patterns in our tile table

And we have our number digits (0–9), starting from position 48 through to 57. This also allows us to use normal text values in our code when specifying numbers (see figure 6.9).

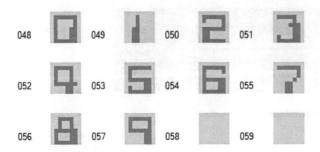

Figure 6.9   Numeric patterns in our tile table

You can use one of the tile editors in chapter 2 to make your tile set; these tile patterns are also already defined in the file megablast.chr included in the download pack for this chapter. We have already added the code to include this file in our game earlier in this chapter.

6.7   *Displaying the title screen*

Now that we have the NES console set up and we have defined the tile patterns we are going to use, we can use these tile patterns to display a title screen for our game. To keep things simple, we will just use the text characters we have in our tile set but introduce different sections of our palette to make the screen look more interesting. We could define the whole screen and copy all the bytes, but as most of the title screen will be blank with a couple of sections of text, it makes sense to just clear the screen and only write the sections of text separately.

Let's start by defining a new function, called `display_title_screen`, and add it to our megablast.s file. As this function needs to write to several PPU video memory locations, we will first wait for the current screen rendering to complete and then disable rendering so we can safely write the screen. Then we will call our useful `clear_nametable` function to clear the screen, and for the moment, we will end our function by waiting for our changes to be drawn to the screen.

Listing 6.14   **Starting the display title screen function (megablast.s)**

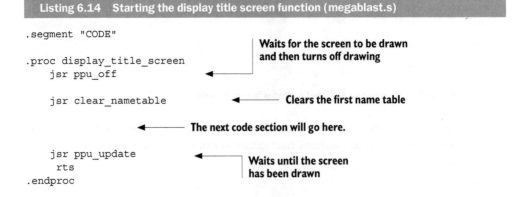

Now that we have the shell of the function started, we can add some code to write two sections of text to the screen. Writing a section of text to the screen is something that we will want to do a few times, so let's add another function called `write_text` to the end of our neslib.s library source file.

The function `write_text` writes a section of text to the screen, with the end of the text being indicated by a zero value. Before calling the function, the zero-page memory location labeled with `text_address` points to the text data to write to the screen, and the PPU address has been set.

Listing 6.15 Writing text to the screen (neslib.s)

```
.segment "ZEROPAGE"

text_address:      .res 2          ◄──────┐ Sets to the address of
                                            the text to write

.segment "CODE"
.proc write_text
    ldy #0                  Gets the byte at the
loop:                       current source address
    lda (text_address),y  ◄──────────────┐    Exits when we encounter a
    beq exit              ◄───────────────┘    zero in the text
    sta PPU_VRAM_IO       ◄──────┐ Writes the byte to
    iny                            video memory
    jmp loop
exit:
    rts
.endproc
```

Now, going back to our `display_title_screen` function earlier, we can add our code to call this new function and display two text strings on the screen: one to display the name of our game (Mega Blast) and another to display the Press Fire to Begin message.

To achieve this, we define our two text messages using the `.byte` instruction. As our tile characters match the normal ASCII character set, we can just have the text sequence we want in between double quotes, which the assembler will turn into a sequence of individual bytes. We end each text sequence with a 0, so we have a way for our `write_text` function to know that it has reached the end of the text. Before we call the `write_text` function, we need to set up two items:

- Set the location on the screen we want the text to be written to, which we do by setting the address of the first tile location on the screen:
  - We use our previously defined `NAME_TABLE_0_ADDRESS` value, which has the video memory address of the first tile on the screen.
  - To this we add 4 * 32, which will place our text on the fifth line of tiles down the screen.
  - And then we add the value 6 to start the text 7 tiles from the left-hand side of the screen.

- This calculation (which needs to be surrounded in brackets) is calculated by the assembler, and then the calculated address is what is stored in the game code. You could work out this value yourself, but using this method makes the code a lot more readable, and it is easier to change the row and column values without having to get out a calculator.
- We use the `vram_set_address` macro we defined earlier to set the video RAM address we want to write to.
  - Set the location in memory where our text sequence is stored using the macro we defined to set up a memory address in a zero-page address pointer.

To make it so that our title text can be displayed in a different color but still use the same tile patterns as the press play text, we change the attribute values for the tiles the title text is drawn to.

Every 8 bytes of the attribute table define the colors for 32 × 4 tiles. Our text is located on the fifth row, so we want to set the second 8-byte block of the attribute table. The value we use is 01, which means the color for the text will use the second of our tile palette sets. Whereas the first palette entries use three shades of purple/pink, the second set of entries uses three shades of green as follows:

- $19 = medium green
- $29 = light green
- $39 = pale green

Each of our alphabet and number font characters have all their pixels set as the first color entry, so each of the title text characters will be displayed using medium green ($19), and the Press Play text characters will be displayed using dark pink ($15).

Listing 6.16   Completing the display title screen function (megablast.s)

```
.segment "ZEROPAGE"

paddr: .res 2                       ◄──  16-bit address
                                         pointer
.segment "CODE"

title_text:
.byte "M E G A   B L A S T",0

press_play_text:
.byte "PRESS FIRE TO BEGIN",0

title_attributes:
.byte %00000101,%00000101,%00000101,%00000101
.byte %00000101,%00000101,%00000101,%00000101

.proc display_title_screen
    jsr ppu_off              ◄──  Waits for the screen to be
                                  drawn and then turn off
```

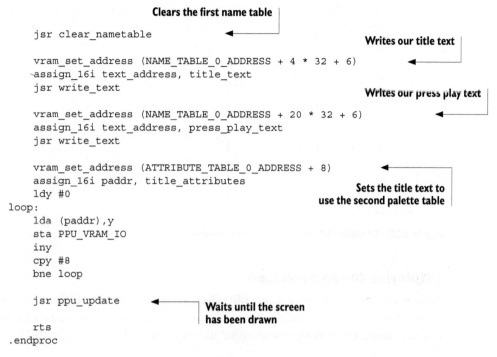

Clears the first name table

```
    jsr clear_nametable

    vram_set_address (NAME_TABLE_0_ADDRESS + 4 * 32 + 6)
    assign_16i text_address, title_text
    jsr write_text

    vram_set_address (NAME_TABLE_0_ADDRESS + 20 * 32 + 6)
    assign_16i text_address, press_play_text
    jsr write_text

    vram_set_address (ATTRIBUTE_TABLE_0_ADDRESS + 8)
    assign_16i paddr, title_attributes
    ldy #0
loop:
    lda (paddr),y
    sta PPU_VRAM_IO
    iny
    cpy #8
    bne loop

    jsr ppu_update

    rts
.endproc
```

Writes our title text

Writes our press play text

Sets the title text to use the second palette table

Waits until the screen has been drawn

Now that we have finished our function to draw our title screen, we need to call it from our main function. Add the code near the end of our main function as follows.

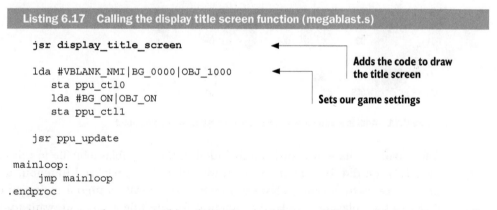

Listing 6.17 Calling the display title screen function (megablast.s)

```
    jsr display_title_screen

    lda #VBLANK_NMI|BG_0000|OBJ_1000
    sta ppu_ctl0
    lda #BG_ON|OBJ_ON
    sta ppu_ctl1

    jsr ppu_update

mainloop:
    jmp mainloop
.endproc
```

Adds the code to draw the title screen

Sets our game settings

At this stage, we have enough code to do a quick test and try out our progress so far in an emulator. Create the NES ROM using the `.\compile.bat` (or `.\compile.sh`) command (via a command line/terminal session). If you get any errors, check your code against the listings we have gone through or download the chapter code to compare. Once it compiles, open the NES ROM in an emulator, and you should get a screen like the one shown in figure 6.10.

Figure 6.10   **Example ROM running on an NES emulator**

6.8   *Displaying the game screen*

Before we finish this chapter, we will add a simple background layout for our main game screen. To make a nice mountainscape as a background and to be able to display our lives later, let's add some additional tile patterns as shown in figure 6.11.

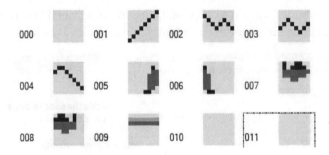

Figure 6.11   **Adding some more tile patterns for our game background**

These patterns have already been included in the megablast.chr file in this chapter's files. Like we did for our title screen, we will add a specialized function, `display_game_screen`, to our megablast.s source file, which will set up our main game screen ready to start playing. Unlike the function for the title screen, we want to output a section of tiles that are not text, so we will define a block of byte data and copy that to video RAM in one go.

Listing 6.18   **Displaying the main game screen (megablast.s)**

```
.segment "RODATA"

game_screen_mountain:
```

◄———   **Puts the data in our data segment of the ROM**

```
.byte 001,002,003,004,001,002,003,004,001,002,003,004,001,002,003,004
.byte 001,002,003,004,001,002,003,004,001,002,003,004,001,002,003,004

game_screen_scoreline:
.byte "SCORE 0000000"

.segment "CODE"
.proc display_game_screen
    jsr ppu_off

    jsr clear_nametable

    vram_set_address (NAME_TABLE_0_ADDRESS + 22 * 32)
    assign_16i paddr, game_screen_mountain
    ldy #0
loop:
    lda (paddr),y
    sta PPU_VRAM_IO
    iny
    cpy #32
    bne loop

    vram_set_address (NAME_TABLE_0_ADDRESS + 26 * 32)
    ldy #0
    lda #9
loop2:
    sta PPU_VRAM_IO
    iny
    cpy #32
    bne loop2

    assign_16i paddr, game_screen_scoreline
    ldy #0
loop3:
    lda (paddr),y
    sta PPU_VRAM_IO
    iny
    cpy #13
    bne loop3

    jsr ppu_update
    rts
.endproc
```

- **Waits for the screen to be drawn and then turn off drawing**
- **Clears the first name table**
- **Output mountain line**
- **Draws a baseline**
- **Tile number to repeat**
- **Outputs the score section on the next line**
- **Waits until the screen has been drawn**

Now we need to add a bit of code to our main function so that we wait for one of the buttons on the controller to be pressed and then call the display_game_screen function.

Listing 6.19 Waiting for a gamepad button (megablast.s)

```
    jsr display_title_screen

    ; set our game settings
    lda #VBLANK_NMI|BG_0000|OBJ_1000
        sta ppu_ctl0
```

- **Draws the title screen**

```
        lda #BG_ON|OBJ_ON
        sta ppu_ctl1

    jsr ppu_update

titleloop:
    jsr gamepad_poll
    lda gamepad
    and #PAD_A|PAD_B|PAD_START|PAD_SELECT
    beq titleloop

    jsr display_game_screen

  mainloop:
      jmp mainloop
```

Waits for a gamepad button to be pressed

Draws the game screen

Compile the game into an NES ROM, and load it into the emulator. You should be able to press one of the buttons on the gamepad, and the main game screen will be shown as in figure 6.12.

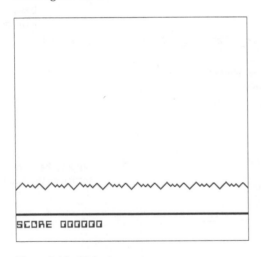

Figure 6.12   Main game screen

Summary

- The NES can display 13 different colors from a palette of 52 for background tiles on screen at one time.
- NES sprites have their own color palettes, allowing another 12 colors for a total of 25 colors on screen at one time.
- The NES can display background graphics made up of 32 × 24 tiles or a resolution of 256 × 224 pixels.
- NTSC NES consoles refresh the screen 60 times per second, but the top and bottom 8 pixels are not shown on the screen.

- PAL NES consoles refresh the screen 50 times per second, which can change the timing of your game.

- In addition to defining functions that can be called from your code, you can also create macros that will repeat common sections of code, saving typing and improving readability.

- You can use the same tile patterns in different places on the screen but point them to a different set of palette entries using the attribute table, which will make them use a different set of colors.

- Tile layouts can be set based on data ending in a terminating byte (e.g., 0), a fixed length of tile number values, or by repeating a tile multiple times.

Move and shoot

7

This chapter covers

- How the NES handles player objects (sprites)
- Defining patterns for our player and bullet
- Controlling the timing of movement and gameplay
- Getting objects moving on the screen
- Testing the gamepad direction and moving the player's ship left or right
- Testing the gamepad fire button and placing a bullet on the screen
- Moving the current player's bullet up the screen

In the last chapter, we drew our background graphics for both the title screen and the main game screen. In this chapter, we can look at how you display the player objects onscreen using special objects provided by the NES hardware called sprites.

We will use the sprites to display our player's ship onscreen and allow the player to move it left and right using the game controller. Then we will use another sprite to display the player's bullet that will be triggered by the player pressing one of the action buttons on the game controller and then moving up to the top of the screen.

7.1   NES sprites

Rather than having to draw moving objects on the screen by changing the individual pixels that are displayed, the NES PPU allows the programmer to define up to 64 objects, called *sprites*, that sit either in front of or behind the tile patterns. The NES PPU then determines what needs to be displayed and renders the final pattern to the screen.

You can think of the tile background and each of the sprite objects as sheets of stacked paper, with holes in them where they don't have any pixels set (see figure 7.1). The PPU will determine where each of the sprites and tile patterns overlap and then determine which pixel pattern to display. Both tiles and sprites will show any objects or tiles under them where they have blank pixels.

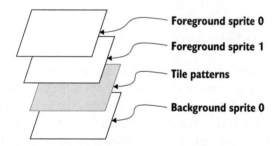

Foreground sprite 0

Foreground sprite 1

Tile patterns

Background sprite 0

Figure 7.1   Sprite and tile background layers

The sprites can be drawn in two different modes, with each sprite either being formed from one 8 × 8 pattern, making an 8 × 8 sprite, or from two 8 × 8 patterns, making an 8 × 16 sprite. The sprite pattern mode cannot be selected for each sprite individually, so all sprites are either 8 × 8 or 8 × 16 at any one time. To ensure the NES PPU can keep up with displaying the screen, it will not draw more than eight sprites in a horizontal row. Sprites are drawn in number order (i.e., from 0–63), making sprite 0 the one that is drawn first, followed by 1, 2, etc. until sprite 63.

Each sprite has 4 bytes allocated to it in the OAM table that control where it is placed onscreen, what tile pattern(s) it uses, whether it is displayed behind or in front of the tile background, whether to flip the pattern it uses horizontally and/or vertically, and what sprite palette to use (see table 7.1).

Table 7.1　The 4 bytes allocated to each sprite in the OAM

Byte	Details
0	Stores the y-coordinate of the top left of the sprite minus 1
1	The index number of the tile pattern to use in either the sprite table for 8 × 8 sprites or both the tile pattern and sprite tables for 8 × 16 sprites
	Note: There is only one index value available, so for 8 × 16 sprites, even sprites will get their two patterns from the first pattern table, and odd sprites will get their two patterns from the second pattern table.
2	Stores the attributes of the sprite, made up of the following sections:
	Bits 0–1—Indicates which of the four sprite color palette tables to use
	Bit 5—Indicates whether this sprite has priority over the background
	Bit 6—Indicates whether to flip the sprite pattern horizontally
	Bit 7—Indicates whether to flip the sprite pattern vertically
3	Stores the x-coordinate of the top left of the sprite minus 1

To change these values for each of the sprites, you can either write changes directly to sprite video RAM 1 byte at a time or transfer the entire OAM table (256 bytes long) with a single PPU command (sprite DMA transfer). In most cases, it is preferable to use the single PPU sprite DMA transfer command to copy the OAM data directly from CPU memory during the vBlank period, rather than writing the bytes individually, as it will save lots of CPU cycles that could be used for executing other changes to video memory that need to be completed during the vBlank period.

Like the background tile patterns, sprite patterns are made up of 2 bytes per 8-pixel row, thus allowing the values 0 to 3 for each pixel. A value of 0 will not be drawn and will show the sprite or background tile pixel underneath. Values 1 to 3 determine which of the entries from the sprite palette table allocated to the sprite (in byte 2) to use to display the pixel's color.

Thus, sprites allow another $3 \times 4 = 12$ colors to be displayed on the screen. These colors are in addition to the colors used by the tile background, allowing a potential 25 total colors displayed on the screen at once. Any palette table can reuse a color used by another palette table.

7.2　*Defining patterns for our player and bullet*

Let's define the patterns we need to draw the player's ship and the player's bullet. The player's ship is larger than 8 × 8 pixels, so we will need four patterns and thus four sprites to display it (see figure 7.2).

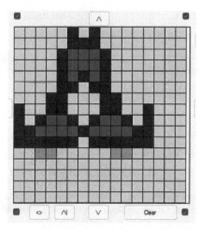

Figure 7.2   Player's ship made up of four 8 × 8 patterns

The player's laser is much smaller, so we only need a single sprite pattern and a single sprite to display it. You can use one of the pattern editors specified in chapter 2 to make some tiles like the ones in figure 7.3, or you can use the megablast.chr file provided as part of this chapter's files.

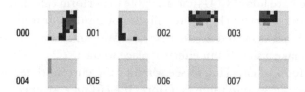

Figure 7.3   Player's ship and player's bullet patterns

7.3   *Controlling timing*

One very important part of creating any game is how the various components will move and react in relation to each other (i.e., the timing). For our game, we want the player's ship to move at a certain speed and the player's bullets to move at another speed; later, the various enemy objects will also move at different speeds.

The NES does not have a clock that provides the time of the day (unless one is provided in the game cartridge; see chapter 16). Most NES games use the vBlank interrupt, which occurs 60 times a second on NTSC NES consoles and 50 times a second on PAL NES consoles, to control timing.

Quite a lot of original NES titles do not consider the different number of vBlanks between the NTSC and PAL console models, so the same game will run at a different speed (~17% slower on PAL NES consoles). To simplify things, let's initially use the same logic for both NTSC and PAL consoles and introduce a simple time counter that we can use as the basis of our timing. The first thing to do is add two zero-page variables to our megablast.s source file—one to hold the current time value and another to store the value that the time value was the last time we checked, as follows.

Listing 7.1   Adding time variables (megablast.s)

```
.segment "ZEROPAGE"

time: .res 1
lasttime: .res 1
```

To update the time variable, we add a single line to our existing NMI function that increases the time counter by one each time the NMI function is called at every vBlank.

Listing 7.2   Incrementing the time counter in NMI routine (megablast.s)

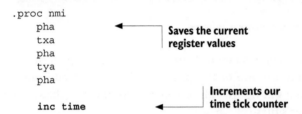

```
.proc nmi
     pha                    ◄─────┐  Saves the current
     txa                          │  register values
     pha
     tya
     pha
                                  ┌  Increments our
                                  │  time tick counter
     inc time              ◄──────┘
```

In our main game loop, we have lots of CPU time available to perform calculations, but we don't want them performed too quickly, so we will start by timing our initial actions based on whether a vBlank has occurred as our base tick. We can add more complex timings later, but this will make a simple but effective place to start.

Let's extend our main loop by checking to see whether the current time value has changed by comparing it to our second value that stores the last time we checked. This way, we will only proceed to the next section of code when the time value has changed.

Listing 7.3   Extending the main loop (megablast.s)

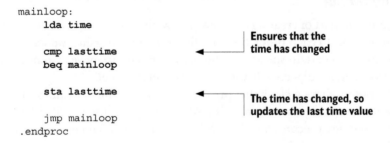

```
mainloop:
     lda time
                                      ┌  Ensures that the
     cmp lasttime         ◄───────────┘  time has changed
     beq mainloop

     sta lasttime         ◄───────┐  The time has changed, so
                                  └  updates the last time value
     jmp mainloop
.endproc
```

7.4   *Moving the player's ship*

Now that we have defined the shapes for the player's ship and bullet, we can start by placing the player's ship on our game screen and then add some logic that allows the player to move the ship left and right using the gamepad (see figure 7.4).

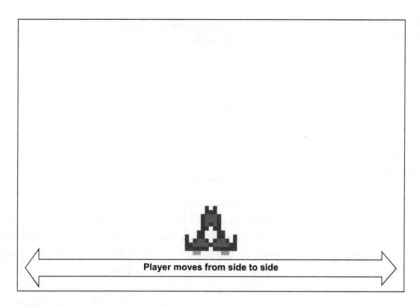

Figure 7.4 Player's ship movement

The first thing to do is place our player's ship on screen after the main game screen has been drawn. As the player's ship is made up of four 8 × 8 patterns, we need to set up four sprites. We could store these values in a set of bytes and copy them into the sprite table, but for our example here, we will set the values one by one to make it clearer what values control which parts of the sprites.

We first set the Y position of each of the four sprites used for the main ship and then the pattern number each part will use (patterns 0–3), clear their attributes to zero, and finally set each sprite's X position.

Listing 7.4 Placing the player's ship sprite on the screen (megablast.s)

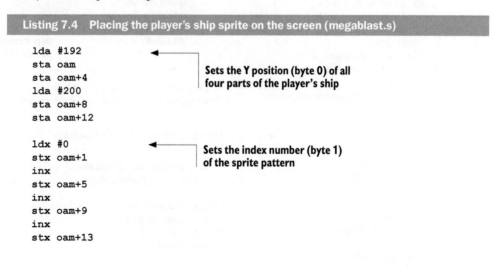

```
lda #192
sta oam
sta oam+4         ◀────────   Sets the Y position (byte 0) of all
lda #200                      four parts of the player's ship
sta oam+8
sta oam+12

ldx #0
stx oam+1         ◀────────   Sets the index number (byte 1)
inx                           of the sprite pattern
stx oam+5
inx
stx oam+9
inx
stx oam+13
```

```
lda #%00000000          ◄──┐   Sets the sprite attributes
sta oam+2                  │   (byte 2))
sta oam+6
sta oam+10
sta oam+14

lda #120                ◄──┐   Sets the X position (byte 3) of all
sta oam+3                  │   four parts of the player's ship
sta oam+11
lda #128
sta oam+7
sta oam+15              ──┐    Waits until the changes have
                          │    been displayed on the screen
jsr ppu_update          ◄─┘
```

Next, we will add a new function that will handle detecting the input from the player by reading the game controller and then adjusting the player's ship position depending on which direction the player has selected. In the routine, we first poll the gamepad to see what buttons are currently pressed; then we have two sections that handle detecting whether the player has pressed the gamepad's left or right buttons. If the player presses the left button, we first see if the player's ship is already on the left-hand side of the screen; if not, we adjust the player's X position and update the four sprites that make up the player's ship. If the player presses the right button, we first see if the player's ship is already on the right-hand side of the screen; if not, we adjust the player's X position and update the four sprites that make up the player's ship.

Listing 7.5   Handling player actions (megablast.s)

```
.segment "CODE"         ──   Checks the gamepad to see
                             what is currently selected

.proc player_actions         Sees if the bit
    jsr gamepad_poll    ◄──  indicating the
    lda gamepad              player has selected
    and #PAD_L          ◄──  left is set          Gets the current X
    beq not_gamepad_left                          position of the ship
        lda oam + 3     ◄──────────────
        cmp #0          ◄──  Checks to see if the player's ship is
        beq not_gamepad_left   already at the left-hand side of the screen

        sec
        sbc #2          ◄──  Subtracts 2 from the ship's X position

        sta oam + 3     ◄──  Updates the four sprites that
        sta oam + 11         make up the player's ship
        clc
        adc #8          ◄──  Adjusts the X position
        sta oam + 7          of the two sprites that
        sta oam + 15         form the right-hand
                             side of the ship
not_gamepad_left:
    lda gamepad
```

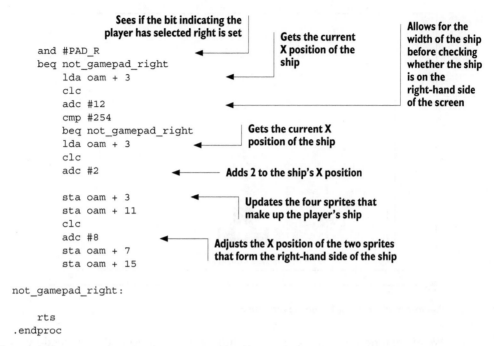

```
        and #PAD_R
        beq not_gamepad_right
            lda oam + 3
            clc
            adc #12
            cmp #254
            beq not_gamepad_right
            lda oam + 3
            clc
            adc #2

            sta oam + 3
            sta oam + 11
            clc
            adc #8
            sta oam + 7
            sta oam + 15

not_gamepad_right:

    rts
.endproc
```

Inside our adjusted main game loop, we need to add a call to our new function as follows:

```
        sta lasttime

        jsr player_actions

        jmp mainloop
.endproc
```

Let's check our progress so far in an emulator. Use the `.\compile.bat` (or `.\compile.sh`) command (via a command line/terminal session) to create our NES ROM file. If you get any errors, check your code against the listings we have gone through or download the chapter code to compare. Once the assembler has finished, run the megablast.nes ROM in an emulator, and you should see the player's ship and be able to move it left and right using the game controller.

7.5 *Firing a player bullet*

We now have the player's ship moving from side to side. Next we can add even more action by detecting when the player has pressed one of the action buttons, which causes a bullet to fire up the screen (see figure 7.5).

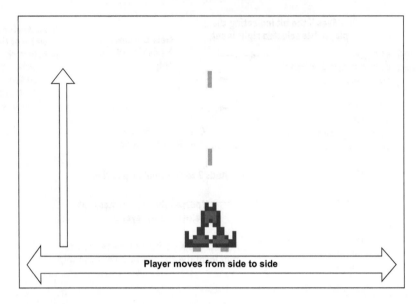

Figure 7.5   Player fires bullets up the screen

We will extend the `player_actions` function we started in the last section:

- Check to see if our player bullet is already on the screen.
- If not, then detect whether the A button on the controller has been pressed.
- Then place the bullet on the screen near the front of the player's ship.

Listing 7.6   Detecting whether the player has pressed the fire button (megablast.s)

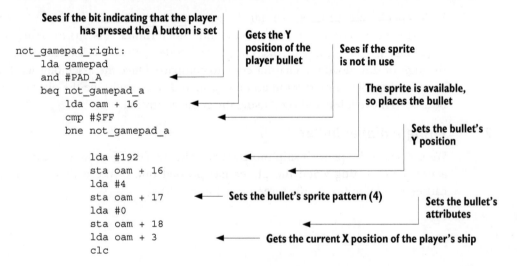

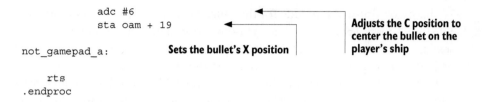

```
        adc #6
        sta oam + 19
```

Adjusts the C position to center the bullet on the player's ship

`not_gamepad_a:`   Sets the bullet's X position

```
    rts
.endproc
```

7.6 Moving the player's bullet

We have detected when the player has pressed the A button and placed the bullet sprite on the screen. Now we need to make the bullet move up the screen and disappear once it reaches the top (so it can be fired again).

Let's create a new function to handle moving the player bullet. If it is currently on screen, then we detect whether it has reached the top of the screen. We first get the bullet sprite's Y position. If it is equal to $ff, then it is not on the screen, and we can exit. Otherwise, we subtract 4 from the bullet's current Y position and update the sprite's Y position. If we get an overflow and end up going less than zero, then the bullet has gone off the top of the screen. We then set the bullet's Y position to $ff, which will remove it from the screen.

Listing 7.7   Moving the player's bullet (megablast.s)

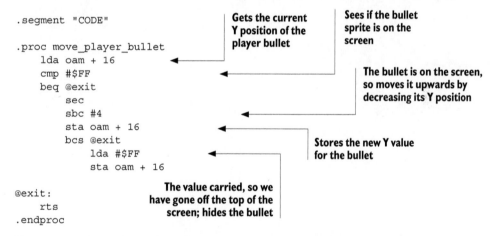

```
.segment "CODE"

.proc move_player_bullet
    lda oam + 16
    cmp #$FF
    beq @exit
        sec
        sbc #4
        sta oam + 16
        bcs @exit
            lda #$FF
            sta oam + 16

@exit:
    rts
.endproc
```

Gets the current Y position of the player bullet

Sees if the bullet sprite is on the screen

The bullet is on the screen, so moves it upwards by decreasing its Y position

Stores the new Y value for the bullet

The value carried, so we have gone off the top of the screen; hides the bullet

Now we need to call this function in our main loop as follows.

Listing 7.8   Adding the call to `move_player_bullet` (megablast.s)

```
    jsr player_actions
    jsr move_player_bullet

    jmp mainloop
.endproc
```

We have now finished our code for this chapter, so it's time to try it out in an emulator. Use the .\compile.bat (or .\compile.sh) command (via a command line/terminal session) to create our NES ROM file. If you get any errors, check your code against the listings we have gone through, or download the chapter code to compare.

Once the assembler has finished, run the megablast.nes ROM in an emulator. You should see the player's ship and be able to move it left and right using the game controller, and you should also be able to fire a bullet up the screen.

Summary

- The NES can display up to 64 sprites on the screen that can appear either in front of or behind the tile patterns.
- Only eight sprites will be displayed on the screen in any one horizontal line.
- Sprites have their own color palette tables, so they can be used to display an additional 12 colors on the screen (bringing the total to 25).
- Sprites can be either 8 × 8 using a single pattern or 8 × 16 using two patterns.
- Game timing is an important part of game design, and the programmer needs to remember that systems from different regions run at different speeds.

Enemy movement 8

This chapter covers

- Generating random numbers
- Adding the logic to generate and display new enemy asteroids
- Making the asteroids move down toward the player
- Removing asteroids as they reach the bottom of the screen

In previous chapters, we placed the player's ship on the screen and allowed the player to move the ship and fire bullets. Now we need to introduce some enemy objects for the player to shoot at and dodge away from as they move down the screen. Just like in the original *Astro Smash* game, our main enemy objects will be asteroids of various sizes that move down the screen at different speeds.

8.1   *Generating random numbers*

Before we start working directly on the enemy objects, it would be nice to have some randomness as to when and where any new enemies appear. To do this, we need to make a new function that will create random numbers that we can call at various places in our game.

It is not actually that easy to generate truly random numbers on any computer, but we can generate some random-like number sequences based on a formula. The key, especially with 8-bit computers, is to not have the formula take up too many of our precious CPU cycles. Here we will cover two random number routines, one based on shifting values and the other based on merging two linear number sequences together.

The randomness of both routines relies on a set of starting values, called seeds, but if these numbers are the same every time, you will get the same sequence of random numbers. So the seeds need to somehow be set randomly as well. This does pose a challenge, but a good way around this is to include a random value from an external factor. One of those external factors is the human player who starts the game. To start the game, the player needs to press a button on the game controller, and they will do so after a different amount of time from when the title screen is displayed. We can use this human randomness to create the seed values that our random number functions will use.

In the previous chapter, we introduced a time counter, but it was only 8 bits in size. To aid in ensuring that we have a complex-enough seed value for our random numbers, let's increase that to a 16-bit time counter. Find where we declare the time variable in our zero-page memory, and increase its size to 2 bytes as follows.

> **Listing 8.1   Increasing the size of our time variable (megablast.s)**

```
.segment "ZEROPAGE"

time: .res 2
lasttime: .res 1
```

Then, in our existing NMI routine, extend the code that increases the time counter to use the second 8-bit counter. When our first 8-bit counter reaches 255 and is incremented again, it will become zero. When our first 8-bit counter reaches zero, we increment our second 8-bit value. This makes our time counter a total of 16-bits as follows:

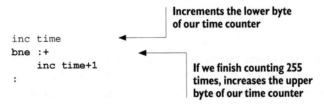

```
inc time                     ◄── Increments the lower byte
bne :+                           of our time counter
    inc time+1               ◄──
:                                If we finish counting 255
                                 times, increases the upper
                                 byte of our time counter
```

The best place to put our new random functions will be as part of our shared library, so add the following code to the neslib.s file. The first random function is a very simple shift-based random number generator.

Listing 8.2   Adding random functions to our shared library (neslib.s)

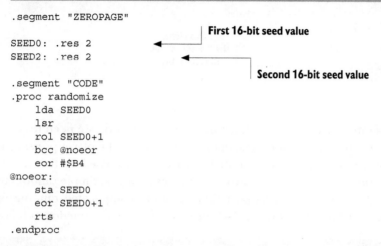

```
.segment "ZEROPAGE"

SEED0:  .res 2
SEED2:  .res 2

.segment "CODE"
.proc randomize
    lda SEED0
    lsr
    rol SEED0+1
    bcc @noeor
    eor #$B4
@noeor:
    sta SEED0
    eor SEED0+1
    rts
.endproc
```

First 16-bit seed value

Second 16-bit seed value

The second random function is a little bit more complicated but also generates a much better sequence of random numbers. It uses two linear frequency number series and merges them to form the final number. This is a software version of a concept called a Linear-Feedback Shift Register, for those wanting to research further.

It will return two 8-bit numbers, one in the A register (the low value) and the other in the Y register (the high value):

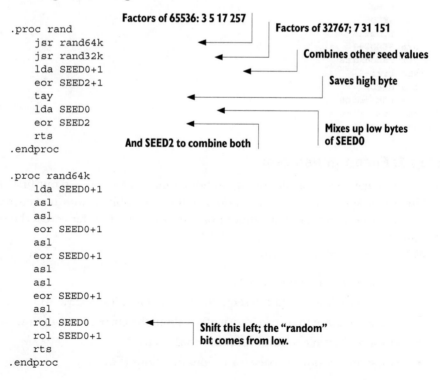

```
.proc rand
    jsr rand64k
    jsr rand32k
    lda SEED0+1
    eor SEED2+1
    tay
    lda SEED0
    eor SEED2
    rts
.endproc

.proc rand64k
    lda SEED0+1
    asl
    asl
    eor SEED0+1
    asl
    eor SEED0+1
    asl
    asl
    eor SEED0+1
    asl
    rol SEED0
    rol SEED0+1
    rts
.endproc
```

Factors of 65536: 3 5 17 257

Factors of 32767; 7 31 151

Combines other seed values

Saves high byte

Mixes up low bytes of SEED0

And SEED2 to combine both

Shift this left; the "random" bit comes from low.

```
.proc rand32k
    lda SEED2+1
    asl
    eor SEED2+1
    asl
    asl
    ror SEED2
    rol SEED2+1
    rts
.endproc
```

Shift this right;
the "random" bit
comes from high.

Most importantly, for the random functions to work properly, we need to set the seed values with a starting value. After we exit the title screen by the player pressing a button on the game controller, we set the initial two seed values based on the time that has passed since the title screen was shown. Then we use our first simple random function to generate the two other seed values that the more complicated random function uses. Add this code just after our `titleloop` label in our main function as follows.

> **Listing 8.3 Setting the random seed values (megablast.s)**

```
titleloop:
    jsr gamepad_poll
    lda gamepad
    and #PAD_A|PAD_B|PAD_START|PAD_SELECT
    beq titleloop

    lda time
    sta SEED0
    lda time+1
    sta SEED0+1
    jsr randomize
    sbc time+1
    sta SEED2
    jsr randomize
    sbc time
    sta SEED2+1
```

8.2 Step 1: Enemy generation

Now that we have a way of generating random numbers, we can add our first enemies, making them appear based on a random number, combined with our current difficulty level. We can use another random value to work out how far across the screen it will appear.

We will need some variables to

- Store our current level (`level`)
- Keep track of the animation sequence for our enemies (`animate`)
- Have some space to record information about the current enemies (`enemydata`)
- Have a cooldown countdown (`enemycooldown`)
- Have some temporary space for various functions (`temp`)

In our main game code file, megablast.s, locate the zero-page area, and add five new variables, called `level`, `animate`, `enemydata`, `enemycooldown`, and `temp`, as follows.

Listing 8.4   Adding five new variables (megablast.s)

```
.segment "ZEROPAGE"

time: .res 2
lasttime: .res 1
level: .res 1
animate: .res 1
enemydata: .res 20
enemycooldown: .res 1
temp: .res 10
```

Now we need a little bit more setup. We need to initialize our `level` and `enemydata` variables when a new game is started; a good spot is just before we display the game screen as follows:

```
lda #1              ◄─────── Setup ready for a new game
sta level
jsr setup_level

jsr display_game_screen    ◄──────┤ Draws the game screen
```

We haven't implemented the function `setup_level` mentioned in that section of code, so we had better add that to our megablast.s file and use it to clear the `enemydata` variable and set the initial value of the `enemycooldown` variable.

Listing 8.5   Function to set up for a new level (megablast.s)

```
.segment "CODE"

.proc setup_level
    lda #0          ◄─────── Clears enemy data
    ldx #0
@loop:
    sta enemydata,x
    inx
    cpx #20
    bne @loop
    lda #20         ◄──────┤ Sets an initial
    sta enemycooldown       │ enemy cooldown
    rts
.endproc
```

Now that we have everything set up, we can start on a new function called `spawn_enemies` that will set up and create new enemies on the screen, based on both the current level and a random value. At the start of the routine, we decrement our cooldown period, only proceeding to see if an enemy should appear if it is zero. This allows us to control how often new enemies appear. Later we will tie this to our level of difficulty.

Listing 8.6   Spawning enemies (megablast.s)

```
.segment "CODE"

.proc spawn_enemies
    ldx enemycooldown                          Decrements an enemy cool down
    dex
    stx enemycooldown
    cpx #0
    beq :+
        rts
    :
```

In our next section, we set a short cooldown so that if our random values do not lead to an enemy appearing, we will check again the next time this function is entered. We then call our random number function, and if the number returned is less than our current level multiplied by 4, we move on to create a new enemy on the screen:

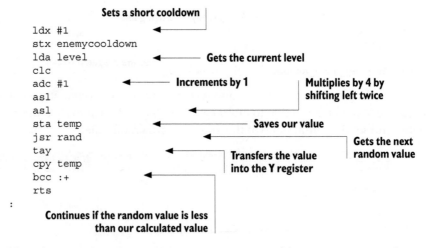

```
                        Sets a short cooldown
    ldx #1
    stx enemycooldown
    lda level                      Gets the current level
    clc
    adc #1              Increments by 1        Multiplies by 4 by
    asl                                        shifting left twice
    asl
    sta temp                       Saves our value
    jsr rand                                   Gets the next
    tay                            Transfers the value    random value
    cpy temp                       into the Y register
    bcc :+
    rts
:
        Continues if the random value is less
            than our calculated value
```

Now that we are going to create a new enemy object, we set a new, longer cooldown period so that another enemy won't be created straight away. Then we search our `enemydata` list for an enemy that is not currently on screen. If an enemy is not on the screen, then its position in our `enemydata` variable will be zero. If there are already 10 enemies on screen, we will exit without trying to create a new one:

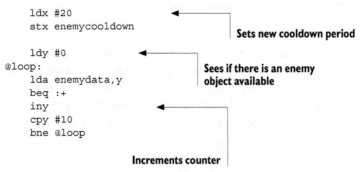

```
    ldx #20
    stx enemycooldown
                                   Sets new cooldown period
    ldy #0
@loop:                             Sees if there is an enemy
    lda enemydata,y                object available
    beq :+
    iny
    cpy #10
    bne @loop

        Increments counter
```

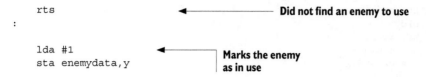

```
        rts
:

        lda #1
        sta enemydata,y
```

Once we know which enemy we want to use, we use its index number to calculate the first sprite it will use. As each enemy will use up to four sprites, and each sprite uses 4 bytes of OAM memory, we need to multiply our enemy number by 4 × 4 = 16 and then add 20 to skip the first five sprites that we use for both the player's ship and the player's bullet:

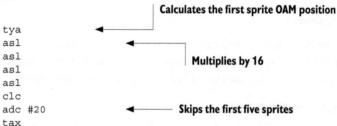

```
        tya
        asl
        asl
        asl
        asl
        clc
        adc #20
        tax
```

Now that we have worked out the first sprite that will make up our enemy, we can set up the 4 bytes needed to put each sprite on the screen, the Y position, sprite pattern number, sprite attributes, and finally the X position:

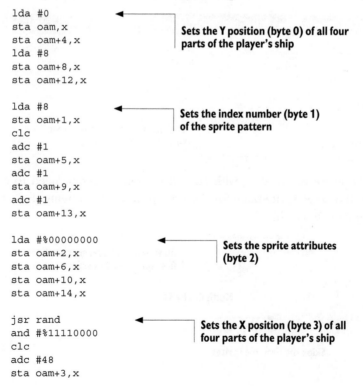

```
        lda #0
        sta oam,x
        sta oam+4,x
        lda #8
        sta oam+8,x
        sta oam+12,x

        lda #8
        sta oam+1,x
        clc
        adc #1
        sta oam+5,x
        adc #1
        sta oam+9,x
        adc #1
        sta oam+13,x

        lda #%00000000
        sta oam+2,x
        sta oam+6,x
        sta oam+10,x
        sta oam+14,x

        jsr rand
        and #%11110000
        clc
        adc #48
        sta oam+3,x
```

```
      sta oam+11,x
      clc
      adc #8
      sta oam+7,x
      sta oam+15,x

      rts
.endproc
```

With our new `spawn_enemies` function created, we need to call it from our game loop as follows:

```
      jsr player_actions
      jsr move_player_bullet
      jsr spawn_enemies
```

We have now created a `spawn enemies` function that will create a single type of enemy onscreen. For the moment, we only have one type of enemy appearing; in a later chapter, we will add more enemy types to add more variety to the gameplay.

8.3   *Step 2: Enemy movement*

Now that enemies can be created on screen, we need to add another function called `move_enemies` to make each active enemy move down the screen until it reaches the ground. At the start of our function, we initialize our loop counter and check the entry for the current enemy in our `enemydata` variable.

Listing 8.7   Moving enemies (megablast.s)

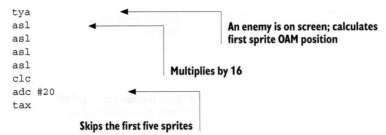

```
.segment "CODE"

.proc move_enemies

      ldy #0
      lda #0
@loop:
      lda enemydata,y          The enemy is not on the screen,
      beq @skip                so skips to the next one
```

Once we know we are dealing with an active enemy, we first need to calculate the position in the OAM sprite table for the first sprite for the enemy (like we did in the `spawn_enemies` function):

```
      tya
      asl                      An enemy is on screen; calculates
      asl                      first sprite OAM position
      asl
      asl
      clc                      Multiplies by 16
      adc #20
      tax

Skips the first five sprites
```

Now that we have our first sprite position, we can get its current Y position and make the enemy move down the screen by increasing it. Before continuing, we check whether the enemy has reached the bottom of the screen. If it has, we hide the four sprites and handle our next enemy:

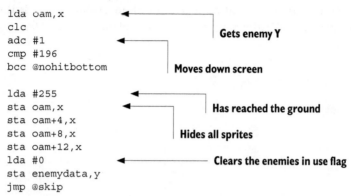

```
lda oam,x          ◀────              Gets enemy Y
clc
adc #1             ◀────
cmp #196
bcc @nohitbottom            Moves down screen

lda #255           ◀────
sta oam,x          ◀────              Has reached the ground
sta oam+4,x
sta oam+8,x                 Hides all sprites
sta oam+12,x
lda #0             ◀────────────      Clears the enemies in use flag
sta enemydata,y
jmp @skip
```

We have now adjusted the Y position of our enemy, so we can write the changes back to the four sprites that make up the enemy:

```
@nohitbottom:
    sta oam,x          ◀──────  Saves the new Y position
    sta oam+4,x
    clc
    adc #8
    sta oam+8,x
    sta oam+12,x
```

Finally, we have the end of our loop, where we increment our loop counter and exit if we have moved all relevant enemies:

```
@skip:
    iny                ◀──────  Goes to the next enemy
    cpy #10
    bne @loop

    rts
.endproc
```

We have now completed our function to move our enemies, so we can call it from our main game loop as follows.

Listing 8.8 Adding call to `move_enemies` inside our main loop (megablast.s)

```
jsr player_actions
jsr move_player_bullet
jsr spawn_enemies
jsr move_enemies
```

Our code is now ready to build using our compile script, and the ROM file can be tested in the NES emulator. From your terminal, execute our build command `.\compile.bat` (or `./compile.sh`) and correct any errors displayed by the assembler.

Upon starting the game, we should be able to move the player's ship from left to right, and enemy meteors should appear at random positions across the top of the screen. Then they will move down until they hit the planet's surface (see figure 8.1).

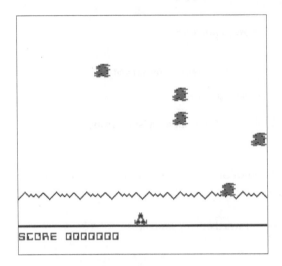

Figure 8.1   Our game so far

In chapter 12, we will improve on the simple enemy movement we have implemented and make it more advanced.

Summary

- It is hard to create truly random numbers on 8-bit systems, especially when trying not to take up too much computational time to generate them.
- To make random numbers even more random, it is a good idea to introduce an external random factor from the person playing the game.
- Breaking logic into different functions makes it easier to understand and modify later.
- The enemies in our game will be displayed using up to 4 separate sprites, so allowing for 10 enemies, we will use up to 40 of the 64 available sprites for enemies.
- We have only introduced one type of enemy so far; in later chapters, we will add more enemy types and make their movement more complex.

Collision detection

9

In most games, especially action games, there will be the need to know when one or more objects collide with each other. Because our sample game is a shoot-em-up, we need to know when our enemy objects encounter both our player and any player's bullets. At this stage, our enemies are all a fixed size, but later we will introduce more enemies of different sizes, so we will need to take this into account with the collision detection routine we will introduce in this chapter.

153

9.1   *Object collision detection*

Our first step is to write a function that works out whether two objects of different sizes have hit each other. How do we check whether two objects have hit each other? It requires a little bit of math. In the interest of simplicity and saving calculation time, instead of working out whether the actual pixels of two objects are touching, we treat all objects as rectangles. What we are trying to do is work out whether two rectangles intersect, as shown in figure 9.1.

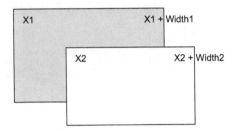

Figure 9.1   Detecting the collision of two objects

Let's break down the problem into some smaller steps, first by picking one direction. It doesn't matter whether we look at each object's X or Y positions (if we stick with one direction at a time).

The best way to ensure a collision detection routine takes up as little time as possible is to check for negative results first and immediately exit the routine. That way, as little code as possible is executed before determining that two objects are not touching (see figure 9.2).

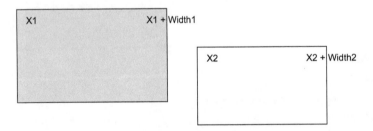

Figure 9.2 Second object to the right of the first object

Looking at figure 9.2, if the X coordinate of the second object (X2) is larger than or equal to the X coordinate of the first object (X1) plus its width (Width1), then the objects will not be touching. Thus, objects are not touching when (X1 + Width1) is smaller than (X2). For our next test, we reverse the object's positions as shown in figure 9.3.

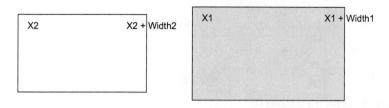

Figure 9.3 First object to the right of the second object

This time, the second object is to the left of the first object, and to test for that, we want to know if the X coordinate of the second object (X2) plus its width (Width2) is less than the X coordinate of the first object (X1). Thus, objects are not touching when (X2 + Width2) is smaller than (X1).

If we get past these two tests, then the two objects are intersecting on their X coordinates. We then repeat the same two tests with each object's Y coordinates but using heights instead of widths.

Now we need to turn these concepts into a function we can use in our game called collision_detection, which we can add to our neslib.s function library. The first thing we need to do is define the memory for the parameters that will be passed to the function. We need 8 bytes of memory to hold the X and Y positions of both objects and their respective width and heights.

Listing 9.1 Collision detection function (neslib.s)

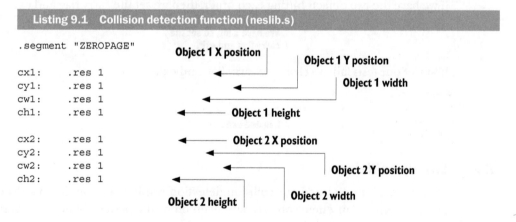

Now we can start the collision detection function and first test whether the two objects' X positions and widths coincide:

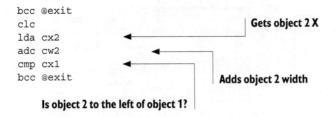

```
bcc @exit
clc
lda cx2
adc cw2
cmp cx1
bcc @exit
```

Once we know the two objects are intersecting on their X positions, we need to test again to see if they are intersecting on their Y positions:

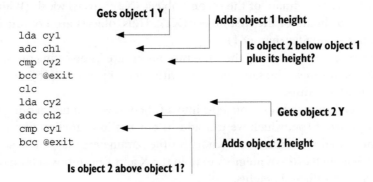

```
lda cy1
adc ch1
cmp cy2
bcc @exit
clc
lda cy2
adc ch2
cmp cy1
bcc @exit
```

If we have the two objects hitting each other, then we set the carry flag and exit:

```
sec
rts
```

If any of our tests fail, we clear the carry flag and exit:

```
@exit:
    clc
    rts
.endproc
```

9.2   Enemy collisions

Now that we have finished our collision detection routine, let's put it to use by detecting when any of our enemy objects have been hit by the player's bullet. The best place to put this code is inside our existing routine that moves the enemies. This way, we can use our existing loop and code that only moves them when they are on screen. Otherwise, we would need to loop through the enemies to check for any collisions, which would use up a lot of our processing time.

> TIP   On systems where we have limited processing resources, ensure that we are not wasting time looping through the same list more than once. Grouping several tests and actions into a single loop will be the most efficient use of processing time.

First, at the start of our `move_enemies` function, we add setting up the collision detection variables for the current position, width, and height of the player bullet. Doing it at the start of the routine, outside of the loop, means this code is only executed once. It's only a few commands and thus processor cycles, but if we did this inside the loop moving the enemies, that small number of cycles would be used every time through the loop. This is a good mindset to keep when making games for 8-bit systems.

Listing 9.2 Setup for collision detection of bullet with meteors (megablast.s)

```
.segment "CODE"

.proc move_enemies                    Gets bullet Y

    lda oam+16          ◄─────┘            Gets bullet X
    sta cy1
    lda oam+19          ◄─────────────┘
    sta cx1
    lda #4              ◄──────── The bullet is 4 pixels high.
    sta ch1
    lda #1              ◄──────── The bullet is 1 pixel wide.
    sta cw1
```

After checking whether the player bullet is on screen, we need to set up and call the collision detection routine for each enemy on screen. Following the code that stores the new position of the enemy, we first check that the player bullet is on screen:

```
@nohitbottom:
    sta oam,x           ◄──────── Saves the new Y position
    sta oam+4,x
    clc
    adc #8
    sta oam+8,x
    sta oam+12,x

    lda oam+16
    cmp #$FF            ◄──────── Is the player bullet on the screen?
    beq @skip
```

Next we get the X and Y positions of the enemy and store them in the parameters for the collision detection function. We also set the width and height hard-coded value for now (we will expand on this in chapter 12):

```
    lda oam,x           ◄──────── Gets the enemy Y position
    sta cy2
    lda oam+3,x         ◄──────── Gets the enemy X position
    sta cx2
    lda #14             ◄──────── Sets the enemy width and height
    sta cw2
    sta ch2
    jsr collision_test
    bcc @skip
```

In our final section of code, after the collision detection routine has returned with the carry flag set, our bullet has hit the enemy object. Now we remove the bullet and enemy from the screen and reset the enemy's data flag in the enemy data table:

```
        lda #$ff
        sta oam+16                          ◄─────────── Erases the player bullet
        sta oam,x                           ◄──────┐
        sta oam+4,x                                │ Erases the enemy
        sta oam+8,x
        sta oam+12,x
        lda #0                              ◄─────── Clears the enemy's data flag
        sta enemydata,y

@skip:
        iny                                 ◄─────── Goes to the next enemy
        cpy #10
        bne @loop

        rts
.endproc
```

Once you have added this section of code, you can use the `.\compile.bat` (or `.\compile.sh`) command in a terminal session to turn the code into an NES ROM file that you can try out in your chosen emulator (see figure 9.4). If you get any errors, check back through the code listings in the chapter for any typing mistakes. If you get stuck, see the complete code that is included in this chapter's support files.

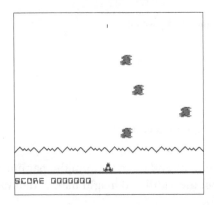

Figure 9.4 *Mega Blast* **running on an emulator**

Summary

- For collision detection on 8-bit systems, it's best to treat all objects as rectangles and work out whether they intersect.
- Ensuring that items that will be the same for each iteration of a loop are initialized before the loop will reduce the number of processor cycles needed.
- Placing collision detection inside an existing loop will decrease the number of processor cycles needed.

Keeping score

10

This chapter covers

- Recording the player's points score
- Adding to the player's score
- Subtracting from the player's score
- Displaying the score on screen
- Checking whether the player has beaten the current high score

In the previous chapter, we added collision detection to our game and detected when our player's bullet encountered any of our enemy objects. Next we will work through how we keep track of and change the player's score.

Our *Mega Blast* game is based on *Astro Smash* for the Intellivision, and in that game, you increase your score by shooting various enemies and decrease your score if any of the enemies make it to the ground. This is another good reason it makes a good example game, as we get to cover both increasing and decreasing the player's score.

10.1 *Keeping track of the player's score*

Every good shoot-em-up needs a way to keep track of the player's score, so we will need to allow our players to rack up points as they progress through the game's levels. We could just use some bytes of RAM and add values to them to increase the score, but we need to think about how the score will be displayed on the screen. We only have so much time in our NMI routine (where we write all changes to the screen), so to cut down the amount of time required to calculate and display the digits of the score, we will use a special method to keep track of each of the digits of the score.

We will use 3 bytes of RAM, and instead of storing the values 0 to 255 in each one, we will store the values 0 to 99 in each one. This will mean that each byte will store two digits of our score and allow for a zero to always be required to the right of the score; then we will be able to have scores from 0 to 9,999,990 points. This should be enough for our needs in this game, but if you have a higher-scoring game, you just need to add more bytes, each one adding two digits.

On a Z80 or normal 6502 processor, there are commands to help with this type of approach to storing numbers, called binary-coded decimal (BCD). Unfortunately, Nintendo removed these extra commands from the custom 6502 that is included in the NES to either save space or make the processor different enough so it didn't have to pay a license. Not to worry, as by doing some extra math when we add or remove our score values, we avoid using many cycles when we display the score on the screen.

To get started, let's add the storage space for the player's score and a place to store a flag so we know we have changed the score. It should be written to the screen. Find the zero-page memory section in our Megablast.s file, and add some storage space.

Listing 10.1   Adding storage for the player's score (Megablast.s)

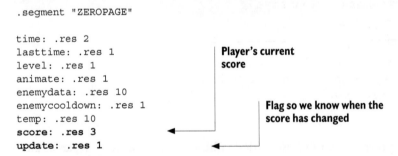

```
.segment "ZEROPAGE"

time: .res 2
lasttime: .res 1          Player's current
level: .res 1             score
animate: .res 1
enemydata: .res 10
enemycooldown: .res 1     Flag so we know when the
temp: .res 10             score has changed
score: .res 3
update: .res 1
```

It is very important to also ensure that the player's score is reset when a new game is being started. Now let's find where we get set up ready for a new game, display the game screen in our `main` function, and add the code to reset the player's score.

```
lda #1
sta level        ◄              Setup ready for a
jsr setup_level                 new game

lda #0           ◄              Resets the player's
sta score                       score
sta score+1
sta score+2
                                Draws the game screen
jsr display_game_screen  ◄
```

10.2   *Adding to the player's score*

Next we need to create a function that we can call to add to the player's score. As the 6502 is an 8-bit processor, we need to add the score to the lowest byte and then make sure we carry forward any overflow to the next byte in turn. So we add our increase in score to the lowest byte, and if there is an overflow past 99, we adjust the first byte, subtracting 100 and then adding 1 to our next highest byte. Repeat the carry forward again if you exceed 99 for that byte (see figure 10.1).

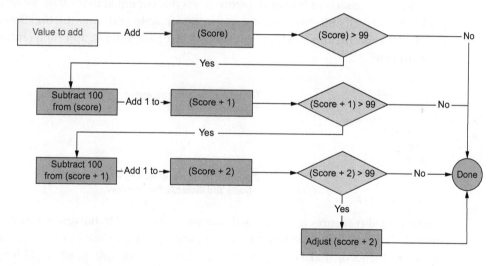

Figure 10.1   Adding to the player's score

This is made a bit more complicated with us only wanting to store the values 0 to 99 in each byte, but let's start by adding a new function called add_score to our Megablast.s file, where our first step is to add to the first byte of the score.

Listing 10.3   Adding a new function, `add_score` (Megablast.s)

```
.segment "CODE"
.proc add_score
    clc
    adc score
    sta score
    cmp #99
    bcc @skip
```

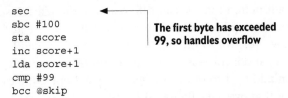

Adds the value in A to the
first byte of the score

If the value of the first byte of the score is less than or equal to 99, then we can jump to our `@skip` label. Otherwise, we need to move on and carry the overflow to our second byte by subtracting 100 from our first byte, updating it, and then adding 1 to our second byte:

```
    sec
    sbc #100
    sta score
    inc score+1
    lda score+1
    cmp #99
    bcc @skip
```

The first byte has exceeded
99, so handles overflow

If the value of the second byte of the score is less than or equal to 99, then we can jump to our `@skip` label. Otherwise, we need to move on again and carry the overflow to our third byte by subtracting 100 from our second byte, updating it, and then adding 1 to our third byte:

```
    sec
    sbc #100
    sta score+1
    inc score+2
    lda score+2
    cmp #99
    bcc @skip
    sec
    sbc #100
    sta score+2
```

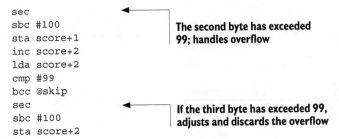

The second byte has exceeded
99; handles overflow

If the third byte has exceeded 99,
adjusts and discards the overflow

This section also ensures that the third byte never exceeds 99, but any overflow will be ignored. This will cause the score to roll around to zero but won't cause any strange display problems or make our game crash. This is an example of where older games could run into problems if the programmer did not account for the player achieving a score larger than the storage space they allocated. To finish off our function, we set our update flag so that we know that the score has changed and should be written to the screen in our NMI function:

```
@skip:
    lda #%000000001
    ora update
    sta update
    rts
.endproc
```

Sets the flag to write the
score to the screen

NOTE This function assumes that no more than 99 (990) will ever be added to the score at one time.

We can now use this new function to increase the player's score every time the player's bullet hits one of the enemy objects. Find the section of code in the move_enemies function where we have determined that the bullet has hit that enemy, and add a call to add_score with A set to a value of 2. This will add 20 to the player's score and signal that the score should be displayed on the screen.

Listing 10.4   Adding to the player's score when hitting an enemy (Megablast.s)

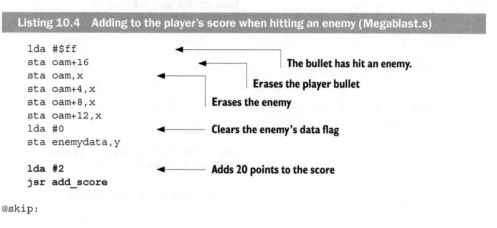

```
        lda #$ff
        sta oam+16                              The bullet has hit an enemy.
        sta oam,x
        sta oam+4,x                             Erases the player bullet
        sta oam+8,x                             Erases the enemy
        sta oam+12,x
        lda #0                                  Clears the enemy's data flag
        sta enemydata,y

        lda #2                                  Adds 20 points to the score
        jsr add_score

@skip:
```

10.3   Subtracting from the player's score

In our game *Mega Blast*, the player can also lose points if any of the enemies make it to the ground, so we also need to create a function that will allow us to subtract from the player's score (see figure 10.2). It is like the add routine in the last section, except our overflows are reversed.

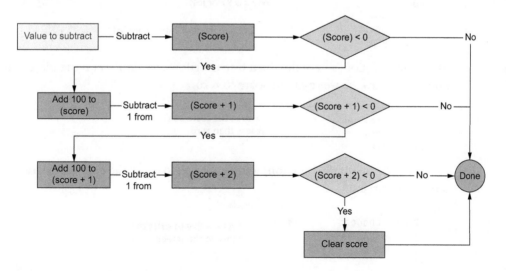

Figure 10.2   Subtracting from the player's score

Add a new function called `subtract_score` to our Megablast.s file, where the first step is to subtract from the first byte of the score.

Listing 10.5 Adding new function, `subtract_score` (Megablast.s)

```
.segment "CODE"
.proc subtract_score
    sta temp          ◄———— Saves our A value
    sec
    lda score         ┌──── Subtracts the value in A from
    sbc temp          ◄──── the first byte of the score
    sta score
    bcs @skip
```

If subtracting from the value of the first byte does not clear the carry flag (i.e., does not go past zero), then we can jump to our `@skip` label. Otherwise, we need to move on and carry the overflow to our second byte by adding 100 to our first byte, updating it, and then subtracting 1 from our second byte:

```
    clc               ┌──── The current value in A is negative, so adds
    adc #100          ◄──── to 100 to ensure we are 99 or less
    sta score
    dec score+1       ◄———— Decrements our second score byte
    bcs @skip
```

If decrementing the value of the second byte does not set the carry flag (i.e., does not go past zero), then we can jump to our `@skip` label. Otherwise, we need to move on again and carry the overflow to our third byte by first adding to our second byte, updating it, and then decrementing our third byte:

```
    clc               ◄────
    lda score+1       ┌──── Adds 100 to ensure
    adc #100          │     byte 2 is 99 or less
    sta score+1
    dec score+2       ◄———— Decrements our third score byte
    bcs @skip
```

In our next section, where the third byte overflows, we don't want the player's score to ever be negative, so we reset our score to zero:

```
    lda #0            ◄────
    sta score+2       ┌──── Ensures the score can't
    sta score+1       │     be less than zero
    sta score
```

Finally, we finish off the function, setting the flag to cause the changed score to be written on the screen:

```
@skip:
    lda #%00000001    ◄──── Sets the flag to write the
    ora update        │     score to the screen
    sta update
    rts
.endproc
```

NOTE This function also assumes that the player's score will never be reduced by more than 99 (990) at any one time.

We can now use this function to subtract from the player's score every time an enemy reaches the base of the screen. Find the section of code in the move_enemies function where we have determined that an enemy has reached the bottom of the screen, and add a call to subtract_score with a set to a value of 1. This will subtract 10 from the player's score and signal that the score should be displayed on the screen.

Listing 10.6   Subtracting from the score if an enemy reaches the bottom (Megablast.s)

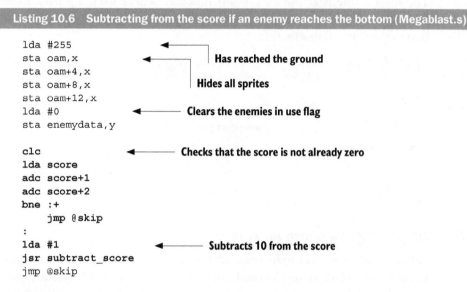

```
        lda #255
        sta oam,x                          Has reached the ground
        sta oam+4,x
        sta oam+8,x                        Hides all sprites
        sta oam+12,x
        lda #0                             Clears the enemies in use flag
        sta enemydata,y

        clc                                Checks that the score is not already zero
        lda score
        adc score+1
        adc score+2
        bne :+
            jmp @skip
        :
        lda #1                             Subtracts 10 from the score
        jsr subtract_score
        jmp @skip
```

@nohitbottom:

As we have added more code to our move_enemies function, we have a couple of branch instructions that now need to jump too far. The first change is near the start of the routine, where we skip the enemy if it is not in use. We need to use a JMP instruction instead of using the BEQ instruction. We do this by reversing the condition to BNE to jump over the next instruction, which we make a JMP instruction, jumping to the original destination.

Listing 10.7   Fixing branch at the start of move_enemies **(neslib.s)**

```
.proc move_enemies

        ; setup for collision detection of bullet with meteors    Gets bullet Y
        lda oam+16
        sta cy1
        lda oam+19                         Gets bullet X
        sta cx1
        lda #4                             The bullet is 4 pixels high.
        sta ch1
        lda #1                             The bullet is 1 pixel wide.
```

```
    sta cw1

    ldy #0
    lda #0
@loop:
    lda enemydata,y
    beq :+
        jmp @skip
    :
```

The second one is at the end of our function, where we jump back to do the next enemy. Once again, we need to reverse the condition so we can skip over a JMP instruction to the original destination.

Listing 10.8   Fixing branch at the end of `move_enemies` **(neslib.s)**

```
@skip:
    iny
    cpy #10        ◄─── Goes to the
    beq :+              next enemy
        jmp @loop
    :

    rts
.endproc
```

10.4   *Displaying the score on screen*

Now that we have a way to increase and decrease our score, we need to write the score to the screen. First, we need to add a new function to our neslib.s library, called `dec99_to_bytes`. This function will take a score counter byte (which contains 0–99) and split it into decimal tens and decimal ones digits so we can write the appropriate tile corresponding to each digit (0–9).

Listing 10.9   Adding `dec99_to_bytes` **function to our library (neslib.s)**

```
.segment "CODE"

.proc dec99_to_bytes
    ldx    #0
    cmp    #50        ◄─────── A = 0–99
    bcc    try20
    sbc    #50
    ldx    #5
    bne    try20

div20:
    inx
    inx
    sbc    #20

try20:
    cmp    #20
```

```
    bcs     div20

try10:
    cmp     #10
    bcc     @finished
    sbc     #10
    inx

@finished:

    rts
.endproc
```

This function uses a smart (and thus fast) division routine to divide the value in the A register by 10, placing the whole result in X as the decimal tens and the remainder in A as the decimal ones.

Now we move on to our function, which will output the current score to the screen. Add a new function called `display_score` to our Megablast.s source file. We start the function by setting the position on the screen where we want to draw the score and then call the `dec99_to_bytes` function we added earlier with the value from the third byte of the score. We write the two values in the X and A registers to our temp memory space.

> **Listing 10.10** Adding a `display_score` function (Megablast.s)

```
.segment "CODE"

.proc display_score
    vram_set_address (NAME_TABLE_0_ADDRESS + 27 * 32 + 6)

    lda score+2          ◀──────   Transforms each decimal
    jsr dec99_to_bytes             digit of the score
    stx temp
    sta temp+1
```

We then repeat the same call but use the value from the second byte of the score:

```
    lda score+1
    jsr dec99_to_bytes
    stx temp+2
    sta temp+3
```

Again, with the first byte of the score, this has our six score digits in left to right order in our "temp" memory space ready to write to the screen:

```
    lda score
    jsr dec99_to_bytes
    stx temp+4
    sta temp+5
```

We then loop through each of the 6 bytes we wrote to the temp memory space, adding 48 (the starting position of our 0–9 tile characters) and then writing it to the screen:

```
    ldx #0                          Writes the six characters
@loop:                              to the screen
    lda temp,x
    clc
    adc #48
    sta PPU_VRAM_IO
    inx
    cpx #6
    bne @loop
    lda #48                         Writes a trailing zero
    sta PPU_VRAM_IO

    vram_clear_address
    rts
.endproc
```

Now that we have finished our `display_score` routine, we can add it to our NMI routine, just after the place where we write our palette to video memory. We only call the `display_score` function if the update flag has been set.

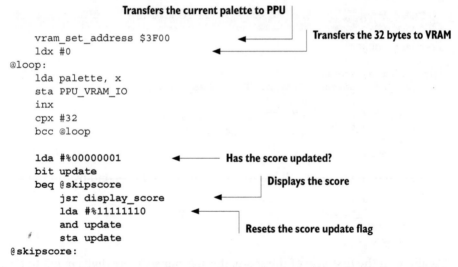

Listing 10.11　Calling the `display_score` function (Megablast.s)

```
                          Transfers the current palette to PPU
                                                      Transfers the 32 bytes to VRAM
    vram_set_address $3F00
    ldx #0
@loop:
    lda palette, x
    sta PPU_VRAM_IO
    inx
    cpx #32
    bcc @loop

    lda #%00000001              Has the score updated?
    bit update
    beq @skipscore              Displays the score
        jsr display_score
        lda #%11111110
        and update
        sta update              Resets the score update flag
@skipscore:
```

This would be a good time to test the code that we have so far. Open a terminal session, and run the `.\compile.bat` (or `.\compile.sh`) script. If you get any errors, check back through the listings for any typing errors or refer to the downloadable code for this chapter. Run the NES ROM in your emulator, and you should be able to shoot enemies, gaining points, but every time an enemy reaches the ground, the point total will decrease (see figure 10.3).

Figure 10.3   Score updating on screen

10.5   *Beating the high score*

To give our shoot-em-up game a goal for the player to strive for, we can add a high
score that the player can try to beat. We will need some space to hold the current high
score. We will only have one high score for this example to keep it simple, but this
could be expanded into a full high score table that allows the player to enter their ini-
tials at a later stage.

Find the zero-page section of our Megablast.s file, and add some space for our high
score. We only need the bytes for the high score itself, and we will reuse the update flag
we put in place for updating the score on the screen.

Listing 10.12   Adding storage space for our high score (Megablast.s)

```
.segment "ZEROPAGE"

time: .res 2
lasttime: .res 1
level: .res 1
animate: .res 1
enemydata: .res 10
enemycooldown: .res 1
temp: .res 10
score: .res 3
update: .res 1
highscore: .res 3
```

We need an initial high score to beat, so let's find our `main` function, and right at the
start, set the second byte of our high score to 1, which will make our initial high score
to beat 1,000.

Listing 10.13   Setting an initial high score (Megablast.s)

```
.segment "CODE"

.proc main

    lda #1          ◄────── Sets the initial high score to 1,000
    sta highscore+1
```

Next we can add a `display_highscore` function that will display the high score on the screen. This is almost identical to our `display_score` function, but the display location is different, and we are getting the score value from our high score variable.

For testing purposes, we will display the high score at the top of the main game screen. Later, we will move it to just display on the title screen once the player reaches game over.

Listing 10.14   Displaying the high score on the screen (Megablast.s)

```
.segment "CODE"

.proc display_highscore
    vram_set_address (NAME_TABLE_0_ADDRESS + 1 * 32 + 13)

    lda highscore+2     ◄────── Transforms each decimal
    jsr dec99_to_bytes         digit of the high score
    stx temp
    sta temp+1

    lda highscore+1
    jsr dec99_to_bytes
    stx temp+2
    sta temp+3

    lda highscore
    jsr dec99_to_bytes
    stx temp+4
    sta temp+5

    ldx #0              ◄────── Writes the six characters
@loop:                         to the screen
    lda temp,x
    clc
    adc #48
    sta PPU_VRAM_IO
    inx
    cpx #6
    bne @loop
    lda #48             ◄────── Writes a trailing zero
    sta PPU_VRAM_IO

    vram_clear_address
    rts
.endproc
```

This needs to be called from our NMI routine but should only write the changes to the screen when we have set the update flag. We used bit 0 as the flag for updating the score, and we will use bit 1 as the flag for updating the high score.

Listing 10.15 Calling `display_highscore` from our NMI routine (Megablast.s)

```
    lda #%00000001
    bit update            ◄────      Has the score updated?
    beq @skipscore
        jsr display_score     ◄────── Displays the score
        lda #%11111110    ◄────
        and update                   Resets the score
        sta update                   update flag
@skipscore:
    lda #%00000010    ◄────     Has the high score
    bit update                  been updated?
    beq @skiphighscore
        jsr display_highscore   ◄────
        lda #%11111101    ◄────      Displays the high
        and update                   score
        sta update
@skiphighscore:
        Resets the high score update flag
```

The last thing we need to do is extend our `add_score` function to check whether the player's score has exceeded the current high score. We do this by comparing each of the bytes of the score and the high score, exiting if the score is less than the high score value and updating the high score if the score is higher.

Listing 10.16 Updating the high score (Megablast.s)

```
@skip:
    lda #%000000001   ◄────     Sets a flag to write the
    ora update                  score to the screen
    sta update

    lda highscore+2
    cmp score+2
    bcc @highscore
    bne @nothighscore

    lda highscore+1
    cmp score+1
    bcc @highscore
    bne @nothighscore

    lda highscore
    cmp score
    bcs @nothighscore

@highscore:
    lda score
    sta highscore
    lda score+1
```

```
        sta highscore+1
        lda score+2
        sta highscore+2

        lda #%00000010          ◄────┐  Sets a flag to write the
        ora update                   │  high score to the screen
        sta update

@nothighscore:
        rts
.endproc
```

Once you have made these changes, you can open a terminal session and use the
`.\compile.bat` (or `./compile.sh`) script. If you get any errors, check back through
the listings for any typing errors or refer to the downloadable code for this chapter.
Run the NES ROM in your emulator, and you should now see the high score display at
the top of the screen once you have scored more than 1,000 points (see figure 10.4).

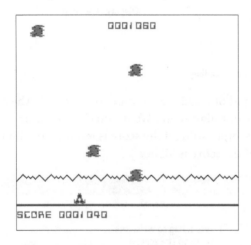

Figure 10.4   Beating the high score

Summary

- The binary-coded decimal instructions that are normally available on a 6502 processor are not available on the NES, so we use some math to add a similar calculation to our game.
- Our *Mega Blast* game makes a good example for scoring, as the player can both gain and lose points with the `add_score` and `subtract_score` functions.
- The add and subtract functions we created in this chapter are limited to an increase or decrease of at most 99 at any one time, as our overflow logic only allows for a single value to be carried.
- Using 3 bytes of memory and having a trailing zero, we can have player scores from 0 to 9,999,990.

Player collisions and lives

11

This chapter covers

- Handling the player's ship colliding with enemies
- Animating the player's death sequence
- Displaying the current player's lives
- Handling the game-over message

In this chapter, we are going to cover handling the collision between the player and enemies, animating the player's death sequence, and displaying the number of lives the player has remaining. Of course, once the player has run out of lives, we need to show Game Over on the screen, returning to our game intro screen so the player can view the high score and start a new game.

11.1 *Player collisions*

First, we need to detect if any of the enemy objects have hit the player's ship. The best place to do this is in our existing enemy object loop, located in the `move_enemies` function in our Megablast.s source file.

Before we add the collision detection, we will need a lives counter so we know how many lives the player has left, as well as a way to know when the player has died and keep track of the animation of the player's death sequence. Find our zero-page memory section, and add two new variables, called `lives` and `player_dead`.

Listing 11.1 Adding a memory variable for player's death sequence (Megablast.s)

```
.segment "ZEROPAGE"

time: .res 2
lasttime: .res 1
level: .res 1
animate: .res 1
enemydata: .res 10
enemycooldown: .res 1
temp: .res 10
score: .res 3
update: .res 1
highscore: .res 3
lives: .res 1
player_dead: .res 1
```

Keeps track of how many lives the player has

Is the player dead? If so, how far through the death animation sequence are we?

We also need to set the number of lives the player starts with, so find where we reset the player's score in the `main` function, and then add some code to set the player's lives to 5, reset our `player_dead` variable to zero, and then use another bit of our `update` flag so that we will know later when to write the changes to the screen.

Listing 11.2 Setting the player's starting lives and resetting the dead flag (Megablast.s)

```
    lda #0
    sta score
    sta score+1
    sta score+2

    lda #5
    sta lives
    lda #0
    sta player_dead

    jsr display_game_screen
```

Resets the player's score

Sets the player's starting lives

Resets our player_dead flag

Draws the game screen

We already have a section of code that detects when an enemy has reached the ground in which we remove the enemy from the screen and decrease the player's score. After this code, we add a section to see if the enemy object has hit the player. In the first part, we make sure the player is not currently dead; then we get the enemy's Y position, add on the enemy's height, and see if we are past the top of the player's ship.

Listing 11.3   Has an enemy hit the player? (Megablast.s)

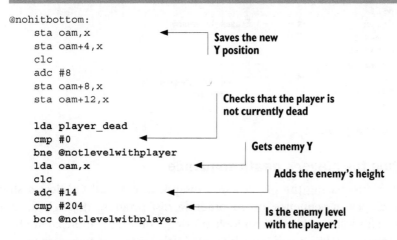

```
@nohitbottom:
    sta oam,x
    sta oam+4,x
    clc
    adc #8
    sta oam+8,x
    sta oam+12,x

    lda player_dead
    cmp #0
    bne @notlevelwithplayer
    lda oam,x
    clc
    adc #14
    cmp #204
    bcc @notlevelwithplayer
```

- Saves the new Y position
- Checks that the player is not currently dead
- Gets enemy Y
- Adds the enemy's height
- Is the enemy level with the player?

If the player is not already dead, and the enemy is at the player's Y position, we check whether the enemy is overlapping with the player's ship. If it is to the right or left of the player, we continue as normal; otherwise, we have hit the player:

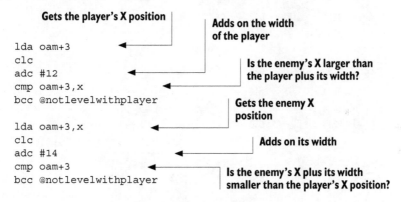

```
    lda oam+3
    clc
    adc #12
    cmp oam+3,x
    bcc @notlevelwithplayer

    lda oam+3,x
    clc
    adc #14
    cmp oam+3
    bcc @notlevelwithplayer
```

- Gets the player's X position
- Adds on the width of the player
- Is the enemy's X larger than the player plus its width?
- Gets the enemy X position
- Adds on its width
- Is the enemy's X plus its width smaller than the player's X position?

Now that we have determined that our enemy object has hit the player, we decrease the player's life counter, set the flag to redraw the player's lives onscreen, and mark the player as currently dead:

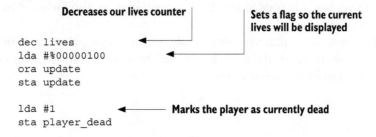

```
    dec lives
    lda #%00000100
    ora update
    sta update

    lda #1
    sta player_dead
```

- Decreases our lives counter
- Sets a flag so the current lives will be displayed
- Marks the player as currently dead

Finally, we need to erase our enemy object and clear its data flag:

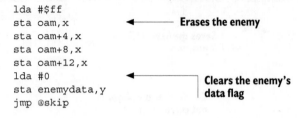

```
lda #$ff
sta oam,x          ◄──────── Erases the enemy
sta oam+4,x
sta oam+8,x
sta oam+12,x
lda #0             ◄────────┐ Clears the enemy's
sta enemydata,y             │ data flag
jmp @skip
```

```
@notlevelwithplayer:
```

11.2   Animating the player's death sequence

Rather than just having the player's ship disappear, it would be nice to show some different shapes in sequence or, in other words, progress through an animation sequence. This will also allow us to look at using a different color palette for the animation sequence, adding some much-needed color variation to our game (see figure 11.1).

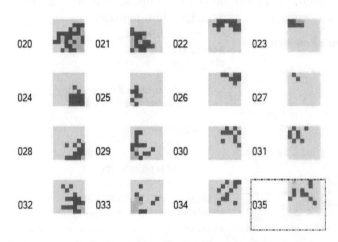

Figure 11.1   Adding player explosion shapes to sprite patterns

Using your tile editor of choice, add 16 new patterns, which will allow the player ship explosion to be shown in four stages. The new patterns are also included in the download files for this chapter.

With these new sprite patterns, we can add an alternative palette for our explosion shapes. Find the default_palette section at the end of our Megablast.s file, and change the second sprite palette entry.

Listing 11.4   Changing the second sprite palette entry (Megablast.s)

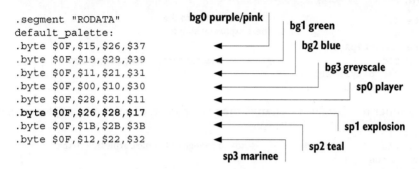

```
.segment "RODATA"
default_palette:
.byte $0F,$15,$26,$37
.byte $0F,$19,$29,$39
.byte $0F,$11,$21,$31
.byte $0F,$00,$10,$30
.byte $0F,$28,$21,$11
.byte $0F,$26,$28,$17
.byte $0F,$1B,$2B,$3B
.byte $0F,$12,$22,$32
```

bg0 purple/pink
bg1 green
bg2 blue
bg3 greyscale
sp0 player
sp1 explosion
sp2 teal
sp3 marinee

Before we start adding to our `player_actions` function, we will add a simple function that will set the patterns the player's ship is using. It takes the starting pattern in the X register, setting each of the four sprites used for the player's ship and, in turn, incrementing X after each one.

Listing 11.5   Setting player shape (Megablast.s)

```
.proc set_player_shape
    stx oam+1
    inx
    stx oam+5
    inx
    stx oam+9
    inx
    stx oam+13
    rts
.endproc
```

Now we can start adding to our `player_actions` function to handle when the player has died, progressing through four stages of animation and then resetting back to the start of the current level. In the first section, we check whether the player is dead, and if not, skip to our original code; otherwise, if the `player_dead` variable has a value of 1, then we set the player to its initial explosion shape.

Listing 11.6   Animating the player's death (Megablast.s)

```
.proc player_actions
    lda player_dead
    beq @continue
    cmp #1
    bne @notstep1
    ldx #20
    jsr set_player_shape
    lda #$00000001
    sta oam+2
    sta oam+6
    sta oam+10
    sta oam+14
    jmp @nextstep
```

The player is flagged as dead, so sets initial shape

Sets the first explosion pattern

Selects the second palette

We wait another four frames and then change the player's shape to the next explosion pattern:

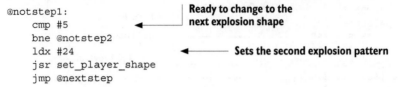

```
@notstep1:
    cmp #5
    bne @notstep2
    ldx #24
    jsr set_player_shape
    jmp @nextstep
```

Ready to change to the next explosion shape

Sets the second explosion pattern

After another five frames, we change the player's shape to the next explosion pattern:

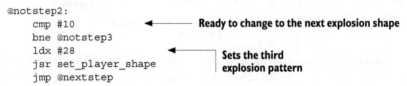

```
@notstep2:
    cmp #10
    bne @notstep3
    ldx #28
    jsr set_player_shape
    jmp @nextstep
```

Ready to change to the next explosion shape

Sets the third explosion pattern

Again, after another five frames, we change the player's shape to the next explosion pattern:

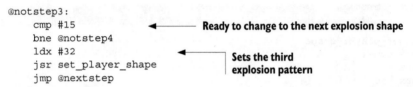

```
@notstep3:
    cmp #15
    bne @notstep4
    ldx #32
    jsr set_player_shape
    jmp @nextstep
```

Ready to change to the next explosion shape

Sets the third explosion pattern

After another five frames, we have now finished the animation of the player's death sequence. We need to check whether we have run out of lives and do our end-of-game sequence. We won't do it in this function; however, we will return and add some code to our main game loop shortly to handle Game Over:

The explosion is finished, so resets player

```
@notstep4:
    cmp #20
    bne @nextstep
    lda lives
    cmp #0
    bne @notgameover
    rts
.endproc
```

Checks for game over

Exits this function if out of lives

If the player still has lives left, we need to reset the game back to the start of the current level. Calling our setup_level function, redisplay the player, and clear the player_ dead flag. The final bit of code increments the player_dead flag so it progresses through the animation stages:

Resets all enemy objects

```
@notgameover:
    jsr setup_level
    jsr display_player
    lda #0
    sta player_dead
```

Displays the player at the starting position

Clears the player's dead flag

```
    rts
@nextstep:
    inc player_dead
    rts
@continue:
```

We need to expand on our `setup_level` function we created in an earlier chapter to ensure that any sprites that are being used for enemies are removed from the screen.

```
.segment "CODE"

.proc setup_level
    lda #0              ◄──────── Clears enemy data
    ldx #0
@loop:
    sta enemydata,x
    inx
    cpx #10
    bne @loop
    lda #20             ◄──────── Sets initial enemy cooldown
    sta enemycooldown

    lda #$ff            ◄──────── Hides all enemy sprites
    ldx #0
@loop2:
    sta oam+20,x
    inx
    cpx #160
    bne @loop2
    rts
.endproc
```

Additionally, we need to move the code we used to put the player on the screen to its own function called `display_player`.

```
.segment "CODE"

.proc display_player
    lda #196            ◄──────── Sets the Y position (byte 0) of all
    sta oam                       four parts of the player's ship
    sta oam+4
    lda #204
    sta oam+8
    sta oam+12

    ldx #0              ◄──────── Sets the index number (byte 1)
    stx oam+1                     of the sprite pattern
    inx
    stx oam+5
    inx
```

```
        stx oam+9
        inx
        stx oam+13

        lda #%00000000          ◄────┐   Sets the sprite
        sta oam+2                     │   attributes (byte 2)
        sta oam+6
        sta oam+10
        sta oam+14

        lda #120                ◄────┐   Sets the X position (byte 3) of all
        sta oam+3                    │   four parts of the player's ship
        sta oam+11
        lda #128
        sta oam+7
        sta oam+15
        rts
.endproc
```

Then replace the code after the call to `display_game_screen` in our `main` function with a call to this new function.

Listing 11.9   Simplifying game setup (Megablast.s)

```
    jsr display_game_screen

    jsr display_player          ◄──────   Displays the player's ship

    jsr ppu_update

mainloop:
```

11.3   *Handling game over*

Now we need to handle when the player has run out of lives, displaying a game-over message for a short time before returning to the title screen of the game. We add this to our main game loop, first displaying our game-over message, then waiting for a period before returning to the title screen.

Listing 11.10   Handling the game-over message (Megablast.s)

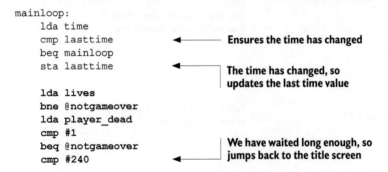

```
mainloop:
    lda time
    cmp lasttime                ◄────────   Ensures the time has changed
    beq mainloop
    sta lasttime                ◄────┐   The time has changed, so
                                     │   updates the last time value
    lda lives
    bne @notgameover
    lda player_dead
    cmp #1
    beq @notgameover            ◄────┐   We have waited long enough, so
    cmp #240                          │   jumps back to the title screen
```

```
      beq resetgame
      cmp #20
      bne @notgameoversetup
      lda #%00001000
      ora update
      sta update
@notgameoversetup:
      inc player_dead
      jmp mainloop
@notgameover:

      jsr player_actions
      jsr move_player_bullet
      jsr spawn_enemies
      jsr move_enemies

      jmp mainloop
```

◀── **Signals to display the game-over message**

We jump back to a new label called `resetgame` and add this just before we display the title screen earlier in our main function. To make sure all sprites are hidden, we also add a call to a new `clear_sprites` function:

```
resetgame:
    jsr clear_sprites

    jsr display_title_screen
```

◀── **Draws the title screen**

Add the `clear_sprites` function to our `neslib.s` function library file, as that will be useful in more programs going forward.

Listing 11.11 Adding a `clear_sprites` function to our library (neslib.s)

```
.segment "CODE"
.proc clear_sprites
    ;
    lda #255
    ldx #0
clear_oam:
    sta oam,x
    inx
    inx
    inx
    inx
    bne clear_oam

    rts
.endproc
```

◀── **Places all sprites offscreen at Y = 255**

To finish, we need to add the code to display our game-over message on the screen to our NMI function. This is triggered by the fourth bit of the update flag.

Listing 11.12   Modifying the NMI to display the game-over message (Megablast.s)

```
@skiphighscore:
    lda #%00001000          ◄──── Does the game-over message
    bit update                    need to be displayed?
    beq @skipgameover
        vram_set_address (NAME_TABLE_0_ADDRESS + 14 * 32 + 7)
        assign_16i text_address, gameovertext
        jsr write_text
        lda #%11110111      ◄──── Resets the game-over
        and update                message update flag
        sta update
@skipgameover:
```

We also need to add our `gameovertext` message; add it anywhere outside of one of the existing functions or with its own `.segment "CODE"` statement:

```
.segment "CODE"

gameovertext:
.byte " G A M E   O V E R",0
```

11.4   *Displaying the player's lives*

One more thing to round out this chapter: we need to display the current number of lives onscreen. To continue making our game more interesting and to increase our programming challenge, let's display the lives as physical player's ship images at the bottom of the screen; the number of ships displayed indicates the number of lives.

When we do this, we need to cater for later when we might score extra lives. There is only so much screen space to display the extra lives, so we will need to limit the number of ships displayed.

The display of the number of lives the player has remaining is made up of our ship pattern tiles, which take up two rows. To make it easier, our code will repeat a little here by drawing the two separate rows of tiles that make up the ships. We must make sure we clear out any previously displayed tiles after the correct number of tiles has been displayed. After first checking that the player has lives left, let's start by drawing the top row of ship tiles matching the number of lives remaining but also only displaying a maximum of eight lives.

Listing 11.13   Displaying player lives (Megablast.s)

```
.segment "CODE"
.proc display_lives
    vram_set_address (NAME_TABLE_0_ADDRESS + 27 * 32 + 14)
    ldx lives
    beq @skip              ◄──── No lives to display
    and #%00000111         ◄──── Limits to a max of 8
@loop:
    lda #5
    sta PPU_VRAM_IO
    lda #6
```

```
    sta PPU_VRAM_IO
    dex
    bne @loop
@skip:
```

At this point, we have displayed the top row of tiles, which show the number of lives remaining. Now we need to write blank tiles to ensure we remove any previous ship tiles:

```
    lda #8              ◄─────────     Blanks out the
    sec                      |         remainder of the row
    sbc lives
    bcc @skip2
    tax
    lda #0
@loop2:
    sta PPU_VRAM_IO
    sta PPU_VRAM_IO
    dex
    bne @loop2
@skip2:
```

That completes the top row of tiles. Now we simply repeat most of this code with two different tiles for the base and end our function:

```
    vram_set_address (NAME_TABLE_0_ADDRESS + 28 * 32 + 14)
    ldx lives
    beq @skip3              ◄──────┐
    and #%00000111      ◄───────┐  │
@loop3:                         |  |          No lives to display
    lda #7                      |
    sta PPU_VRAM_IO             |              Limits to a max of 8
    lda #8
    sta PPU_VRAM_IO
    dex
    bne @loop3
@skip3:

    lda #8              ◄─────────     Blanks out the
    sec                      |         remainder of the row
    sbc lives
    bcc @skip4
    tax
    lda #0
@loop4:
    sta PPU_VRAM_IO
    sta PPU_VRAM_IO
    dex
    bne @loop4
@skip4:

    rts
.endproc
```

We need to add the call to this display routine in two places: when setting up the game screen for the first time and in our NMI routine so that it will change the number of lives displayed. Let's add the call to our `display_lives` function to the end of the `display_game_screen` function.

Listing 11.14   Adding the call to display lives (Megablast.s)

```
    jsr display_lives

    jsr ppu_update          ◄────┐  Waits until the screen
    rts                          │  has been drawn
.endproc
```

Finally, we add the call to display lives in our NMI function when the change in the `update` flag is detected.

Listing 11.15   Calling display lives from the NMI function (Megablast.s)

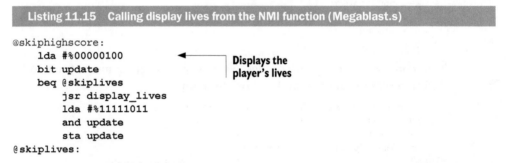

```
@skiphighscore:
    lda #%00000100          ◄────┐  Displays the
    bit update                   │  player's lives
    beq @skiplives
        jsr display_lives
        lda #%11111011
        and update
        sta update
@skiplives:
```

Now we can test all of our hard work. Open a terminal session, and use our `.\compile.bat` (or `.\compile.sh`) script to turn our code into an NES ROM and try it out in your emulator.

This now makes our game playable, with all the basic action elements in place. In the next chapter, we will add some enhancements to our enemy objects to make the game more challenging and fun.

Summary

- Using character animations made up of several frames can greatly enhance the visual appeal of your game.
- When we displayed our lives, we used a technique of repeating characters representing the player's ship, but we had to ensure that we never exceeded a maximum value. This underpins the need to always consider what checks you need to add so that a routine won't exceed physical bounds.
- We looked at using a second palette for the explosion animation of the player character, which allowed another three colors to be added to what was being displayed on the screen.
- Rather than just returning straight to the title screen when the player ran out of lives, we displayed a game-over message for a period of time first.

More enemies 12

This chapter covers
- Defining more enemy types
- Keeping track of enemies
- Changing our enemy spawn code
- Changing our enemy movement code
- Making our smart bomb smarter

So far, our game only has one type of enemy, which always moves the same way. This does not present much of a challenge to the gamer and does not make the game very interesting.

In this chapter, we are going to look at how we define different types of enemies in our game code. Then we will look at how we will keep track of more information about each enemy. This will allow us to make the enemies move in different directions and patterns and to introduce some animation.

12.1   *Defining more enemy types*

To make our game more interesting, let's add some more enemy types with different looks and behaviors. Our first step will be to include a table in our code that defines the different attributes each type of enemy will have. Some of these attributes could include

- The starting shape/pattern entry for the enemy
- The ending shape/pattern entry for the enemy, assuming that a sequence of patterns is in order in the pattern table so that we can animate through them
- The number of tile patterns and thus sprites that the enemy needs
- Any starting change in X (i.e., how fast it will move horizontally with the initial direction being randomly chosen)
- Any starting change in Y (i.e., how fast it will move vertically)
- The score the player will receive when the enemy is destroyed
- The width and height of the enemy object to use with our collision detection routine

Let's define the ones we will use in table 12.1.

Table 12.1   Enemy definition table

Name	Bytes	Description
Starting shape	1	Starting sprite pattern number
Ending shape	1	Ending sprite pattern number
Patterns	1	Number of patterns (and sprites) used
DX	1	Any starting change in X (we will randomly choose the direction)
DY	1	Any starting change in Y
Score	1	The value added to the player's score when destroyed
Width	1	The width of our enemy for collision detection
Height	1	The height of our enemy for collision detection
Attributes	1	The sprite attributes to use (mainly used here to set the palette)

Each enemy definition in our NES ROM will be 9 bytes long. For the moment, we will add a smaller meteor, a smart bomb, and a third type that will cater to animating the explosion of enemies, rather than them just disappearing.

Our NES sprite pattern table already includes 2 × 4 patterns for the large meteor and four patterns for the smart bomb, but we need to add some more patterns for the small meteor and a different explosion sequence to use with enemies. Using your chosen tile editing tool, add patterns like those shown in figure 12.1 (or you can use the updated Megablast.chr file included in the files for this chapter).

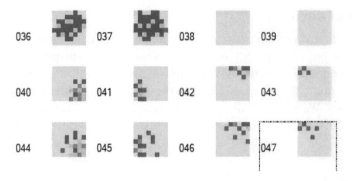

Figure 12.1   Adding small meteor and enemy explosion shapes

I have left two blank patterns after the small meteor in case we want to add more animation steps later. Now we can add the enemy source data table to our Megablast.s source file. We add a line for each enemy type we want to define and add a byte for each corresponding to table 12.1. To enable using different colors for the different enemies, we can modify our `default_palette` data for the last two sprite palettes as follows.

Listing 12.1   Changing our palette tables (megablast.s)

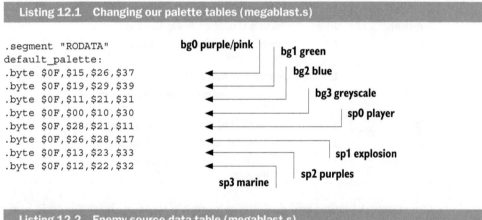

```
.segment "RODATA"
default_palette:
.byte $0F,$15,$26,$37
.byte $0F,$19,$29,$39
.byte $0F,$11,$21,$31
.byte $0F,$00,$10,$30
.byte $0F,$28,$21,$11
.byte $0F,$26,$28,$17
.byte $0F,$13,$23,$33
.byte $0F,$12,$22,$32
```

bg0 purple/pink
bg1 green
bg2 blue
bg3 greyscale
sp0 player
sp1 explosion
sp2 purples
sp3 marine

Listing 12.2   Enemy source data table (megablast.s)

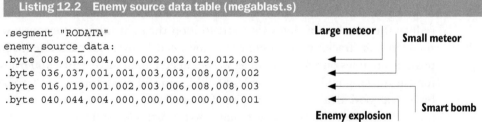

```
.segment "RODATA"
enemy_source_data:
.byte 008,012,004,000,002,002,012,012,003
.byte 036,037,001,001,003,003,008,007,002
.byte 016,019,001,002,003,006,008,008,003
.byte 040,044,004,000,000,000,000,000,001
```

Large meteor
Small meteor
Enemy explosion
Smart bomb

12.2   *Keeping track of enemies*

Our table in RAM for each of our active enemies needs to have the same information as in our ROM table but with an additional value so we know what type of enemy it is. This means we will need 10 bytes of RAM for each enemy. This will allow us to customize behavior based on the type of enemy in both our spawn and move enemy code sections (see table 12.2). We will copy all the information regarding each enemy to RAM when we create it; that way, we don't have to calculate and look up the information from the ROM table.

Table 12.2   Enemy tracking table

Name	Bytes	Description
Enemy type	1	Type of enemy
		1 = Large meteor
		2 = Small meteor
		3 = Smart bomb
		4 = Explosion
Starting shape	1	Starting sprite pattern number
Ending shape	1	Ending sprite pattern number
Patterns	1	Number of patterns (and sprites) used
DX	1	Any starting change in X (we will randomly choose the direction)
DY	1	Any starting change in Y
Score	1	The value added to the player's score when destroyed
Width	1	The width of our enemy for collision detection
Height	1	The height of our enemy for collision detection
Attributes	1	The sprite attributes to use (mainly used here to set the palette)

The enemy spawning and movement loops are some of the more code-heavy sections of our game, and with limited processing resources, we must consider how we can reduce the number of times we need to loop through things. Previously we used a single byte for tracking each enemy; we now need 10 bytes for each enemy. So with 10 possible enemies on screen at once, we will need a total of $10 \times 10 = 100$ bytes of RAM for our tracking table. Larger tables like this can still be stored in our zero-page area, but it is a good idea to keep zero-page for small variables that you are going to access more often, so let's move our larger table to normal RAM storage. Remove the current enemy data in our zero-page section.

Listing 12.3   Removing the current enemy data declaration (megablast.s)

```
.segment "ZEROPAGE"

time: .res 2
lasttime: .res 1
level: .res 1
animate: .res 1
enemydata: .res 10
enemycooldown: .res 1
temp: .res 10
score: .res 3
update: .res 1
highscore: .res 3
lives: .res 1
player_dead: .res 1
```

Go to the BSS memory section where we placed our current palette sections, and add our new larger enemy data buffer as follows.

Listing 12.4   Adding the enemy data buffer declaration to normal memory (megablast.s)

```
;****************************************************************
; Remainder of normal RAM area
;****************************************************************

.segment "BSS"
palette: .res 32        ◄──────┐  The current palette buffer
enemydata: .res 100            ◄────────┐
                                        │
                    Enemy tracking data │
```

Now that we have changed the size of our enemy data buffer, we need to change where we clear it at the start of a level in our `setup_level` function so that the new size of the buffer is cleared.

Listing 12.5   Clearing the larger enemy data buffer at the start of a level (megablast.s)

```
;****************************************************************
; Get setup for a new level
;****************************************************************
.segment "CODE"

.proc setup_level
    lda #0          ◄─────── Clears the enemy data
    ldx #0
@loop:
    sta enemydata,x
    inx                      Changes the loop to clear
    cpx #100        ◄──────┘ 100 bytes instead of 10
    bne @loop
    lda #20         ◄─────── Sets the initial enemy cooldown
    sta enemycooldown
```

```
        lda #$ff                    ◄─────── Hides all enemy sprites
        ldx #0
@loop2:
        sta oam+20,x
        inx
        cpx #160
        bne @loop2
        rts
.endproc
```

12.3 *Changing our enemy spawn code*

Now that we have worked out how we are going to define various enemies and keep track of them, we can rewrite our spawn_enemies routine to consider these changes. A lot of it will stay the same, but we will work our way through the routine again so that the changes are more obvious.

We start our routine the same way as before, checking that our cooldown period has passed before deciding to create new enemies. Then, once the cooldown period has expired, it stays set to zero, and we will perform our random check each time.

Listing 12.6   Start of our new spawn enemies function (megablast.s)

```
.segment "CODE"

.proc spawn_enemies
    ldx enemycooldown               ◄──┐
    dex                                 ├── Decrements the
    stx enemycooldown                   │   enemy cooldown
    cpx #0
    beq :+
        rts
    :
    ldx #1                          ◄─────── Sets a short cooldown
    stx enemycooldown
```

As before, we call our rand function and decide whether we should create a new enemy. We use the current difficulty level to increase the chance of enemies appearing.

Listing 12.7   Deciding if we should spawn a new enemy (megablast.s)

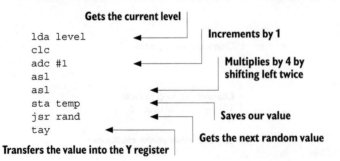

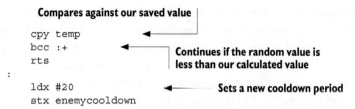

```
cpy temp          ◄──────      Compares against our saved value
bcc :+            ◄──────      Continues if the random value is
rts                            less than our calculated value
:

ldx #20           ◄──────      Sets a new cooldown period
stx enemycooldown
```

In our next section, we have the first change to our previous logic. We need to see if an enemy is available to use, so we loop through our 10 enemy data sets. But now that our enemy data is larger, we need to skip 10 bytes instead of 1.

We could just call `iny` 10 times to increment Y, or we could add 10 to Y. Either way is valid, and which way to choose comes down to a few factors:

- Available registers
- Speed of execution
- ROM space used (size of code)

As an exercise, let's go through the thought process of how we would choose how to create this code.

TIP Find a table of 6502 instruction timings here: https://www.nesdev.org/wiki/6502_cycle_times

One approach would be to call `iny` 10 times, which takes 10 bytes of ROM and takes $2 \times 10 = 20$ cycles to execute, so that doesn't sound too bad so far. Alternatively, another approach would use the A register: transfer Y into A (1 byte, 2 cycles), clear carry (1 byte, 2 cycles), add 10 to A (2 bytes, 2 cycles), and transfer A into Y (1 byte, 2 cycles). This code, even though it seems much more complicated, uses 5 bytes of ROM and only takes $2 + 2 + 2 = 6$ cycles to execute. So let's use this one in our code as follows.

Listing 12.8   Finding an enemy to use (megablast.s)

```
        ; now see if the is an enemy object available
        ldy #0            ◄──────
        sty temp                     Initializes our loop
@loop:                               counter
        lda enemydata,y
        beq :+
        tya               ◄──────
        clc                          Increases the
        adc #10                      counter by 10
        tay
        inc temp
        lda temp
        cmp #10
        bne @loop
        rts               ◄──────
:                                    Did not find an
                                     enemy to use
```

Now that we have determined that we will display an enemy and that we have an enemy available, we need to work out what type of enemy will appear. We have defined three types of enemies: a normal meteor, a small meteor, and a smart bomb. We probably don't want the same chance of each type of enemy; that is, we would want to see a variety of the two meteor sizes, with smart bombs appearing less frequently (as, by their very nature, they will be smarter and more of a challenge for the player).

Using our random function, we get a single random value, and if the lower 4 bits are set, we will display a smart bomb—this should result in a 1 in 16 chance. If we have not selected a smart bomb and then bit 0 is set, we will select a small meteor; otherwise, we will select a large meteor.

Listing 12.9   Determining the type of enemy to select (megablast.s)

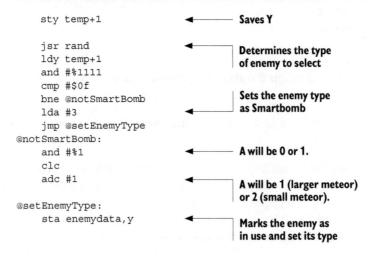

```
            sty temp+1              ◄────── Saves Y

            jsr rand                ◄
            ldy temp+1                      Determines the type
            and #%1111                      of enemy to select
            cmp #$0f
            bne @notSmartBomb               Sets the enemy type
            lda #3                  ◄────── as Smartbomb
            jmp @setEnemyType
@notSmartBomb:
            and #%1                 ◄────── A will be 0 or 1.
            clc
            adc #1                  ◄
                                            A will be 1 (larger meteor)
                                            or 2 (small meteor).
@setEnemyType:
            sta enemydata,y         ◄
                                            Marks the enemy as
                                            in use and set its type
```

Now that we have selected the type of enemy, we need to copy its data from our ROM table into our RAM enemy data table.

Listing 12.10   Copying the enemy data (megablast.s)

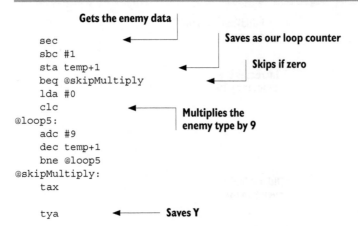

```
        Gets the enemy data
                                            Saves as our loop counter
            sec                     ◄
            sbc #1
            sta temp+1              ◄        Skips if zero
            beq @skipMultiply       ◄
            lda #0
            clc                     ◄
@loop5:                                     Multiplies the
            adc #9                          enemy type by 9
            dec temp+1
            bne @loop5
@skipMultiply:
            tax

            tya                     ◄────── Saves Y
```

```
        pha

        iny

        lda #9                              Now copies 8 bytes
        sta temp+1
@loop4:
        lda enemy_source_data,x
        sta enemydata,y
        inx
        iny
        dec temp+1
        bne @loop4

        pla                                 Restores Y
        tay
        lda enemydata,y
```

Next we calculate the starting position in the OAM sprite table of the sprite we want to use.

Listing 12.11   Calculating the sprite OAM position (megablast.s)

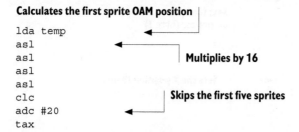

Calculates the first sprite OAM position

```
        lda temp
        asl
        asl                                 Multiplies by 16
        asl
        asl
        clc                                 Skips the first five sprites
        adc #20
        tax
```

If our enemy definition has a change in X velocity (DX), then we do another random call to see if it will start to the left instead of the right.

Listing 12.12   Whether the X direction of the enemy should be reversed (megablast.s)

```
        lda enemydata+4,y
        beq @noAdjustX
        sty temp+1
        jsr rand
        ldy temp+1
        and #%1
        beq @noAdjustX
        lda enemydata+4,y
        eor #$ff                            Makes negative
        clc
        adc #$01
        sta enemydata+4,y

@noAdjustX:
```

Now, depending on whether our enemy is made up of one or four sprites, we have a section of code dealing with each as follows.

Listing 12.13   Setting up the enemy sprite if it uses one sprite (megablast.s)

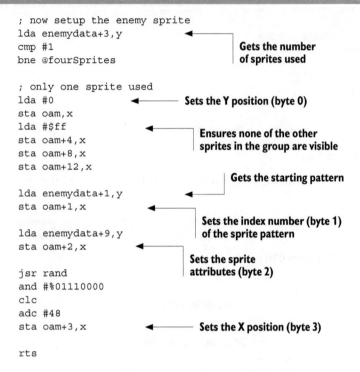

```
; now setup the enemy sprite
lda enemydata+3,y                          Gets the number
cmp #1                                      of sprites used
bne @fourSprites

; only one sprite used
lda #0                        Sets the Y position (byte 0)
sta oam,x
lda #$ff                      Ensures none of the other
sta oam+4,x                   sprites in the group are visible
sta oam+8,x
sta oam+12,x
                              Gets the starting pattern
lda enemydata+1,y
sta oam+1,x
                              Sets the index number (byte 1)
lda enemydata+9,y             of the sprite pattern
sta oam+2,x
                              Sets the sprite
jsr rand                      attributes (byte 2)
and #%01110000
clc
adc #48
sta oam+3,x                   Sets the X position (byte 3)

rts
```

Listing 12.14   Setting up an enemy using four sprites (megablast.s)

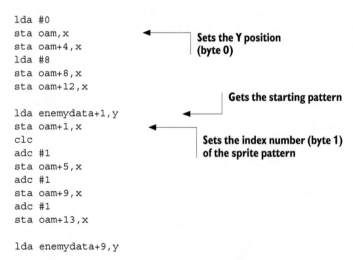

```
@fourSprites:

lda #0
sta oam,x                     Sets the Y position
sta oam+4,x                   (byte 0)
lda #8
sta oam+8,x
sta oam+12,x
                              Gets the starting pattern
lda enemydata+1,y
sta oam+1,x
clc                           Sets the index number (byte 1)
adc #1                        of the sprite pattern
sta oam+5,x
adc #1
sta oam+9,x
adc #1
sta oam+13,x

lda enemydata+9,y
```

```
    sta oam+2,x        ◄──────── Sets the sprite attributes (byte 2)
    sta oam+6,x
    sta oam+10,x
    sta oam+14,x

    jsr rand
    and #%11110000
    clc
    adc #48
    sta oam+3,x        ◄──────── Sets the X position (byte 3)
    sta oam+11,x
    clc
    adc #8
    sta oam+7,x
    sta oam+15,x

    rts
.endproc
```

12.4 *Changing our enemy movement code*

Now we need to rewrite our move_enemies routine to consider our extra enemy data,
movement, and behavior. We start the routine the same way as previously, setting up
for the collision detection with the player's bullet. As we need to use the X and Y registers for other tasks inside the main loop, we can use a zero-page memory location
(temp + 2) as our loop counter as follows.

Listing 12.15   Start of our new `move_enemies` routine (megablast.s)

```
.segment "CODE"

.proc move_enemies

    ; setup for collision detection of bullet with enemies
    lda oam+16        ◄┐
    sta cy1            │ Gets bullet Y
    lda oam+19        ◄┘
    sta cx1            │ Gets bullet X
    lda #4            ◄┘
    sta ch1            │ The bullet is 4 pixels high.
    lda #1            ◄┘
    sta cw1            │ The bullet is 1 pixel wide.

    ldy #0
    lda #0
    sta temp+2        ◄──────── Initializes the loop counter
@loop:
    lda enemydata,y
    bne :+
        jmp @skip
    :
```

Next we work out the starting sprite used for this enemy as follows.

Listing 12.16 Working out the starting sprite for the enemy (megablast.s)

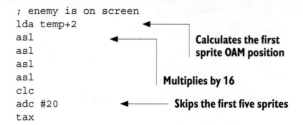

```
; enemy is on screen
lda temp+2
asl
asl
asl
asl
clc
adc #20
tax
```

Calculates the first sprite OAM position

Multiplies by 16

Skips the first five sprites

We are now ready to start moving our enemy object based on its stored settings. First, if the enemy has a change in X (DX) defined in its enemy data, then we adjust the enemy's X position.

Listing 12.17 Adjusting the enemy's X position (megablast.s)

```
lda enemydata+4,y
beq @noMoveX
    clc
    adc oam+3,x
    sta oam+3,x
    sta oam+11,x
    clc
    adc #8
    sta oam+7,x
    sta oam+15,x
```

Adjusts the enemy X

```
@noMoveX:
```

Next, we adjust the enemy's Y position using the change in Y (DY) defined in its enemy data. We also check whether the enemy has reached the ground, taking into account its height, and if so, we remove it from the screen and subtract 10 points from the score (if the score is not already zero).

Listing 12.18 Adjusting the enemy's Y position (megablast.s)

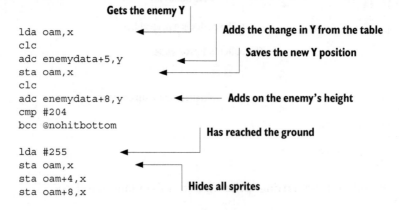

Gets the enemy Y

Adds the change in Y from the table

Saves the new Y position

```
lda oam,x
clc
adc enemydata+5,y
sta oam,x
clc
adc enemydata+8,y
cmp #204
bcc @nohitbottom

lda #255
sta oam,x
sta oam+4,x
sta oam+8,x
```

Adds on the enemy's height

Has reached the ground

Hides all sprites

```
sta oam+12,x
lda #0
sta enemydata,y          Clears the enemies
                         in-use flag

clc                      Checks that the score
lda score                is not already zero
adc score+1
adc score+2
bne :+
    jmp @skip
:
lda #1                   Subtracts 10
jsr subtract_score       from the score
jmp @skip
```

@nohitbottom:

The enemy is now in its new position on the screen; if it is an enemy with multiple sprites, we need to update the Y position of the other sprites. Then we need to check if it is level with the player's ship and whether it has collided with the player. If so, we need to decrease the player's lives, remove the enemy from the screen, and mark the player as dead.

Listing 12.19 Checking for collision with the player's ship

```
lda enemydata+3,y
cmp #1
beq :+                   Does the enemy only
lda oam,x                have one pattern?
sta oam+4,x
clc
adc #8                   Updates the other
sta oam+8,x              sprite Y positions
sta oam+12,x
:
    lda player_dead      Checks that the player
    cmp #0               is not currently dead
    bne @notlevelwithplayer
```

If the player is currently alive, check whether the enemy is at the same level as the player's ship:

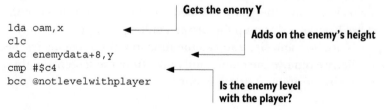

```
lda oam,x                Gets the enemy Y
clc                              Adds on the enemy's height
adc enemydata+8,y
cmp #$c4
bcc @notlevelwithplayer
                         Is the enemy level
                         with the player?
```

Now compare the X position of the enemy and the player's ship, considering the width of both objects:

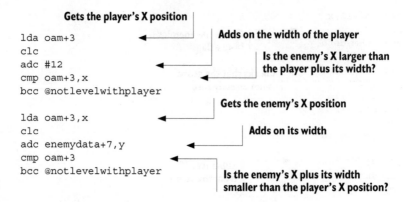

If the player has been hit, decrease the player's lives, set the flag so that the number of lives displayed on the screen is changed, and mark the player as currently dead:

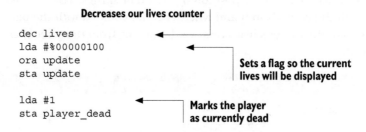

Remove the enemy sprites from the screen, and clear the enemy's data flag:

```
lda #$ff
sta oam,x              ◄───────  Erases the enemy
sta oam+4,x
sta oam+8,x
sta oam+12,x
lda #0                 ◄───────  Clears the enemy's data flag
sta enemydata,y
jmp @skip
```

```
@notlevelwithplayer:
```

If the enemy has not hit the player and the player's bullet is on the screen, then we need to check whether they have collided. To do this, we use our `collision_test` function; we have already set up the player's bullet position, so we only need to set up the enemy's position and size and call the function. If the enemy has been hit by the player's bullet, we remove the enemy and bullet from the screen and then increase the player's score by the amount stored in our enemy data.

Listing 12.20   Checking for a collision with the player's bullet (megablast.s)

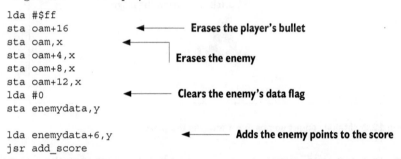

```
lda oam+16
cmp #$ff           ◄──┐     Is the player's
beq @skip             │     bullet onscreen?

lda oam,x          ◄─────── Gets the enemy Y position
sta cy2
lda oam+3,x        ◄─────── Gets the enemy X position
sta cx2
lda enemydata+7,y  ◄─────── Sets the enemy width
sta cw2
lda enemydata+8,y  ◄─────── Sets the enemy height
sta ch2
jsr collision_test
bcc @skip
```

If the bullet has hit the enemy, remove the bullet and enemy sprites, clear the enemy data flag, and add to the player's score:

```
lda #$ff
sta oam+16         ◄─────── Erases the player's bullet
sta oam,x          ◄──┐
sta oam+4,x           │    Erases the enemy
sta oam+8,x
sta oam+12,x
lda #0             ◄─────── Clears the enemy's data flag
sta enemydata,y

lda enemydata+6,y  ◄─────── Adds the enemy points to the score
jsr add_score
```

Now, to finish off our `move_enemies` function, we move to our next enemy data section, increment our counter, and check whether we have gone through all our enemies.

Listing 12.21   Finish of our `move_enemies` loop and function (megablast.s)

```
@skip:
    tya            ◄─────── Goes to the next enemy
    clc
    adc #10
    tay
    inc temp+2
    lda temp+2
    cmp #10
    beq :+
        jmp @loop
    :

    rts
.endproc
```

Now is a probably a good time to compile and test the code so far. The game should now display and move three different enemy types, some of which move left and right as well as down, all at different movement speeds.

12.5   *Making our smart bomb smarter*

Other than moving at a slightly different speed, our smart bomb is not very smart. The idea with the smart bomb is that, in addition to moving quite fast, it will try to move closer to the player when it can (see figure 12.2).

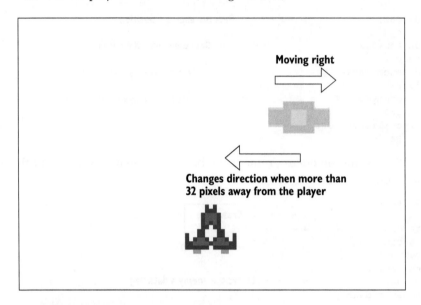

Figure 12.2   Making smart bombs move towards the player

Revisiting our move_enemies function, just before we change the enemy's X position (see listing 12.17), we add some code limited to the smart bomb enemy. If the smart bomb is moving away from the player and is a certain distance (32 pixels) away, then we want it to change direction so that it is moving toward the player. First, if the smart bomb is moving to the left, then we check if the smart bomb is to the left of the player, and then, if it is more than 32 pixels to the left of the player, we change its direction so that it will start moving to the right.

Listing 12.22   Is the smart bomb to the left of the player? (megablast.s)

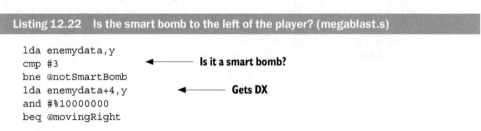

```
lda enemydata,y
cmp #3                ◄─────── Is it a smart bomb?
bne @notSmartBomb
lda enemydata+4,y     ◄─────── Gets DX
and #%10000000
beq @movingRight
```

The smart bomb is moving to the left. Is it to the left of the player's ship?

```
lda oam+3                                    Gets player X
cmp oam+3,x
bcc @notSmartBomb                            Is the smart bomb to
                                             the left of the player?
```

The smart bomb is to the left of the player:

```
sec
sbc oam+3,x
cmp #32
bcc @notSmartBomb
lda enemydata+4,y
eor #$ff                 Makes negative
clc
adc #$01
sta enemydata+4,y
jmp @notSmartBomb
```

Extending this further, we do similar logic. If the smart bomb is moving to the right, we check if the smart bomb is to the right of the player; then, if it is more than 32 pixels to the right of the player (also considering the player's width), we change its direction so that it will move to the left.

Listing 12.23   Is the smart bomb to the right of the player? (megablast.s)

```
@movingRight:
    ; smart bomb moving right
    lda oam+3                    Gets player X
    clc
    adc #12                      Adjusts for the width of the player
    cmp oam+3,x
    bcs @notSmartBomb            Is the smart bomb to the
    lda oam+3,x                  right of the player?
    sec
    sbc oam+3                    Gets the difference between the two
    cmp #44
    bcc @notSmartBomb            Is it within 32 pixels?
    lda enemydata+4,y
    eor #$ff                     Makes negative
    clc
    adc #$01
    sta enemydata+4,y
```

```
@notSmartBomb:
```

Now you can compile the source code and run it in the emulator, and when a smart bomb appears, it should change direction, trying to move closer to the player. They move very fast, so you must be on your toes to either dodge them or shoot them before they hit you.

Summary

- We included a table in our NES ROM that defines the different attributes each type of enemy will have.
- Enemy objects can now move left and right as well as down the screen, at different speeds, and as one of three different types.
- Our table in RAM for each of our active enemies needs to have the same information as in our ROM table but with an additional value so we know what type of enemy it is.
- There are often multiple ways of achieving a section of logic in code, so looking at how long the code takes to run versus how readable it is should be taken into account.
- We introduce some intelligence for our smart bomb enemy, making it move toward the player's ship.

Animations and more
13

This chapter covers

- Animating our enemies
- Adding background animation
- Visualizing a bigger explosion when an enemy mine hits the ground
- Progressing to the next level of difficulty

We now have a mostly playable game, but it still lacks excitement and doesn't really show some of the abilities of the NES hardware. We will use this chapter to add some items to make the game more interesting, including animations for both our enemies and the background, shaking the screen and fast cycling some colors when one of the enemy mines hits the planet's surface, and finally allowing the player to progress to the next level of difficulty.

13.1 *Enemy animations*

In our previous chapter, we added starting and ending pattern numbers to both our enemy definition table and our in-memory tracking table. In this section, we will add to our code to use this information to progress each of the enemies through an animation sequence.

Before we get into our main code changes, let's adjust some more of our default palette values so our meteor enemies are using a base brown color. Find our `default_palette` section, and make the following changes.

Listing 13.1 Adjusting sprite colors (Megablast.s)

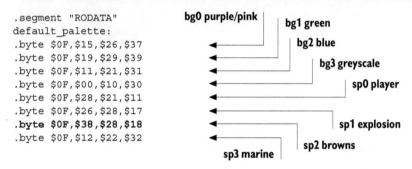

```
.segment "RODATA"
default_palette:
.byte $0F,$15,$26,$37
.byte $0F,$19,$29,$39
.byte $0F,$11,$21,$31
.byte $0F,$00,$10,$30
.byte $0F,$28,$21,$11
.byte $0F,$26,$28,$17
.byte $0F,$38,$28,$18
.byte $0F,$12,$22,$32
```

bg0 purple/pink · bg1 green · bg2 blue · bg3 greyscale · sp0 player · sp1 explosion · sp2 browns · sp3 marine

Now let's get into our code changes. We already have our `move_enemies` function that loops through each of the enemies that are currently onscreen, so we will add a section to that to animate each enemy through different patterns. Find the `move_enemies` function and the section where we have just finished updating the enemy's Y position; we will add our code there as follows.

Listing 13.2 Animating each enemy (Megablast.s)

```
@nohitbottom:

    lda enemydata+3,y
    cmp #1                    ◄─────── Does the enemy only have one pattern?
    beq :+
    lda oam,x                 ◄─────── Updates the other sprite Y positions
    sta oam+4,x
    clc
    adc #8
    sta oam+8,x
    sta oam+12,x
:
```

After finding the code, the first thing we want to do is make sure that we don't change the patterns too quickly, so we make sure that at least four time ticks have passed before changing the enemy's pattern:

```
lda time
and #%11                    ◄──────── Only animates every four frames
bne @noanimate
```

Next we check to see if the enemy has more than one pattern. There's no point in animating it if it only has a single pattern:

```
; does the enemy have more than one pattern?
lda enemydata+1,y           ◄
cmp enemydata+2,y               │ Gets the starting pattern
beq @noanimate
```

Then we split our code depending on whether the enemy uses a single sprite or four sprites:

```
lda enemydata+3,y
cmp #1                      ◄──────── Does the enemy only have one sprite?
beq @singleSprite
```

If the enemy uses four sprites, we get the first sprite's current pattern and add 4, and then we check that we haven't gone past the enemy's last sprite pattern. If we have, we reset back to the starting pattern:

```
lda oam+1,x                 ◄           Gets the first sprite
clc                                     │ pattern number
adc #4 ; go to the next pattern
cmp enemydata+2,y
beq :+
bcc :+                                  Past the end pattern,
    lda enemydata+1,y       ◄           so gets the starting pattern
:
```

We have worked out the next pattern of the first sprite, so we update it and then add 1 for each subsequent sprite and set them:

```
sta oam+1,x
clc
adc #1
sta oam+5,x                 ◄──────── Updates the other patterns
clc
adc #1
sta oam+9,x
clc
adc #1
sta oam+13,x
jmp @noanimate
```

If our sprite only has a single sprite, we only need to increment the pattern by 1. Check whether we have gone past the end pattern, and if so, reset back to the starting one:

```
@singleSprite:
    lda oam+1,x             ◄           Gets the first sprite
    clc                                 │ pattern number
    adc #1                  ◄
    cmp enemydata+2,y
    beq :+                              Goes to the next pattern
```

```
    bcc :+
        lda enemydata+1,y
    :
    sta oam+1,x
```

◄ ┐ **Past the end pattern, so**
  │ **gets the starting pattern**

```
@noanimate:
```

Now is a good time to compile the code and test it in the emulator. You should be able to see the different enemies cycling through their patterns. Much better!

13.2 Background animations

Just like the animation of our enemies, adding some animation to items in the background will add some more excitement to our game. Plus, of course, it's a good way to show some more ways to manipulate graphics on the NES.

The main restriction for background animation is the limited number of changes that can be written to video memory every frame (especially for NTSC consoles; see section 6.5), so we need to focus on simple changes such as changing which tiles are displayed at locations on the screen or changing the colors being used. We will try both techniques in this section, but before we get into the specific parts, we need to add some more tile patterns to our background characters. Either use one of the editors to add the tile patterns shown in figure 13.1 to our background tile set, or download the updated megablast.chr included in this chapter's files.

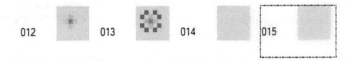

012   013   014   015

Figure 13.1 Adding some new shapes to our pattern table

13.2.1 Changing tile patterns

Our first technique is changing which tile patterns are displayed on the screen. This is possible to do on the NES, but care must be taken to limit the number of changes to video memory needed.

We will start by randomly placing a small number of star (*) characters across the open area of the screen, keeping a list of name table addresses, so we know where each star is. Then we will randomly swap the pattern where each star is located so they will animate. As we will be calculating a 16-bit memory address for each star's location using a random column and row, we need to add a new macro that will add an 8-bit number to a 16-bit number as follows.

Listing 13.3 Adding `add_16_8` macro (macros.s)

```
;**********************************************************************
; Adds an 8-bit value to a 16-bit value
;**********************************************************************
.macro add_16_8 dest, value

    lda value
      bmi :+
      clc
      adc dest
      sta dest
      lda dest+1
      adc #0
      sta dest+1
        jmp :++
    :

      clc
      adc dest
      sta dest
      lda dest+1
      adc #$FF
      sta dest+1
    :

.endmacro
```

The first thing we will need is a RAM table for storing the name table address for each one and then a function to place the stars on the screen in random locations. At the start of the function, we clear out our existing table of star locations.

Listing 13.4 Randomly displaying star characters (Megablast.s)

```
;**************************************************************
; Randomly display star characters
;**************************************************************

.segment "ZEROPAGE"

starlocations:    .res 10*2          ◄──────── 2 bytes per star

.segment "CODE"

.proc place_stars
    lda #0          ◄──────── Clears star locations
    ldx #0
@loop:
    sta starlocations,x
    inx
    cpx #20
    bne @loop
```

Now that we have cleared our star locations, we can loop through each one of our 10 stars and call our `rand` function to get a random value. We get the lower 4 bits and add 1 to get a number from 1 to 16. This will be our screen row:

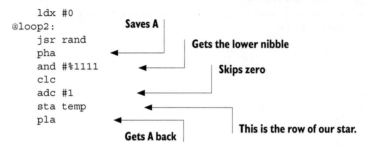

```
    ldx #0
@loop2:
    jsr rand
    pha
    and #%1111
    clc
    adc #1
    sta temp
    pla
```

Saves A

Gets the lower nibble

Skips zero

This is the row of our star.

Gets A back

We then use the upper 4-bits, multiplied by 2 to get a number from 0 to 31. This will be our screen column:

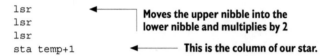

```
    lsr
    lsr
    lsr
    sta temp+1
```

Moves the upper nibble into the lower nibble and multiplies by 2

This is the column of our star.

We now have the row and column where our star will be displayed, so starting from the second row, we add 32 until we reach our chosen row:

```
    assign_16i paddr, NAME_TABLE_0_ADDRESS+64
@loop3:
    add_16_8 paddr, #32
    dec temp
    bne @loop3
```

Starts from the second row

Adds 32 for each row

Then we add the column value, and we have our final screen location:

```
    add_16_8 paddr, temp+1
```

Adds the column

We use our macro that sets the screen position from a 16-bit variable and then write the pattern for our star to the screen:

```
    vram_set_address_i paddr
    lda #12
    sta PPU_VRAM_IO
```

Output star pattern

Next we need to save our calculated address for later so we can make the star patterns change:

```
    lda paddr
    sta starlocations,x
    lda paddr+1
    sta starlocations+1,x
```

Saves our address for later

Finally, we increment X to point to our next star location entry, and if we haven't run out of stars, jump back to the start of our loop:

```
    inx
    inx
    cpx #20
    beq :+
        jmp @loop2
    :

    rts
.endproc
```

Find our `display_game_screen` function, and add a call to our new `place_stars` function as follows.

Listing 13.5   Calling our `place_stars` function (megablast.s)

```
    jsr display_lives

    jsr place_stars

    jsr ppu_update        ◄──────────   Waits until the screen
    rts                                 has been drawn
.endproc
```

This is a good spot to compile your code and run the result in the emulator. You should see 10 stars placed randomly on the screen in different locations each time you start a game (see figure 13.2).

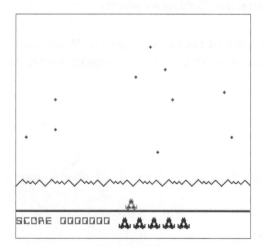

Figure 13.2   Now we have stars.

Now that we have some stars being displayed, we want to introduce some animation so that the stars twinkle. We will add a function that will be called from our NMI routine to animate the pattern each star is displayed with, using the name table locations we stored when placing the stars onscreen. It is very important that any code called from the NMI routine is as fast as possible, as we only have a limited amount of time before the PPU will be ready to start drawing the screen again.

Our routine will first check whether enough time has passed. We don't want to update the shape of our stars at every update, as we wouldn't be able to see them change shape.

Listing 13.6   Adding a function to animate stars (Megablast.s)

```
;****************************************************************
; Randomly animate stars by changing their pattern
;****************************************************************

.segment "CODE"

.proc animate_stars
    lda time
    and #%11
    beq :+
        rts          ◄──────── Any change every four ticks
    :
```

Next we check to see if the star locations have been set by making sure the locations are nonzero. We do not want to cause any problems by trying to write to the wrong location in video memory:

```
    ldx #0
    lda starlocations,x
    bne @loop
        rts          ◄──────── Skips processing if there are no stars
@loop:
```

For each star location, we used our stored values to set the VRAM address. I am not using any of the macros, as I want to directly see which statements we are using and thus how many cycles:

```
    lda PPU_STATUS
    lda starlocations+1,x
    sta PPU_VRAM_ADDRESS2
    lda starlocations,x
    sta PPU_VRAM_ADDRESS2
```

Using our time counter, we grab the third bit to determine whether we want to show our first or second star pattern:

```
    lda time
    lsr
    lsr
    and #%1          ◄──────── Uses the third bit of time
    clc                        to control our pattern
    adc #12
    sta PPU_VRAM_IO
```

Finally, we update X to point to our next star location, check whether we have processed all stars, and if not, jump back to the start of our loop:

```
        inx
        inx
        cpx #20
        bne @loop
        rts
.endproc
```

We now have our new `animate_stars` function, so we need to call it from our NMI function as follows.

Listing 13.7 Adding call to animate stars to the NMI function (megablast.s)

```
@skipgameover:

        jsr animate_stars

        lda #0              ◄─────── Writes current scroll and control settings
        sta PPU_VRAM_ADDRESS1
        sta PPU_VRAM_ADDRESS1
```

There is one more thing to tidy up. We want to clear our star locations when we go back to our title screen; otherwise, the stars will appear on the title screen as well. We will do this in our `display_title_screen` function by adding a loop to clear each of the positions in our `starlocations` variable as follows.

Listing 13.8 Clearing star locations (megablast.s)

```
        vram_set_address (ATTRIBUTE_TABLE_0_ADDRESS + 8)  ◄─┐
        assign_16i paddr, title_attributes                 │
        ldy #0                              Sets the title text to use
loop:                                       the second palette entries
        lda (paddr),y
        sta PPU_VRAM_IO
        iny
        cpy #8
        bne loop

        lda #0              ◄─────── Clears the star locations
        ldx #0
@loop:
        sta starlocations,x
        inx
        cpx #20
        bne @loop

        jsr ppu_update      ◄─────┐ Waits until the screen
                                   │ has been drawn
        rts
.endproc
```

This is a good spot to compile your code and run the result in the emulator. You should see 10 stars placed randomly on the screen in different locations each time you start a game, but now they should change between our two star patterns, making them twinkle.

13.2.2 Changing the palette

Our second technique is changing larger amounts of the screen by changing the entries in one or more sections of the palette. Any changes to the palette entries change every place on the screen where that palette is used and can be used to produce some quite pleasing visual effects.

We could use this technique to animate stars as well, but for our example, we will swap the first two entries in the first tile palette table inside our `main` loop. This will make anything that uses those two palette tables alternate between the two colors (i.e., they will flash). This will make the player's score, the extra lives display, and the base of the planet change. Find the end of our `main` function, and add the following code.

Listing 13.9   Swapping two colors in the first palette table (megablast.s)

```
    jsr player_actions
    jsr move_player_bullet
    jsr spawn_enemies
    jsr move_enemies

    lda time
    and #%111
    bne @nopalettechange
        ldx palette+1
        lda palette+2
        sta palette+1
        stx palette+2

@nopalettechange:

    jmp mainloop
.endproc
```

This is all we need to do to make changes to the palette and thus to the colors being used. Any tile that points to that palette and uses either of the first two colors will be affected. The code we added when we first created the `NMI` function copies all the entries in our palette table that we have stored in RAM to the PPU, so we only need to change one or more entries in our RAM table, and it will take effect on the screen automatically.

This is a good spot to compile your code and run the result in the emulator. The player's score and extra lives and the planet's surface change color, which livens things up even more. This technique can be used to produce some very complex animation for little cost by carefully designing patterns using two colors and either swapping or progressing through several colors.

13.3   Shaking things up

We are going to cover two more techniques to add even more visual excitement to our game. To make our enemy smart bombs a little bit more exciting, we will make the screen flash and shake when a mine hits the planet's surface. This will allow us to cover changing the shared background color and using the screen position registers to move the screen around (i.e., make it shake).

13.3.1   Changing the shared background color

For our first visual effect, we will rapidly change the shared background color being used between black and white, and to get started, we need to add a variable to keep track of how many times we want to flash the screen, which will also act as a trigger to start flashing the screen. In our ZEROPAGE variable area, add a new variable called flash as follows.

> **Listing 13.10   Adding the `flash` zero-page variable (megablast.s)**

```
;*****************************************************************
; 6502 Zero Page Memory (256 bytes)
;*****************************************************************

.segment "ZEROPAGE"

time: .res 2
lasttime: .res 1
level: .res 1
animate: .res 1
enemycooldown: .res 1
temp: .res 10
score: .res 3
update: .res 1
highscore: .res 3
lives: .res 1
player_dead: .res 1
flash: .res 1
```

Next we need to update the background palette color if the flash variable is not zero, so just after the palette change code we added to our main function earlier in this chapter, add the following code. In this section of code, we first check to see if our flash variable is larger than zero; if it is, we decrease its value by 1. Then we check the current background color; if it is already black ($0f), then we set it to white ($30) and jump back to the start of our mainloop. Otherwise, we set the background color to black ($0f). This makes sure that when our flash variable is set to zero, the background is reset to black.

```
@nopalettechange:

    lda flash
    beq @noflash
        dec flash
        lda palette
        cmp #$0f
        bne @noflash
            lda #$30
            sta palette
            sta palette+16
            jmp mainloop
@noflash:
    lda #$f
    sta palette
    sta palette+16

    jmp mainloop
.endproc
```

Note that we set the first background color for each of the pattern and sprite palette tables, as since we write the whole palette table to VRAM every NMI, all the background color bytes are sent to VRAM, and the NES PPU will set the common background to the last value written to the first background color of either the tile or sprite palette sets. That is, if our shared background color was black ($0f) and we only set the first background color to white ($30), then when our copy loop reached the first background color for the sprites, the shared background color would be reset back to black.

Now we need to trigger flashing the screen by giving our flash variable a value whenever a smart bomb reaches the ground. Inside our move_enemies function where we handle an enemy reaching the ground, add some code to set our flash variable as follows.

```
    bcc @nohitbottom

    lda #255          ◄──────── Has reached the ground
    sta oam,x         ◄──────┐
    sta oam+4,x              │
    sta oam+8,x              │ Hides all sprites
    sta oam+12,x

    lda enemydata,y
    cmp #3
    bne @notSmartBomb2
        lda #32
        sta flash
```

```
@notSmartBomb2:

    lda #0
    sta enemydata,y
```

Clears the enemies in-use flag

This is a good spot to compile your code and run the result in the emulator. Play the game until a smart bomb appears, and let it hit the ground. The screen should flash white for several seconds.

13.3.2 *Using the scroll registers*

In chapter 6, we saw that the NES can have up to four name tables (normally there are only two name tables, but an additional two can be provided in the game cartridge) that determine what tile is displayed at each location on the screen. They are arranged in a 2 × 2 grid. What is displayed onscreen is determined by the position of the top-left corner of a view box (see figure 13.3).

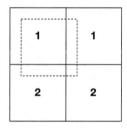

Figure 13.3   Screen view box

The position of the view box is determined by the value stored in two PPU registers called the horizontal and vertical scroll position registers. So far, we have set these two registers to zero, so only tiles displayed in the top-left name table have appeared onscreen.

We are going to alternate between the values 0 and 4 for both the horizontal and vertical scroll registers once per frame for the period we set in a variable. This will make the screen appear to be shaking back and forth. First, we need another variable, so in our shared ZEROPAGE area, add another variable called shake as follows.

Listing 13.13   Adding shake ZEROPAGE variable (megablast.s)

```
;****************************************************************
; 6502 Zero Page Memory (256 bytes)
;****************************************************************

.segment "ZEROPAGE"

time: .res 2
lasttime: .res 1
level: .res 1
animate: .res 1
enemycooldown: .res 1
```

```
temp: .res 10
score: .res 3
update: .res 1
highscore: .res 3
lives: .res 1
player_dead: .res 1
flash: .res 1
shake: .res 1
```

Then, in our NMI function, we need to replace the code where we set the two PPU scroll registers to 0 with code that looks at whether our shake variable has a value. Then we must set both horizontal and vertical scroll registers to 4 if our shake variable is an odd number, as follows.

Listing 13.14   Setting scroll registers if shake variable is not zero (megablast.s)

```
    jsr animate_stars

    ; write current scroll and control settings
    lda shake
    beq :+                          Shakes the screen
        dec shake                   from side to side
        and #%1
        asl a
        asl a
    :
    sta PPU_VRAM_ADDRESS1
    sta PPU_VRAM_ADDRESS1
    lda ppu_ctl0                    Writes the current
    sta PPU_CONTROL                 screen settings
    lda ppu_ctl1
    sta PPU_MASK
```

Next, we need to trigger the shaking of the screen when our smart bomb enemy reaches the bottom of the screen. In the same place in our move_enemies function, set the shake variable at the same time that we set the flash variable, as follows.

Listing 13.15   Setting shake variable (megablast.s)

```
    lda enemydata,y
    cmp #3
    bne @notSmartBomb2
        lda #32
        sta flash
        sta shake

@notSmartBomb2:
```

This is a good spot to compile your code and run the result in the emulator. Play the game until a smart bomb appears, and let it hit the ground. The screen should both flash white and shake for several seconds.

13.4 Level progression

Our final enhancement to our game for this chapter is to introduce the concept of level progression so that not only does the challenge for the player increase, but there is also some sense of progression. Let's make each level progress by the number of enemies that have appeared from the start of the level, whether they are destroyed or not. It would also be nice to have a visual indication that a new level has started. And, of course, we want our game to get harder the more levels the player manages to progress through. The first thing we will need is a way to keep track of how many enemies have appeared and add a counter for displaying our level, so we will need some more variables added to our ZEROPAGE code section as follows.

Listing 13.16 Adding `enemycount` variable to zero page (megablast.s)

```
;****************************************************************
; 6502 Zero Page Memory (256 bytes)
;****************************************************************

.segment "ZEROPAGE"

time: .res 2
lasttime: .res 1
level: .res 1
animate: .res 1
enemycooldown: .res 1
temp: .res 10
score: .res 3
update: .res 1
highscore: .res 3
lives: .res 1
player_dead: .res 1
flash: .res 1
shake: .res 1
enemycount: .res 1
displaylevel: .res 1
```

In our `setup_level` function, we need to make sure that it is reset to zero at the start of a level and set an update flag and counter so that we can display a start of level display as follows.

Listing 13.17 Resetting our enemy count (megablast.s)

```
    lda #$ff
    ldx #0              ◄──────┐  Hides all enemy
@loop2:                        │  sprites
    sta oam+20,x
    inx
    cpx #160
    bne @loop2

    lda #0              ◄──────┐  Resets our
    sta enemycount              │  enemy count
```

```
    lda #64
    sta displaylevel
    lda #%00010000
    ora update
    sta update
    rts
.endproc
```

Sets a flag so the current
level will be displayed

We will update our enemy count in our `spawn_enemies` function where we have determined that an enemy will be displayed but before we have selected what type of enemy will appear. We increment the count, and when it reaches 40, we increase the level and trigger the level display message as follows.

Listing 13.18   Progressing enemy count (megablast.s)

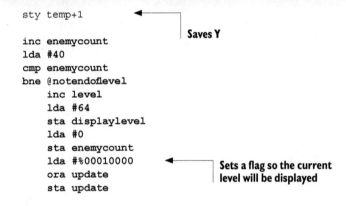

```
    sty temp+1

    inc enemycount
    lda #40
    cmp enemycount
    bne @notendoflevel
        inc level
        lda #64
        sta displaylevel
        lda #0
        sta enemycount
        lda #%00010000
        ora update
        sta update

@notendoflevel:
```

Saves Y

Sets a flag so the current
level will be displayed

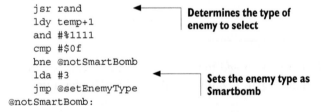

```
    jsr rand
    ldy temp+1
    and #%1111
    cmp #$0f
    bne @notSmartBomb
    lda #3
    jmp @setEnemyType
@notSmartBomb:
```

Determines the type of
enemy to select

Sets the enemy type as
Smartbomb

We need to add a section of code to our `main` function to decrease our `displaylevel` counter and, when it reaches zero, trigger the level display message to be removed from the screen, as the following listing shows.

Listing 13.19   Checking for removing the level display (megablast.s)

```
    jsr player_actions
    jsr move_player_bullet
    jsr spawn_enemies
    jsr move_enemies
```

```
lda displaylevel
beq @nodisplaylevelcountdown
    dec displaylevel
    bne @nodisplaylevelcountdown
    lda #%00100000          ◄────────┐  Signals to erase
    ora update                        │  level message
    sta update

@nodisplaylevelcountdown:

    lda time
    and #%111
    bne @nopalettechange
```

Also, in our `main` function, we need to trigger the display of the level at the start of the game and replace/update the section of code just after we reset the player's score to zero, as shown in the next listing.

Listing 13.20 Displaying the level at the start of the game (megablast.s)

```
lda #1              ◄────────┐
sta level                     │  Setup ready for a
jsr setup_level               │  new game

lda #0          ◄────────┐
sta score                 │  Resets the
sta score+1               │  player's score
sta score+2

lda #5          ◄──────── Sets the player's starting lives
sta lives
lda #0          ◄──────── Resets our player_dead flag
sta player_dead

jsr display_game_screen    ◄──────── Draws the game screen

jsr display_player         ◄──────── Displays the player's ship

lda #64
sta displaylevel
lda #%00010001      ◄────────┐  Sets a flag so the current score
ora update                    │  and level will be displayed
sta update

jsr ppu_update
```

Our last step is to implement the code to both display and remove the level display message from the screen in our `NMI` function, as shown next.

Listing 13.21 Displaying and removing the level display message (megablast.s)

```
lda #%00001000      ◄────────┐
bit update                    │  Does the game-over message
beq @skipgameover             │  need to be displayed?
```

```
        vram_set_address (NAME_TABLE_0_ADDRESS + 14 * 32 + 7)
        assign_16i text_address, gameovertext
        jsr write_text
        lda #%11110111          ◄───────  Resets the game over
        and update                         message update flag
        sta update
@skipgameover:
                                ┌── Does the level message
    lda #%00010000     ◄────────┘    need to be displayed?
    bit update
    beq @skipdisplaylevel
        vram_set_address (NAME_TABLE_0_ADDRESS + 14 * 32 + 9)
        assign_16i text_address, leveltext
        jsr write_text
        lda level           ◄──────  Transforms each decimal
        jsr dec99_to_bytes          digit of the level
        stx temp
        sta temp+1
        lda temp
        clc
        adc #48
        sta PPU_VRAM_IO
        lda temp+1
        clc
        adc #48
        sta PPU_VRAM_IO
        lda #%11101111      ◄──────  Resets the level
        and update                   message update flag
        sta update
@skipdisplaylevel:
```

Now remove the level display:

```
                                ┌── Does the level message
    lda #%00100000     ◄────────┘    need to be removed?
    bit update
    beq @skipremovedisplaylevel
        vram_set_address (NAME_TABLE_0_ADDRESS + 14 * 32 + 9)
        ldx #0
        lda #0
        :
            sta PPU_VRAM_IO
            inx
            cpx #18
            bne :-

        lda #%11011111      ◄──────  Resets the level
        and update                   message update flag
        sta update
@skipremovedisplaylevel:

    jsr animate_stars
```

Just above the nmi function, we need to add the definition for the leveltext reference we just used that will contain the text to be displayed.

Listing 13.22   Adding level display text (megablast.s)

```
;****************************************************************
; NMI Routine - called every vBlank
;****************************************************************

.segment "CODE"

gameovertext:
.byte " G A M E   O V E R",0

leveltext:
.byte " L E V E L  ",0

.proc nmi
```

This is a good spot to compile your code and run the result in the emulator. The level display should briefly show when you start the game, if you lose a life, or if you progress to the next level (see figure 13.4). Our increase in level will make the enemies appear faster, gradually making the game harder.

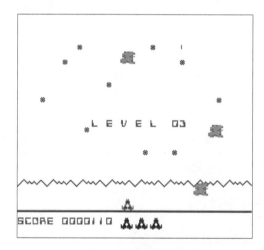

Figure 13.4   Level progression

Summary

- The NES will display all background tiles that fall within a view area controlled by two scroll registers.
- Changing an entry in a palette table will change the color of every element on the screen that uses that palette entry.
- There is only limited time to write changes to the PPU after the NMI interrupt has been raised.
- Changing first entries in either of the background or sprite palette tables will set the current background color for all palette entries.

Sound effects

14

This chapter covers

- The sound capabilities of the NES console
- Creating sound effects in FamiStudio
- Adding the music/sound effects engine to our game
- Using sound effects in our game

We now have lots of gameplay features in our game and have learned several techniques for using the NES graphical hardware, but our game is silent. We need to add some sound to our game so that we can hear our main ship's laser firing, enemies moving, explosions, and more. This will make our game even more compelling and fun to play, and we will get to learn about the distinctive sound capabilities of the NES hardware.

14.1 NES sound capabilities

The NES has a custom audio processor unit (APU) that has quite a distinctive sound, mainly due to the type of waveforms that can be generated. The APU has five channels: two pulse wave generators, a triangle wave, a noise generator, and a delta modulation channel for playing digital sound samples. The ability to play digital sound samples on an 8-bit system was particularly advanced for the time when the console was released.

The ability to not just set a pitch for each channel but also to partially control the shape of the waveform generated and how long it will last and potentially repeat frees up the CPU. In most 8-bit systems that have simpler sound chips, the CPU needs to constantly control the pitch and volume of each channel.

In practice, dedicating the CPU to controlling the sound waveform does result in more complex and better-sounding results. Earlier NES titles used the APU waveform controller, whereas later titles used more CPU cycles and even more sound channels in cartridge hardware to improve sound performance. The APU has its own internal clock and will continue to play each channel's currently programmed waveform, decrementing each channel length counter until it is zero.

14.1.1 Pulse wave channels

The APU has two channels that act as pulse wave generators, also known as square wave generators (see figure 14.1). Sound engines such as those from FamiTracker and Fami-Studio can allow more complex waveforms. A square wave is rich in harmonics and sounds quite harsh, but it makes any music generated more interesting.

Figure 14.1 APU pulse or square wave

Each of these channels can produce a variable-width pulse signal (tone) controlled by a volume envelope, length, and sweep units:

- *Envelope control*—Controlling the envelope of a sound means controlling the volume. The volume could be set once or set in several steps.
- *Length*—This is the width or time the selected note will be played.
- *Sweep*—A note can either be swept up or down, which means the note frequency will be changed over the length of the note by a set amount (see figure 14.2).

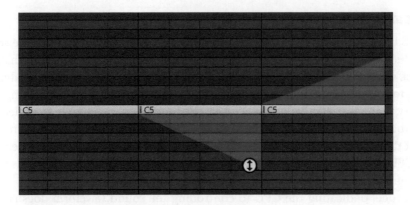

Figure 14.2　Normal, swept down, swept up notes

14.1.2　Triangle channel

The APU has a single triangle wave channel. You can't directly control the volume, but the length can be set. You do have an indirect way of setting the volume to either half or full using a setting called the PCM level. Setting it to Max will cause the triangle volume to be around half of its normal level. A triangle waveform sounds more rounded (like a sine wave) than a square wave and gives its output quite an "electronic" sound; it is often used for bass notes (see figure 14.3). The pitch of the triangle channel is one octave below the pulse channels.

Figure 14.3　APU triangle wave

14.1.3　Noise channel

The noise channel produces noise using a random number generator. The volume, envelope shape, and length can be set.

The random fluctuations produced by the noise channel make it useful for "shhh," rumbling, and short-period noise types of sounds (see figure 14.4). This can be used for making explosions or rougher notes or adding drum sounds to music. We will use it to produce some different explosion sounds for our game.

Figure 14.4   Noise generator

14.1.4 Delta modulation channel

The delta modulation channel (DMC) outputs a 7-bit value fed by a stream of 1-bit values that either increase or decrease the current output value. The playback rate can also be controlled and allow a sample to loop.

This allows short, digitally sampled sounds to be played. It is often used to add more specific instrument sounds to music but can also be used to produce speech samples. It does take up a fair bit of space in your game ROM, so it needs to be used sparingly.

Think of them as low-quality MP3 files. In comparison, Apple Music commonly uses 128-bit samples, as compared to the 7 bits available for the NES sound chip.

> **TIP**   If you want more technical details on the APU, see https://www.nesdev .org/wiki/APU.

14.2 Creating some sound effects

We will use FamiStudio to create our sound effects. Open FamiStudio, create a new project, and save it as CH_SFX.fms (or open the project CH_SFX.fms in the downloadable chapter files).

14.2.1 Zap

For our first sound effect, we want a nice laser sound for when the player fires a laser from their ship. The new FamiStudio project will have a single song (Song1) added by default. Click the gear wheel on the right-hand side in the same bar as Song1, and change the details as described next.

We will only have one part to our sound effect, so our song length is 1. Also, set the beats per minute (BPM) to 200 and both notes per pattern and notes per beat to 2 (see figure 14.5). This sets the base scale of each of the notes that we will draw. Once you have entered those figures, it will display nine frames per note. This means it will take nine display frames to play each note. Display frames per second will be either 60 on a NTSC NES or 50 on a PAL NES console.

Figure 14.5   Entering the base values for our zap sound

Now click next to the [Square 1] level (on the left side of the screen), and a pattern (called Pattern 1) will be created. The keyboard section further down the screen will also show Pattern 1 in the same color. Pointing the mouse to the right of the keyboard section in the column of Pattern 1 and using your mouse scroll wheel, you can adjust the size of the column (i.e., make it bigger and easier to see). Note that depending on your operating system, you may need to hold the Ctrl key while using the scroll wheel.

Turn on Recording Mode by clicking the circle button on the top bar. Add a note by clicking on the row marked with a P just up from the C5 indicator on the keyboard in the Editing area. This should give you a single E5 note as shown in figure 14.6.

Figure 14.6   Adding a single note

Don't worry if you put the wrong note in. To change it, simply click and hold the left mouse button on the note, and move it up and down until you have an E5. If you click the Play button at the top of FamiStudio now, just a flat note will be played—so nothing like a laser so far, but we have more to do. Next, right-click on the note, and select Toggle Slide Note from the menu that is displayed (see figure 14.7).

Figure 14.7   Toggle slide note

Once you have selected Toggle Slide Note, the note should look like figure 14.8.

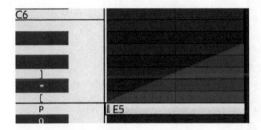

Figure 14.8   E5 slide note

If you click the Play button at the top of FamiStudio, you will hear a reasonably high-pitched sound that goes higher. This sounds more like a siren than a laser zap.

Hold the mouse pointer at the top right of the lighter-colored area, and an up/down arrow symbol will appear. You can then click and drag down until you get to F3 (level with the V on the keyboard to the left). Try playing the note again now, and it should sound much more like a zap sound (see figure 14.9).

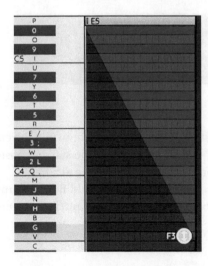

**Figure 14.9
E5 note sliding
to F3 equals a
nice zap sound.**

14.2.2 *Boom*

When an enemy is hit, we want a nice, short explosion sound. Use the plus (+) button at the top of the list of songs on the right-hand side of the screen; a song will be added (called Song1 again). Click on the gear wheel on the right-hand side, and change the details as shown in figure 14.10. We are making a much longer sound, so even though we only have one pattern, inside that pattern, we will have 10 notes.

Figure 14.10   Setting up the details for our boom sound effect

Once you have saved these details by clicking the tick symbol, click next to the Noise row, and a pattern will appear called Pattern 1 next to the Noise row and in the Editing area below. Add four notes—E1, D#1, E1, and D#1—and adjust their lengths to approximately match figure 14.11.

Figure 14.11   Adding notes for our boom sound

To adjust the length of the notes, you need to hold down the Alt key while the cursor is at the end of the note. It is best to add the second note, adjust the starting position of the second one, and then add each additional note and adjust one at a time.

If you click the Play button at the top of FamiStudio, you should hear a sound that, with the up and down in the notes, flips between two different pitches of noise and sounds a bit like a short explosion.

14.2.3 Big boom

When the player's ship or the ground is hit by a smart bomb, we want a much bigger explosion. For this explosion sound, we will use the noise channel again, but we will take advantage of being able to use the slide note functionality to produce a much bigger-sounding explosion.

Use the plus (+) button at the top of the list of songs on the right-hand side of the screen, and a song will be added (called Song1 again). Click on the gear wheel on the right-hand side, and change the details as shown in figure 14.12. This explosion will sound bigger, but it is only one note longer than the previous one.

Figure 14.12   Setting up the details for our big boom sound effect

Once you have saved these details by clicking the tick symbol, click next to the Noise row, and a pattern will appear, called Pattern 1, next to the Noise row and in the Editing area below. Add two notes—G2 and E2—and make the first note three times longer than the second note (see figure 14.13). Then turn both into slide notes, which should make them slide to C3 and A2, respectively. This should produce a longer rising noise sound, followed by a shorter rising sound.

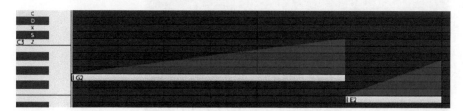

Figure 14.13   Adding two notes to form the two parts of the explosion

14.3   *Adding the sound engine*

We have made some sound effects for our game. Now we need to add them to our game code so we can use them.

14.3.1   *Exporting sound effects*

The first step is to export the sound effects we created using FamiStudio into code we can include in our game. In FamiStudio, with the example sound effects file we made in the previous section open, select [Export] from the toolbar (see figure 14.14) and then select [FamiStudio SFX Code]; your screen should resemble figure 14.15.

Figure 14.14   Exporting our sound effects in FamiStudio

Figure 14.15   FamiStudio export SFX code

In the [Format] field, select CA65 from the three assemblers supported, and then click the tick button (see figure 14.16).

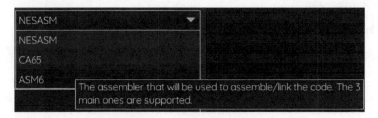

Figure 14.16 FamiStudio export SFX code—selecting assembler

Then make sure you select the same directory where you have the rest of your source code for the chapter, and specify the output file name as megablast-sfx.s. FamiStudio will display a summary window showing how many bytes are needed for each of the sound effects. This will be the space each sound effect will use in the final game ROM (see figure 14.17).

Figure 14.17 Exported sound effects log output

You should end up with a new source file called megablast-sfx.s with contents similar to the following listing.

Listing 14.1   Generated sound effects data (megablast.sfx.s)

```
; This file is for the FamiStudio Sound Engine and was generated by
FamiStudio


.if FAMISTUDIO_CFG_C_BINDINGS
.export _sounds=sounds
.endif

sounds:
```

```
    .word @ntsc
    .word @ntsc
@ntsc:
    .word @sfx_ntsc_zap
    .word @sfx_ntsc_boom
    .word @sfx_ntsc_bigboom

@sfx_ntsc_zap:
    .byte $82,$00,$81,$61,$80,$3f,$89,$f0,$01,$81,$6f,$01,$81,$7c,$01,$81
    .byte $8a,$01,$81,$97,$01,$81,$a5,$01,$81,$b2,$01,$81,$c0,$01,$81,$cd
    .byte $01,$81,$db,$01,$81,$e8,$01,$81,$f6,$01,$82,$01,$81,$03,$01,$81
    .byte $11,$01,$81,$1e,$01,$81,$2c,$01,$81,$39,$01,$81,$3f,$00
@sfx_ntsc_boom:
    .byte $8a,$0e,$89,$3f,$14,$8a,$0f,$0a,$8a,$0e,$06,$8a,$0f,$0c,$00
@sfx_ntsc_bigboom:
    .byte $8a,$0f,$89,$3f,$07,$8a,$0e,$08,$8a,$0d,$08,$8a,$0c,$08,$8a,$0b
    .byte $08,$8a,$0a,$14,$8a,$02,$03,$8a,$01,$04,$8a,$00,$04,$8a,$0f,$04
    .byte $8a,$0e,$04,$8a,$0d,$02,$00

.export sounds
```

14.3.2 *Adding the sound engine code*

Go to the FamiStudio support website (https://famistudio.org), and download the CA65 version of the NES sound engine (see figure 14.18).

Figure 14.18   Downloading the NES sound engine for the CA65 assembler

Inside the compressed file that you download, copy the famistudio_ca65.s file into your project directory. We need to add some settings that will be used by the FamiStudio engine to enable it to work with our code and to indicate what features we want to use.

We start with the setting that specifies that our FamiStudio configuration is external (i.e., specified in our source file rather than the engine itself). Lots of features in the FamiStudio engine can be turned on and off using these configuration settings. The idea is that every feature you turn on uses memory and CPU resources, so you should only enable the ones you are going to use in your project. The other settings we will turn on are listed in table 14.1.

Table 14.1   FamiStudio settings

Setting	Description
DPCM_SUPPORT	Support samples. We didn't use any in this chapter, but turning this on won't use any memory if none of the SFX use samples.
SFX_SUPPORT	Turns on support for sound effects
SFX_STREAMS	This defines the number of sound effects that can be played at once.
EQUALIZER	Allows the relative volume of the sound channel to be controlled
VOLUME_TRACK	For when your sound effects/music control the volume
PITCH_TRACK	Allows notes to control pitch
SLIDE_NOTES	To support notes that slide up or down
VIBRATO	Supports vibrato——notes that change pitch rapidly
ARPEGGIO	Supports arpeggio——notes made up of multiple pitch sections
SMOOTH_VIBRATO	Allows vibrato notes to have a rounder sound (i.e., less harsh)
RELEASE_NOTES	Supports notes that have a release point configured
DPCM_OFF	Where the DPCM samples are located

We also need to indicate what symbols we are using for our zero page, RAM, and code segments, and we need to include both the sound engine file and the file that contains the sound effects data.

We also add a zero-page variable for passing the sound effects channel we want to use. By using different sound effects channels, more than one sound effect can be played at the same time.

Listing 14.2   Including sound engine and sound effects code (megablast.s)

```
;***************************************************************
; Include NES Function Library
;***************************************************************

.include "neslib.s"

;***************************************************************
; Include Sound Engine and Sound Effects Data
;***************************************************************

.segment "CODE"

; FamiStudio config.
FAMISTUDIO_CFG_EXTERNAL        = 1
FAMISTUDIO_CFG_DPCM_SUPPORT    = 1
FAMISTUDIO_CFG_SFX_SUPPORT     = 1
FAMISTUDIO_CFG_SFX_STREAMS     = 2
```

```
FAMISTUDIO_CFG_EQUALIZER      = 1
FAMISTUDIO_USE_VOLUME_TRACK   = 1
FAMISTUDIO_USE_PITCH_TRACK    = 1
FAMISTUDIO_USE_SLIDE_NOTES    = 1
FAMISTUDIO_USE_VIBRATO        = 1
FAMISTUDIO_USE_ARPEGGIO       = 1
FAMISTUDIO_CFG_SMOOTH_VIBRATO = 1
FAMISTUDIO_USE_RELEASE_NOTES  = 1
FAMISTUDIO_DPCM_OFF           = $e000

; CA65-specifc config.
.define FAMISTUDIO_CA65_ZP_SEGMENT    ZEROPAGE
.define FAMISTUDIO_CA65_RAM_SEGMENT   BSS
.define FAMISTUDIO_CA65_CODE_SEGMENT  CODE

.include "famistudio_ca65.s"

.include "megablast-sfx.s"
.segment "ZEROPAGE"

sfx_channel: .res 1
```

Sound effects channel to use

The music engine needs to be initialized before we try to play any sounds. At the start of our main function, we call both the engine's general initialization function and the function to initialize our sound effects.

Listing 14.3   Initializing the sound engine (megablast.s)

```
.segment "CODE"
 .proc main
    ; main application - rendering is currently off
   lda #1
   sta highscore+1

   lda #1              NTSC
   ldx #0
   ldy #0
   jsr famistudio_init

   ldx #.lobyte(sounds)
   ldy #.hibyte(sounds)
   jsr famistudio_sfx_init
```

Sets the initial high score to 1,000

Sets the address of sound effects

In order for our sound effects (and later our music) to be played, we need to add code in our NMI function that will call the sound engine at every frame that the screen is displayed. This will cause the music engine to be called 60 times per second on NTSC machines and 50 times per second on PAL machines. The APU continues playing a note on a channel until its timer reaches zero or it is told to play a different note. The music engine keeps track of which notes should be playing on each channel for the song or sound effect being played. The music engine will also allow a larger music piece to play. Sound effects will override the music notes (on the channels it uses) so you can hear the sound effects, but the music will continue to play afterward. Near the end of our existing NMI routine, add a call to the sound engine as follows.

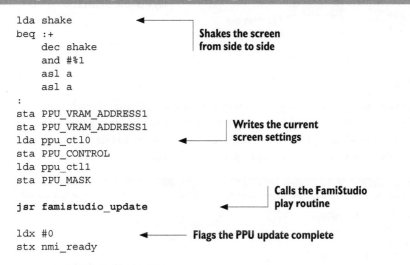

Listing 14.4   Calling the sound engine (megablast.s)

```
        lda shake
        beq :+                          Shakes the screen
            dec shake                   from side to side
            and #%1
            asl a
            asl a
        :
        sta PPU_VRAM_ADDRESS1
        sta PPU_VRAM_ADDRESS1
        lda ppu_ctl0                    Writes the current
        sta PPU_CONTROL                 screen settings
        lda ppu_ctl1
        sta PPU_MASK

        jsr famistudio_update           Calls the FamiStudio
                                        play routine

        ldx #0                          Flags the PPU update complete
        stx nmi_ready
```

14.4   Adding sound effects to our game

We will be adding sound effects at a few different places in our game, so we will add a function to call to play one of our sound effects. We will pass the number of the sound effects we want to play using the A register. The function then will

- Save the current values of the X and Y registers
- Set up the sound engine with the address where the sound effects are located
- Set our selected sound effect as the current one
- Restore the values of the X and Y registers

Listing 14.5   Adding the `Play a sound effect` function (megablast.s)

```
;********************************************************
; Play a sound effect
; a = sound effect to play
; sfx_channel = sound effects channel to use
;********************************************************/
.segment "CODE"

.proc play_sfx                          Saves the sound
    sta temp+9                          effect number
    tya
    pha                     
    txa                                 Saves the current
    pha                                 register values
```

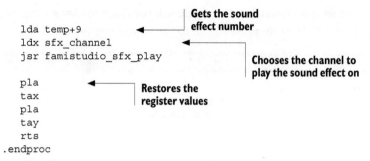

```
        lda temp+9              ◄─────┐  Gets the sound
                                      └── effect number
        ldx sfx_channel         ◄──────────────┐
        jsr famistudio_sfx_play                 │
                                                │  Chooses the channel to
                                                   play the sound effect on
        pla         ◄──────┐  Restores the
        tax                │  register values
        pla
        tay
        rts
.endproc
```

Now we can put the `play_sfx` function to use and call it each time the player fires a
bullet. We add this code to our existing `player_actions` function where we detect
that the player has pressed the fire button on the controller and we have a bullet available. We specify the first sound effects channel for our zap sound.

Listing 14.6   Playing a zap sound when firing a bullet (megablast.s)

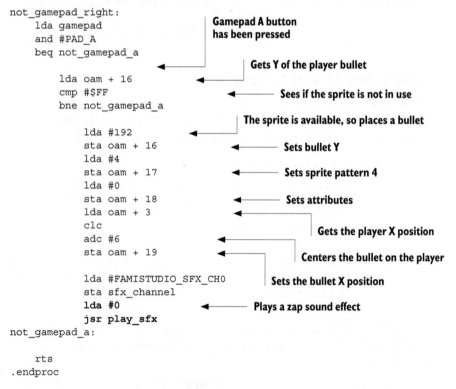

```
not_gamepad_right:
    lda gamepad              Gamepad A button
    and #PAD_A               has been pressed
    beq not_gamepad_a

        lda oam + 16         ◄───────  Gets Y of the player bullet
        cmp #$FF             ◄───────  Sees if the sprite is not in use
        bne not_gamepad_a

            lda #192         ◄───────  The sprite is available, so places a bullet
            sta oam + 16     ◄───────  Sets bullet Y
            lda #4
            sta oam + 17     ◄───────  Sets sprite pattern 4
            lda #0
            sta oam + 18     ◄───────  Sets attributes
            lda oam + 3      ◄───────┐
            clc                      │  Gets the player X position
            adc #6           ◄───────
            sta oam + 19     ◄───────  Centers the bullet on the player

            lda #FAMISTUDIO_SFX_CH0      Sets the bullet X position
            sta sfx_channel
            lda #0           ◄───────  Plays a zap sound effect
            jsr play_sfx
not_gamepad_a:

    rts
.endproc
```

The next sound effect to add will be used when we have hit one of the enemy objects.
Near the end of the `move_enemies` function, just after we add to the player's score
when hitting an enemy, we can play our boom sound effect. We use the second sound
effects channel so that the zap sound from the player firing their next bullet will not
stop the boom sound from being played in full.

Listing 14.7 Playing a boom sound when hitting an enemy (megablast.s)

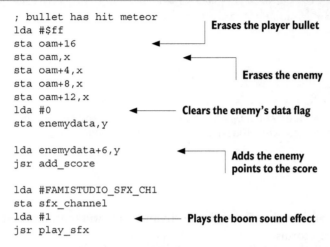

```
; bullet has hit meteor
lda #$ff
sta oam+16                        Erases the player bullet
sta oam,x
sta oam+4,x                       Erases the enemy
sta oam+8,x
sta oam+12,x
lda #0                            Clears the enemy's data flag
sta enemydata,y

lda enemydata+6,y                 Adds the enemy
jsr add_score                     points to the score

lda #FAMISTUDIO_SFX_CH1
sta sfx_channel
lda #1                            Plays the boom sound effect
jsr play_sfx
```

The next sound effect to add is also in the `move_enemies` function, where the player has been hit and has lost a life. We will play the big boom sound effect, but we can reuse the second sound effects channel to make sure it is played straight away.

Listing 14.8 Playing the big boom sound when the player loses a life (megablast.s)

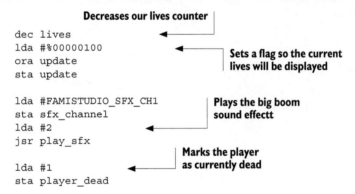

```
                    Decreases our lives counter
dec lives
lda #%00000100                    Sets a flag so the current
ora update                        lives will be displayed
sta update

lda #FAMISTUDIO_SFX_CH1           Plays the big boom
sta sfx_channel                   sound effectt
lda #2
jsr play_sfx
                                  Marks the player
                                  as currently dead
lda #1
sta player_dead
```

One more sound effect to add is when the smart bomb hits the ground. This is also in the `move_enemies` function, where we set the flags to flash and shake the screen.

Listing 14.9 Playing the big boom sound for the smart bomb (megablast.s)

```
lda enemydata,y
cmp #3
bne @notSmartBomb2
    lda #32
    sta flash
    sta shake

    lda #FAMISTUDIO_SFX_CH1
```

```
sta sfx_channel
lda #2          ◄──────── Plays the big boom sound effect
jsr play_sfx
```

@notSmartBomb2:

Exercise 14.1

We have reused the big boom sound effect for the smart bomb hitting the ground. Add another explosion sound effect using FamiStudio; export it, and change the code to use the new sound effect for when the smart bomb hits the ground.

Summary

- The NES hardware has five separate channels that will output sound with different basic waveforms.
- The sound hardware can be programmed directly, but it is much easier to use one of the sound and music creation tools and the playback engines they provide.
- Use the sound engine code provided by the Music and Sound editing tool to output the sound and music.
- Spread sound effects across multiple logical channels so they can be played at the same time.

Music

15

This chapter covers

- Music project structure
- Arpeggios
- Instruments
- Generating music data for our game
- Using music in our game

We have used sound effects to bring our game to life with zap and explosion sounds, but to bring more atmosphere to any game, it is also good to add some music. Music can be played on the title screen or during the game and can change depending on the location or scenario.

I do not purport to have the ability to create original-sounding music, and I usually rely on others to supply such things. But what we will focus on in this chapter is how to use the FamiStudio tool to create or adapt music. We will work with one of the included music examples included with FamiStudio.

We will use the file called Tetris (Tutorial Song).fms during this chapter. It is located in the Demo Songs folder of your FamiStudio's installation directory.

15.1 *Music project structure*

A FamiStudio project consists of four main components (see figure 15.1):

- A list of songs
- A list of instruments (used to define different sounding notes)
- A list of delta pulse code modulation (DPCM; 1-bit digital) samples
- A list of arpeggios (multichord notes)

Figure 15.1   Tetris music project structure

Each song is made up of one or more patterns. A pattern is on one of the five channels supported by the NES APU (more channels can be used with additional hardware provided in the game cartridge; see chapter 16). Each pattern is made up of one or more notes, which are played by an instrument and may refer to an arpeggio, except for DPCM samples, which play the sample itself as the note.

Instruments can have some of their attributes (pitch, volume, and arpeggio) modulated by envelopes. An envelope in sound and music describes how sound changes over time. An instrument could generate notes like a grand piano, an electronic organ, a guitar, or many others.

15.1.1 *Sequencer*

The sequencer allows you to enter/edit and view the patterns that make up your song and the sound channels they are played on (see figure 15.2).

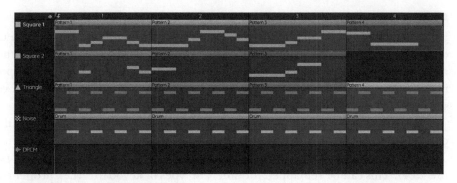

Figure 15.2   Tetris demo song

The thumbnails for each of the patterns are only an approximation of what they contain. The Piano Roll section is where you edit each pattern's detail.

15.1.2 Piano roll

This is where you edit the actual notes that make up the patterns on a single channel. You can adjust each note's envelope and add some special effects (see figure 15.3).

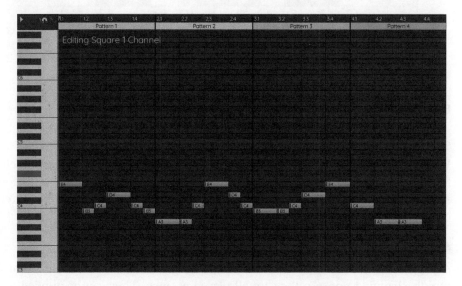

Figure 15.3   The notes using the Square 1 channel for the Tetris song

You can preview the currently selected instrument by clicking on the piano keyboard to the left of the editing area. Each thin vertical black line represents an individual frame, and there are 60 frames per second on NTSC systems and 50 frames per second on PAL systems. Each thicker black vertical line represents a beat (usually four notes by default).

ADDING AND EDITING NOTES

Notes are placed in line with a key on the piano keyboard to the left. Place a note by clicking on a row and then dragging and releasing when you reach the length of the note you require. You can then edit a note by dragging it to another line and positioning or adjusting either its start its end. If an instrument has a release envelope, you can set a release point, which allows a note to fade out rather than just end.

Each note is played by an instrument (see section 15.3). New notes will default to the currently selected instrument (highlighted in bold in the project list to the right).

You can also start [Recording Mode] and play notes using the keyboard (see figure 15.4). This can be remapped for different types of keyboards (i.e., proper external piano keyboards).

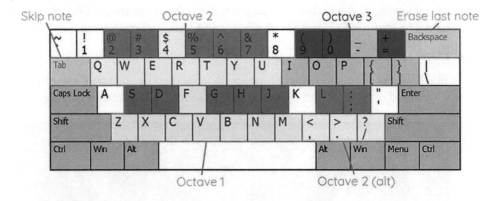

Figure 15.4 Default keyboard mapping

SLIDE NOTES

We saw slide notes in action in the last chapter when generating notes that changed from a starting pitch to an ending pitch over time. You turn a note into a slide note by right-clicking on the note and selecting Slide Note. You can then move the target up or down from the starting pitch.

15.2 *Arpeggios*

Arpeggios are used to simulate chords (playing multiple notes simultaneously) by rapidly changing notes so they are all played at once. They can be applied to a specific note and will override any arpeggio envelope that may be defined in the selected instrument.

> **DEFINITION** An arpeggio (Italian: [ar'peddʒo]) is a type of broken chord in which the notes that compose a chord are individually sounded in a progressive rising or descending order. Arpeggios on keyboard instruments may be called rolled chords.

15.3 Instruments

An instrument allows you to define a standard note sound and structure that you can reuse and play at different pitches. Each instrument can have up to five items applied:

- The duty cycle envelope
- The volume envelope
- The pitch envelope
- The arpeggio envelope
- DPCM samples

An envelope allows an item to vary over the duration of the note as it plays. It can be used to create vibrato or tremolo and change the attack and release of a note.

15.3.1 Envelopes

An envelope in sound and music describes how sound changes over time. A piano key when struck generates an immediate sound that gradually decreases in volume to zero. An envelope can control either volume or pitch (note frequency).

Clicking on one of the [Envelope] icons (Duty Cycle, Volume, Pitch, Arpeggio) of an instrument will display the envelope on the piano roll. You can then change its length and adjust each of its segments up and down.

The example in figure 15.5 shows the volume envelope for the bass instrument in the sample project. This would cause the volume of the sound to drop over the time the note is played.

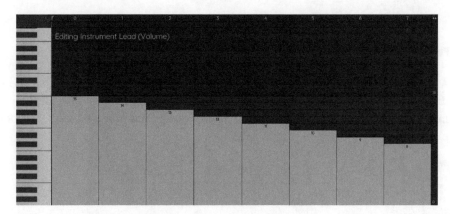

Figure 15.5 Editing the volume envelope of an instrument

15.3.2 DPCM samples

DPCM samples are 1-bit digital samples (Apple Music commonly uses 128-bit samples). They are very low quality but have been put to good use for providing drums and bass.

15.4   *Generating music data*

Once we have one or more songs designed in FamiStudio, the next step is to get the application to generate the code that will be included in our game code. We use the `export songs` function (located at the top of the FamiStudio application), select [FamiStudio Music Code], and set the format to [CA65] to match our selected assembler (see figure 15.6).

Leave both versions of the song selected so we can try each in our game. Select your project folder, and enter the file name as megablast-music.s.

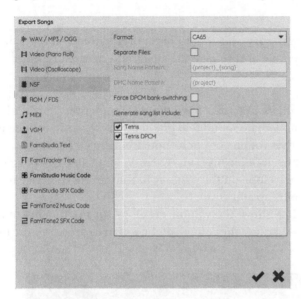

Figure 15.6   Exporting music code from FamiStudio

After clicking the tick button and entering the filename details, FamiStudio should display a dialog showing some details about the music data exported. Your output may vary from figure 15.7 slightly if the sample song has changed since this book was published.

```
Log

Info: Exporting all songs to a single assembly file.
Info: Header size : 33 bytes.
Info: Instruments size : 63 bytes.
Info: Tempo envelopes size : 3 bytes.
Info: Song 'Tetris' size: 185 bytes.
Info: Song 'Tetris DPCM' size: 182 bytes.
Info: Total assembly file size: 466 bytes.
Info: DMC bank 0 file size: 960 bytes.
Info: Volume track is used, you must set FAMISTUDIO_USE_VOLUME_TRACK = 1.
Info: Done!
```

Figure 15.7   Exported music data details

The output window breaks the data into a few sections, which helps us understand how using various features in your songs can affect the size of the output. In this case, both versions of the songs use 185 and 182 bytes each (466 bytes total), but the second version of the song that uses DPCM samples needs an additional 960 bytes for the samples themselves. We obviously don't have any problems with space in our sample game, but in more complex games, managing how much space things use becomes very important.

For the Tetris example file, two output files are created: megablast-music.s contains the main song data, and the file megablast-music.dmc contains the digital samples used by the second song. The .s file will contain code similar to the following.

Listing 15.1   Generated music data (megablast-music.s)

```
; This file is for the FamiStudio Sound Engine
; and was generated by FamiStudio

.if FAMISTUDIO_CFG_C_BINDINGS
.export _music_data_untitled=music_data_untitled
.endif

music_data_untitled:
    .byte 2
    .word @instruments
    .word @samples-4
    .word @song0ch0,@song0ch1,@song0ch2,@song0ch3,@song0ch4 ; 00 : Tetris
    .byte .lobyte(@tempo_env_1_mid), .hibyte(@tempo_env_1_mid), 0, 0
    .word @song1ch0,@song1ch1,@song1ch2,@song1ch3,@song1ch4 ; 01 : Tetris
DPCM
    .byte .lobyte(@tempo_env_1_mid), .hibyte(@tempo_env_1_mid), 0, 0

.export music_data_untitled
.global FAMISTUDIO_DPCM_PTR

@instruments:
    .word @env3,@env4,@env5,@env0 ; 00 : Bass
    .word @env1,@env4,@env5,@env0 ; 01 : Drum
    .word @env2,@env4,@env6,@env0 ; 02 : Lead

@env0:
    .byte $00,$c0,$7f,$00,$02
@env1:
    .byte $00,$cf,$ca,$c5,$c0,$00,$04
@env2:
    .byte $00,$cf,$ce,$cd,$cc,$cb,$ca,$c9,$c8,$00,$08
```

See the generated file for the rest of the code.

15.5   *Using music in our game*

Now that we have some music in the format the FamiStudio engine will understand, we need to add some code so that we can play the music in our game. First we need to include both the music data file and the music DMC samples file in our code so that we can use them. Find where we included the sound effects file in the previous chapter and include the music data file. After that, we include the DMC binary file containing the samples for the second track. We place this in a segment marked DPCM, as the NES APU expects the samples to be in a specific place in memory.

Listing 15.2   Including our music data and music samples (megablast.s)

```
;****************************************************************
; Include Sound Engine, Sound Effects and Music Data
;****************************************************************

.segment "CODE"

; FamiStudio config.
FAMISTUDIO_CFG_EXTERNAL        = 1
FAMISTUDIO_CFG_DPCM_SUPPORT    = 1
FAMISTUDIO_CFG_SFX_SUPPORT     = 1
FAMISTUDIO_CFG_SFX_STREAMS     = 2
FAMISTUDIO_CFG_EQUALIZER       = 1
FAMISTUDIO_USE_VOLUME_TRACK    = 1
FAMISTUDIO_USE_PITCH_TRACK     = 1
FAMISTUDIO_USE_SLIDE_NOTES     = 1
FAMISTUDIO_USE_VIBRATO         = 1
FAMISTUDIO_USE_ARPEGGIO        = 1
FAMISTUDIO_CFG_SMOOTH_VIBRATO  = 1
FAMISTUDIO_USE_RELEASE_NOTES   = 1
FAMISTUDIO_DPCM_OFF            = $e000

; CA65-specifc config.
.define FAMISTUDIO_CA65_ZP_SEGMENT    ZEROPAGE
.define FAMISTUDIO_CA65_RAM_SEGMENT   BSS
.define FAMISTUDIO_CA65_CODE_SEGMENT  CODE

.include "famistudio_ca65.s"

.include "megablast-sfx.s"
.include "megablast-music.s"

.segment "DPCM"
.incbin "megablast-music.dmc"

.segment "ZEROPAGE"
                                      Sound effects channel to use
sfx_channel: .res 1    ◄──────────
```

In that section of code, we referenced a new memory segment, so we need to adjust our megablast.cfg file that controls where the segments are used. We only need to change the SEGMENTS section, adding a new entry called DMC and adjusting the CODE entry so it will be placed after the new entry.

Listing 15.3 Adding a DMC segment to our configuration (megablast.cfg)

```
MEMORY {
  ZP:  start= $00,  size= $0100,type = rw, file= "";
  OAM: start= $0200,size= $0100,type = rw, file= "";
  RAM: start= $0300,size= $0500,type = rw, file= "";
  HDR: start= $0000,size= $0010,type = ro,file= %O,fill= yes, fillval= $00;
  ROM0:start= $8000,size= $4000,type= ro,file= %O, fill= yes, fillval= $00;
  ROM1:start= $C000,size= $2000,type= ro,file= %O, fill= yes, fillval= $00;
  DPCM:start= $e000,size= $1FFA,type= ro,file= %O, fill= yes, fillval= $ff;
  VECTORS: start= $fffa,size= $6, file= %O,fill= yes;
  CHR: start= $0000,size= $2000,type= ro,file= %O, fill= yes, fillval= $00;
}

SEGMENTS {
    ZEROPAGE: load = ZP,  type = zp;
    OAM:      load = OAM, type = bss, align = $100;
    BSS:      load = RAM, type = bss;
    HEADER:   load = HDR, type = ro;
    CODE:     load = ROM0, type = ro, align = $100;
    RODATA:   load = ROM0, type = ro;
    DPCM:     load = DPCM,     type = ro;
    VECTORS:  load = VECTORS, type = ro,  start = $FFFA;
    TILES:    load = CHR, type = ro;
}
```

In chapter 14, we already added calling the FamiStudio update routine to our NMI routine. So we only need to add a new function that can be called from various places in our game, with a parameter specifying the piece of music to play.

Add a new function called play_music to the megablast.s file. In it, we first save our music track number passed in the A register and then save the rest of the registers.

Then we get back the number of the track we want to play into the A register and call the FamiStudio play_music function. This sets up the music to be played, with the update function located in the NMI routine sending the data to the APU based on the timings we built into the music track in the editor.

Listing 15.4 Adding a play_music function (megablast.s)

```
;************************************************************
; Play a music track
; a = number of the music track to play
;************************************************************/
.segment "CODE"

.proc play_music
    sta temp+9          ← Saves the music track number
    tya
    pha                 ← Saves the current
    txa                   register values
    pha

    lda temp+9          ← Gets the music track to play
```

```
      jsr famistudio_music_play

      pla          ◄─────────  Restores the register values
      tax
      pla
      tay
      rts
.endproc
```

In our main function, we need to initialize the music engine so that it knows where the song data is located. We set the X and Y registers to point to the low and high bytes of the location where our music data is located. The label music_data_untitled is located near the top of the megablast-music.s file.

After this, we call the FamiStudio initialization function. This ensures that the music engine knows where to find our music data.

Listing 15.5   Initializing the music engine

```
.segment "CODE"
 .proc main
     ; main application - rendering is currently off
     lda #1
     sta highscore+1              ◄──────────────────┐
                                                       │ Sets the initial high score to 1000
     lda #1                        ◄───────  NTSC
     ldx #.lobyte(music_data_untitled)
     ldy #.hibyte(music_data_untitled)
     jsr famistudio_init

     ldx #.lobyte(sounds)          ◄───────  Sets the address of the sound effects
     ldy #.hibyte(sounds)
     jsr famistudio_sfx_init
```

We should now have everything in place to start our music playing. We will add a call to our new play music function after we have displayed our title screen as follows.

Listing 15.6   Adding the call to play music function (megablast.s)

```
   ; draw the title screen
   jsr display_title_screen

   ; set our game settings
   lda #VBLANK_NMI|BG_0000|OBJ_1000
      sta ppu_ctl0
      lda #BG_ON|OBJ_ON
      sta ppu_ctl1

   jsr ppu_update

   lda #0          ◄───────  Plays the first song
   jsr play_music
```

As our sample contains a second version of the song using samples for drums, we can change to the second song when the player starts the game.

Listing 15.7   **Playing a second song during game play (megablast.s)**

```
; draw the game screen
jsr display_game_screen

; display the player's ship
jsr display_player

lda #64
sta displaylevel
lda #%00010001          ◄──────    Sets a flag so the current score
ora update                         and level will be displayed
sta update

jsr ppu_update

lda #1                  ◄─────── Plays a second song
jsr play_music

mainloop:
```

You should now be able to compile the code and test it out in the emulator. You should hear the first version of the Teris song on the title screen and the second version that uses the DPCM samples during the game.

Exercise 15.1

Choose another one of the FamiStudio sample songs, export it, and try it with this same code. You will need to make sure you pick a song that only uses the original channels built into the NES (*Castlevania 2* and *Silver Surfer*, for example) and change the label name for the start of the music data.

Summary

- A FamiStudio project can contain multiple songs.
- Each song can be made up of one or more patterns.
- Each pattern is made up of multiple notes played by one or more instruments.
- Where you have multiple effects applied to individual notes that you might want to reuse, these can be combined into instruments.
- We use FamiStudio to generate the music data that is then played by the music engine.
- FamiStudio comes with a lot of sample projects to use as examples of what can be achieved.

Where to from here?

16

We have put together a simple game over the course of this book. With a few enhancements, it could be made more interesting and a much more professional title.

Our sample game covers only one genre of video games (i.e., a shoot-em-up). Especially with the NES and its extended capabilities, there are quite a few other genres that can be achieved on the hardware. Once you have finished a game, one of the greatest rewards is to see others playing it, whether that be via a free download ROM, sold online, or produced in physical form, perhaps even with a proper box and manual.

16.1 *Enhancing our game*

Our sample game, *Mega Blast,* is still quite simple and could do with several features added to turn it into a more polished and professional title—and, of course, make it more fun for the player. We have discussed some ideas for improving things as we have worked through the book, but let's expand on these as follows.

16.1.1 *More enemies*

We covered extending the information we stored on each enemy object in chapter 12. To add more variety to the game, it would be good to add some more enemies with slightly different behaviors. New types of enemies could have more complex attack patterns; for example, instead of just coming down the screen toward the player, a new enemy could go across the screen and launch another projectile directly toward the player. This would give the player less reaction time with the reward of a higher point score if they hit the enemy before it fires at the player. The appearance of new enemies could be purely random or perhaps based on how far through the game you are. Another example of a good additional enemy behavior would be to have the larger meteors split into two smaller ones (a bit like *Asteroids*) that continue downward but at different angles from the original meteor.

16.1.2 *Extra lives*

As a player makes progress through a game and their score increases, another reward for the player is earning extra lives. The extra lives are usually added on either a regular points boundary (e.g., 5,000, 10,000, 15,000, etc.) or as a set number of extra lives based on a table of scores that the player needs to pass.

In our sample game, the logic for seeing if the player has beaten the next score and gained an extra life is best added to the `add_score` function. As an example, let us assume that we have another variable called `next_extra_life`, a single byte holding the next score to pass. It only needs to be a single byte, as we are only interested in when the score passes a thousand-score boundary.

Where we declare our other zero-page variables, we need to add a variable called `next_extra_life` that is a single byte in size. Then, in our main function, we initialize the `next_extra_life` variable, where we set up the other game's settings.

Lastly, in our `add_score` function, we add a short section of code to check whether the player's score's thousand digit is equal to or greater than the next extra life variable. If it is, we add 5 to the next extra life variable, increase the player's lives, and set the flag to trigger updating the lives counter onscreen.

Listing 16.1 Awarding the player an extra life (megablast.s)

```
shake: .res 1
enemycount: .res 1
displaylevel: .res 1       Sets the player's
next_extra_life: .res 1    starting lives
lda #5
```

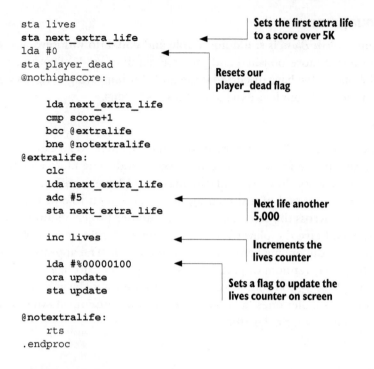

```
        sta lives
        sta next_extra_life          ◄───┐   Sets the first extra life
        lda #0                       ◄──  │   to a score over 5K
        sta player_dead
        @nothighscore:                         Resets our
                                               player_dead flag

            lda next_extra_life
            cmp score+1
            bcc @extralife
            bne @notextralife
        @extralife:
            clc
            lda next_extra_life
            adc #5                   ◄───      Next life another
            sta next_extra_life                5,000

            inc lives                ◄───
                                               Increments the
                                               lives counter
            lda #%00000100           ◄───
            ora update
            sta update                         Sets a flag to update the
                                               lives counter on screen

        @notextralife:
            rts
        .endproc
```

> ### Exercise 16.1
>
> Add an extra life sound effect. In addition to a visual indication of the player gaining an extra life, it would also be good to have a specific sound effect that plays.

16.1.3 *Increased difficulty*

Only the chance of a new enemy appearing changes in our sample game as the player progresses. It would be better for the game to start with the enemies moving more slowly, increasing speed as the player progresses through levels. For other types of games, difficulty might increase based on the number of screens or waves of enemies completed.

16.1.4 *Music*

In our tutorial chapter, we only added a music piece from one of the samples that comes with the FamiStudio software. Selecting or writing a more suitable piece of music will make our game come alive. You could have different music depending on whether the player is on the title screen or in the game. If more distinctive levels with more enemies and different backgrounds have been introduced, you could also have different music pieces matching the style of the levels.

16.1.5 Arcade touches

A few more things to think about adding to give your title a professional touch and make it more compelling would be

High score table—Save more than one high score, and optionally also save the high scores to battery-backed random access memory (RAM) on the cartridge (see appendix B).

Animated title screen—Add some animated background graphics to make it more appealing and perhaps a second alternative screen showing each of the enemy types and the scores they are worth if destroyed.

Gameplay demo—While waiting for the player to start a game, show the game in action. The player's ship could be moved randomly back and forth, constantly shooting, with the enemies appearing as normal, and then the screen could switch back to the main title screen after a brief period of time.

16.2 Extending the NES

One of the reasons the NES had such a long life as a console was that developers could extend the functionality of the console by adding features inside the game cartridge. These include such things as

- More ROM space for code, graphics, and music
- More video memory to allow for additional name tables
- Additional interrupts generated
- Battery-backed memory for saving games
- Additional audio hardware that can provide more sound channels with different capabilities
- An enhanced color attribute table, thus allowing more color detail to be displayed
- Additional processing capabilities (e.g., fast multiplication, scanline interrupts)

16.2.1 What is a mapper?

The term *mapper* comes from the concept of memory mapping where early extended cartridges for the NES console provided additional ROM space for larger games (see figure 16.1). When the Famicom (the Japanese version of the NES) first launched the original games that came with the system, they were limited to either 16K or 32K of ROM for the game code, along with 8K of ROM for the patterns used for the tiles and sprites.

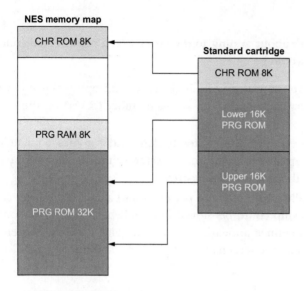

Figure 16.1   Standard NES cartridge memory layout

To create larger, more complex games, additional logic chips were added to the cartridge hardware that allowed the programmer to have more space for both code and patterns using a technique called bank switching. Due to its 8-bit CPU and 16-bit memory, the NES can only access 64K of memory at any one time. But by swapping parts of memory in and out of the 64K memory space, programmers were able to extend the available space for both code and patterns.

These extended cartridges still only had 8K of CHR ROM and 32K of PRG ROM active at any one time, but by writing to a particular memory address, the logic chip inside the cartridge would select different sections of memory as the current CHR ROM or PRG ROM that the NES could use. Different mappers would break the memory segments into different sizes and configurations (see figure 16.2).

There were several add-on chips developed by Nintendo itself that extended the space available using slightly different methods (see the MMC line of mappers detailed in appendix B). Third-party companies also developed their own chips and techniques for extending the available storage space for code and patterns.

How you, the programmer, can use this extra memory changes depending on which mapper you choose. But, in general, they usually set aside one or more memory locations that you write values to and control which memory banks are active, allowing you to use the other capabilities of the mapper. These memory locations work just like the memory locations we used earlier in the book to talk to the video controller and sound processor and read things such as the game controllers. See appendix B for more information on some of the more common mappers from Nintendo, Konami, and more.

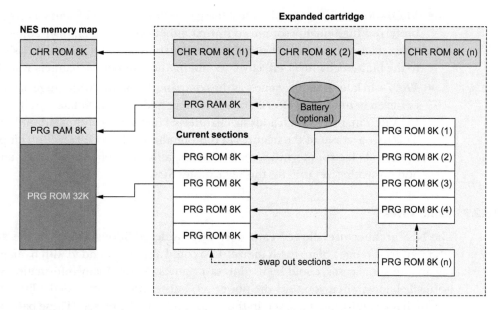

Figure 16.2 Example of expanded NES cartridge memory layout

16.2.2 *More sound*

By default, the NES has five sound channels available: two square waves, one triangle, one noise, and the 1-bit digital sample channel. Using these, musicians were able to create quite complex and compelling original music pieces and sound effects for the early games. But as the games became more complex and more storage space was available in the later cartridges, additional sound channels were provided along with the extra storage space for code and patterns. Some examples of mappers that also provided additional sound channels are as follows:

- *MMC5*—Released by Nintendo, the MMC5 mapper adds two additional pulse wave channels and a PCM channel (digital sound).
- *Namco 163*—Released with several Namco titles, the Namco 163 mapper adds up to an additional eight sound channels that play wave table samples, with each channel having a linear volume control. It only has a limited clock, so using all eight channels reduces the update frequency of the sound values.
- *Sunsoft 5B*—Sunsoft released a single game, *Gimmick!*, that makes use of this mapper's Yamaha YM2149F sound chip. This sound chip is a variant of the General Instruments AY-3-8910 sound chip used in several 8-bit consoles and computers such as the MSX, Amstrad CPC, and Vectrex. This chip has three independent wave channels and a noise channel that can be mixed with one or more of the wave channels.

- *VRC6*—Konami converted quite a few games over to the NES and Famicom and preferred high-quality sound, so its first enhanced sound mapper added three extra channels for sound: two pulse waves and one sawtooth. These work similarly to the built-in channels, effectively doubling the number of channels available.

- *VRC7*—In later Konami games, as the company did on the MSX range of computers, even better sound effects and music were added. To facilitate this, it released the VRC7 mapper, which adds six channels of frequency-modulated (FM) audio. This uses a subset of the features in the Yamaha TM2413 OPLL sound chip used in several electronic synthesizer keyboards, a number of arcade games, and the add-on synthesizer unit for the Sega Master System.

16.2.3   Game saves

The NES architecture allowed cartridges to provide additional RAM (in the $6000-$7fff address range) of up to 8K in size. This could also be extended with bank switching and, in some cases, could be used to save games. As RAM, any information would normally be lost when you turn the power off, but several games added a lithium battery so that any information saved in the RAM would not be erased. These batteries do eventually go flat, but a cartridge can be opened and the battery easily replaced.

A limited number of later games used erasable electronic programmed read-only memory (EEPROM) and were able to keep game saves without using a battery. EEPROMs of the time that the games were released for the NES could only be written to a certain number of times and were very expensive. You can think of EEPROMs as the early (much smaller and slower) version of the memory sticks in common use today.

16.2.4   Extra features

In addition to expanding the amount of space for code and patterns, adding extra sound capabilities, and saving game progress, there were a few mappers that extended the NES's capabilities even further.

FOUR-SCREEN NAME TABLE MIRRORING

The NES as standard only has enough video memory to store two tile name tables but has four virtual name tables with the two real name tables being mirrored either vertically or horizontally. Another enhancement that could be provided in a cartridge was an additional 2K of RAM providing room for another two tile name tables (see figure 16.3).

1	2
3	4

Figure 16.3   Adding an extra 2K of name table RAM allows four separate tables.

IMPROVING ATTRIBUTE TABLE MAPPING

Only being able to change the palette being used for each group of four tiles is one of the more limiting aspects of NES graphics capabilities and leads to a lot of games that look very limited in terms of the number of colors displayed onscreen. The Nintendo MMC5 mapper introduced the concept of extended attributes. Instead of the attribute table being stored with the name tables in normal video memory, it is in the cartridge expansion RAM. Each tile can select its palette and can also select that its tile pattern comes from either the first or the second CHR pattern table.

SCANLINE INTERRUPT

A few mappers added an additional interrupt that triggered each time a scan line was drawn on the screen. While the beam drawing the screen resets back to the start of the next line, there is a very short period where code can be executed. This code can be used to change palette entries or even change the scroll registers to allow only part of the screen to be scrolled (often called split screen scrolling).

16.3 Publishing your finished game

There is nothing greater as a developer of a homebrew title for a classic system such as the NES than having it played and appreciated by as many people as possible. There are different types of NES enthusiasts who have different levels of expectations.

16.3.1 Free ROM download

Some, of course, want everything for free and so will push for a freely available ROM download. For some authors, it is enough just to get gratitude for their efforts. However, rather than give away the whole game freely, you could release a version of your game with limited features, perhaps with fewer levels or a time limit. This way, users can get a sample of what your game is like without you giving away the whole thing.

16.3.2 Online ROM sales

There is no real way to stop people from sharing a ROM once they have downloaded it, but this still does not detract from having a ROM image that users can download for a fee. Many of the online stores you can add to your website can include digital goods, and you can easily add your finished NES ROM as a downloadable purchase.

16.3.3 Physical cartridges

The ultimate repository for your hard work in developing a new game for the NES is to see it published in physical form. Not that many years ago, this was achieved by sacrificing original common NES titles and repurposing both the circuit boards and the case so that they could hold new titles. This, of course, greatly limits the number of copies that can be produced. Most of these titles were published as bare cartridges without a box or manual.

Through the cooperation of a number of these homebrew publishers, a new case mold was created, along with several clone game circuit board designs that supported one or more of the more popular memory mappers (see appendix B). These were swiftly copied by various industrious individuals and companies, and a number of sites offer individual parts so that you can self-publish your titles (see figure 16.4).

Figure 16.4   UNROM printed circuit board (PCB) from Muramasa

SELF-PUBLICATION

To publish a game, you will need an appropriate cartridge, printed circuit board, and electronic components that support the mapper you chose to develop your title for (see table 16.1). The level of complication of the mapper determines the cost of the components needed.

Table 16.1   Physical cartridge component sellers and custom project sites

Name	Link	Notes
Muramasa	http://mng.bz/K9D0	PCBs only
Mouse Byte Labs	http://mng.bz/G9NO	Guide
Game-Tech	http://mng.bz/0IM6	PCBs and Shells
NES Repair Shop	http://mng.bz/z0nQ	Shells
6502 Collective	https://6502collective.com/	PCBs and Shells

In addition, providing a complete original game experience including a physical box and manual will assist in making your title more attractive to collectors. This does increase the amount of funds that will be required depending on the number of copies you make. Recently, many homebrew authors have used Kickstarter to get a known number of copies that are required so that funds are not wasted on unsold copies.

USING AN EXISTING PUBLISHER

Publishing your own titles allows you to control the process and keep any profits, but it does come with a lot of financial risk and requires a large amount of time to produce, assemble, and ship titles to the end consumers. This is where publishers come in, and due to the popularity of retro games and the NES itself, there are a number of publishers who produce very high-quality titles (see table 16.2). They take on the risk of the number of cartridges to produce and handle all the production and sales, with you, the author, receiving an agreed amount per copy sold. As with anything like this, make sure you have a written contract with the publisher and have read all the terms and conditions before committing.

Table 16.2   NES cartridge publishers

Name	Link
Broke Studio	https://www.brokestudio.fr/
CollectorVision	https://www.collectorvision.com/
Infinite NES Lives	https://www.infiniteneslives.com/
Mega Cat Studios	https://megacatstudios.com/
Mind Kids (AliExpress Store)	https://www.aliexpress.com/store/5741092
Morphcat Games	http://morphcat.de/
Limited Run Games	https://limitedrungames.com/
Retro-Bit Publishing	https://retro-bit.com/retro-bit-publishing/

16.4   Other types of games

Throughout this book, we have covered only a simple type of game so we could focus on adding mechanics and discovering the capabilities of the NES hardware. There are many other genres of games that are perfectly suited to the NES, some of which defined popular genres that were expanded on in later systems. As the NES's architecture allowed it to be extended by adding additional hardware to the game cartridges (see appendix B), this also allowed for much larger, more complex titles, with lots of music, samples, and a variety of graphics.

16.4.1   Platformers

One genre of game that the NES represented particularly well and was known for was platformers. These types of games have the player controlling a main character that climbs ladders or jumps between platforms.

The first versions of these sorts of games, like *Jump Man* and *Donkey Kong*, had single screens where the player needed to collect several objects or just make it to the top of the screen (see figure 16.5).

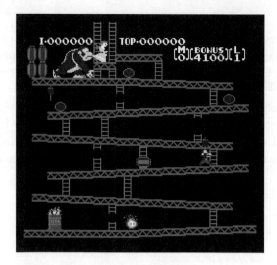

Figure 16.5   *Donkey Kong* **on the NES**

Later games, such as *Megama*n, had several screens that the player could move freely between, working their way past enemies, collecting objects, and working through puzzles (see figure 16.6).

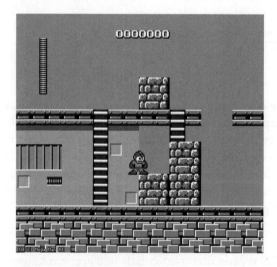

Figure 16.6   *Megaman* **on the NES**

16.4.2 Scrolling platformers

One of leading games that made the Famicom (and the NES after it) so popular was the very first *Super Mario Bros* game (see figure 16.7). This game took advantage of the console's hardware horizontal scrolling capabilities and levels designed around the 16 × 16 square color limitations.

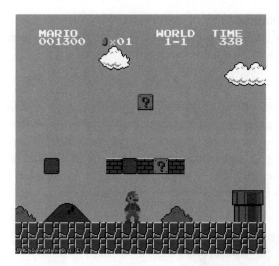

Figure 16.7 *Super Marios Bros* **on the NES**

Like the sequels to the original *Super Mario Bros* game, a few other games also used scrolling screens rather than switching between screens when the player reached the edge of the screen. The vertical name-table mirroring configuration has the two name tables side by side. Then changing the horizontal scroll register allows the next part of the scene to be shown. In the background, the next sections of the view are drawn into the left-hand name table offscreen, and when the end of the right-hand screen is reached, the two name tables are swapped, allowing a continuous, long scrolling area (see figure 16.8).

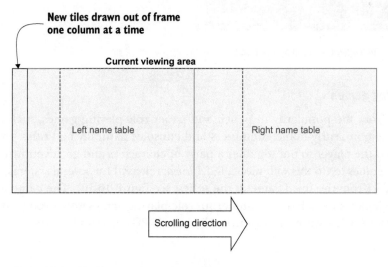

Figure 16.8 **Handling a horizontally scrolling area**

Early games used sprites to display the player's score, as the whole screen had to scroll; later cartridges allowed horizontal interrupts that accommodated partial screen scrolling and even four-way scrolling with fixed score areas.

16.4.3 Action adventures

The NES popularized the action-adventure game type with the *Legend of Zelda* game (see figure 16.9). This style of game owes allegiance to *Adventure* on the Atari 2600, with its top-down view, from which a main character had to search multiple screens for objects that could then be used to get past various enemies and blocked pathways. Some of the later platform games inherited some of the elements introduced in *Zelda*, such as exploration and item collection and reuse of items for puzzles.

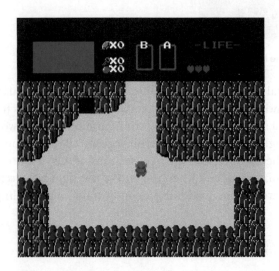

Figure 16.9 *The Legend of Zelda* **on the NES**

16.4.4 Role-playing games

Spawning from the popularity of pencil and paper role-playing games, such as *Dungeons and Dragons*, early home computers and consoles naturally had titles produced that allowed the player to put together a party of characters and go adventuring. One of the first games to do this well was called *Ultima*, released for several systems, including the NES (from the third game in the series; see figure 16.10). The game was very popular in Japan, so much so that numerous role-playing games were produced by Japanese developers (spawning a subgenre called the JRPG) in a similar style.

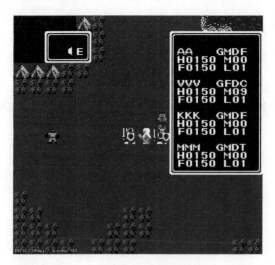

Figure 16.10 *Ultima Exodus* **on the NES**

Summary

- There are quite a few things that can be added to our sample game to make it more polished and compelling for players, such as a high score table, extra difficulty, music, and more arcade touches.

- The NES was popular, and along with its capability to be extended via extra hardware in the game cartridges, it championed several more complex game genres, like platformers and action-adventure games, as well as role-playing games.

- Modern titles for the NES can be published several ways, such as via a free ROM download of a demo or even a full version to allow as many people access to your game as possible, sale of a ROM online, or maybe even produced in physical cartridge form with a proper box and manual to be enjoyed by the many NES enthusiasts and collectors.

- NES cartridges are not limited to 32K of PRG ROM and 8K of CHR ROM; using custom logic chips, more space for code and patterns can be used, allowing much larger and more complex games.

- Not only can cartridges contain more storage, but they can also provide additional sound channels to allow richer music and more sound effects to be played without interrupting other sounds already being played.

- Cartridges can also provide space for progress in games to be saved using either a built-in battery or EEPROM memory.

- There are well over 100 documented mappers that add different capabilities to the NES console, which is one of the main reasons the console enjoyed such a long life.

Installation and setup A

Now that we have looked at the various options for each of the different types of tools that you will need to start developing NES games, we will walk through getting set up on each of the three supported platforms.

A.1 Windows

This section covers the Windows operating system.

A.1.1 Setting up the CC65 Assembler

If you are using one of the Windows platforms, from Windows XP up to Windows 11, you need to go to the cc65 home page and select the Windows Snapshot link at the bottom of the page. Clicking the link will download the ZIP library cc65-snapshot-win32.zip. Most reasonably modern versions of Windows can extract files from ZIP files, in which case you can just right-click the downloaded file and select Extract All from the menu. In the dialog box that is shown, change the directory to C:\cc65, and click the Extract button (see figure A.1).

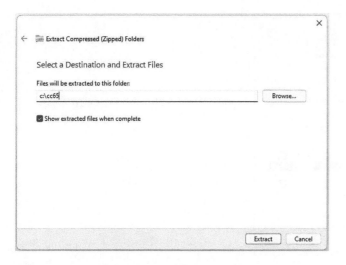

Figure A.1 CC65 install—extracting files

Once complete, you will see a folder named c:\cc65 with contents like those shown in figure A.2.

asminc
bin
cfg
html
include
lib
samples
target

Figure A.2 CC65 folder contents

A.1.2 *Installing and setting up the emulator*

Download the version for Windows from the main website here: https://www.mesen .ca/. Once you have it downloaded, installation is very simple: basically, select a folder (e.g., c:\mesen on Windows systems), and put the application in that folder. When you run it for the first time, it will present a configuration wizard screen that allows you to choose where you want to keep the files Mesen creates (either in your user profile or in the Mesen directory). Select one or more input mappings (game controller types and keyboard layouts) and whether you would like a shortcut placed on your desktop to be able to easily find Mesen later (see figure A.3).

Figure A.3   Mesen configuration wizard

A.1.3   *Installing and setting up the editor*

To download and install Visual Studio Code, use the official site here: https://code .visualstudio.com/. There are several plugins available that support syntax highlighting and build command mapping for the 6502 Assembler. One of the extensions to try is ca65 Macro Assembler Language Support (6502/65816) from Cole Campbell (https://mng.bz/GZwq).

To find this in Visual Studio Code, go to the extensions tab on the left-hand side and type "ca65." The extension should be near the top of the list of items returned. Click on it and then the Install button. You will need to accept and trust the publisher for the extension to be enabled (see figure A.4). This extension not only adds syntax highlighting to Visual Studio Code but will also enable the build command to use the CC65 compiler/assembler to compile your code from within the editor.

Figure A.4   ca65 macro assembler extension

A.1.4 Installing the graphics tool

Download the NES Tile Editor from https://www.electricadventures.net/Pages/Category/34. Then run the included setup program, and it will place a shortcut on the desktop.

A.1.5 Installing the music tool

Download the Windows version of FamiStudio from https://famistudio.org/ (see figure A.5).

Figure A.5 Downloading the Windows installer of FamiStudio

Once you have the download, run the installer (setup.exe) (see figure A.6). A shortcut to FamiStudio and the included demo songs will be added to your Start menu. If you get a warning when installing or if the app crashes when running, check out the documentation section of the website for the fix. Also make sure you download the NES sound engine code for the CA65 Assembler.

Figure A.6 Downloading the NES sound engine for the CA65 Assembler

A.2 Linux

This section covers the Linux operating system.

A.2.1 Setting up the CC65 Assembler

Setting up cc65 on a Linux system involves either downloading a binary (Debian based) or building the project from a Git repository.

DOWNLOADING A BINARY

To download a binary from trikaliotos.net, go to the home page and, follow the instructions: https://spiro.trikaliotis.net/debian.

BUILDING FROM GIT

On a Debian or Ubuntu-based Linux system, you can build the latest version of cc65 on your system using the following commands:

```
sudo apt install build-essential git
mkdir -p ~/develop
cd ~/develop
git clone https://github.com/cc65/cc65.git
cd cc65
nice make -j2
make install PREFIX=~/.local
which cc65
```

If your Linux login account has been configured to run applications built from source and installed for only one user, you need to change the last step to be

```
/home/<username>/.local/bin/cc65
```

If not, then the following needs to be included in your PATH variable:

```
~/.local/bin
```

> **NOTE**   These instructions were current at the time of printing, but if you have issues, the source of the instructions is located here: https://www.nesdev.org/wiki/Installing_CC65.

A.2.2   *Installing and setting up the emulator*

Download the version for Linux (Ubuntu) from the main website at https://www.mesen.ca/, or compile a version for your distribution from the GitHub source code and instructions here: https://github.com/SourMesen/Mesen/. Before installing, you will need the following components installed:

- glibx 2.23+
- Mono 5.18+
- SDL 2

Once you have it downloaded, installation is very simple. Basically, select a folder (e.g., /home/mesen on your system drive), and put the application in that folder. When you run it for the first time, it will present a configuration wizard screen that allows you to choose where you want to keep the files Mesen creates (either in your user profile or in the Mesen directory; see figure A.7). Select one or more input mappings (game controller types and keyboard layouts) and whether you would like a shortcut placed on your desktop to be able to easily find Mesen later.

Figure A.7   Mesen configuration wizard

A.2.3   *Installing and setting up the editor*

To download and install Visual Studio Code, use the official site here: https://code .visualstudio.com/. There are several plugins available that support syntax highlighting and build command mapping for 6502 Assembler. One of the extensions to try is ca65 Macro Assembler Language Support (6502/65816) from Cole Campbell (https://mng.bz/GZwq).

To find this in Visual Studio Code, go to the Extensions tab on the left-hand side, and type "ca65." The extension should be near the top of the list of items returned. Click on it and then the Install button (see figure A.8). You will need to accept and trust the publisher for the extension to be enabled. This extension not only adds syntax highlighting to Visual Studio Code but will also enable the build command to use the CC65 compiler/assembler to compile your code from within the editor (see figure A.8).

Figure A.8   ca65 macro assembler extension

Installing the graphics tool

Download NES Lightbox for Linux (the appropriate version for your environment) from https://github.com/kzurawel/neslightbox. Install the music tool. Download the Linux version of FamiStudio from https://famistudio.org/ (see figure A.9).

Figure A.9   Downloading the Linux installer of FamiStudio

Once you have the download, follow the instructions on the GitHub page. Also make sure you download the NES sound engine code for the CA65 Assembler (see figure A.10).

Figure A.10   Downloading the NES sound engine for the CA65 Assembler

A.3   macOS

This section covers the macOS operating system.

A.3.1   Setting up the CC65 Assembler

To assist with the installation on macOS, the open source site MacPorts has premade packages of the CC65 compiler and assembler. First install MacPorts, following the instructions here: https://www.macports.org/install.php (see figure A.11).

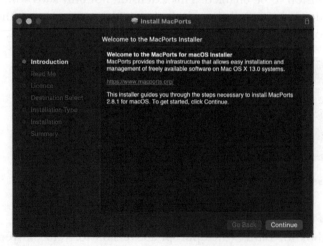

Figure A.11   Installing MacPorts

Once it is installed, open a fresh Terminal session and enter the following command:

```
sudo port install cc65
```

You will need to enter your administrator password to complete the installation. The CC65 executables will be automatically added to the command path, so any scripts can access them by name without needing a direct path.

A.3.2 *Installing and setting up the emulator*

At the time of writing, there was not a build of Mesen for macOS, but the FCEUX emulator has a downloadable installation that you can use here: https://fceux.com/web/download.html. Select the macOS binary; then open it, and drag it into the Applications folder to install.

A.3.3 *Installing and setting up the editor*

To download and install Visual Studio Code, use the official site here: https://code.visualstudio.com/.

There are several plugins available that support syntax highlighting and build command mapping for 6502 Assembler. One of the extensions to try is ca65 Macro Assembler Language Support (6502/65816) from Cole Campbell (https://mng.bz/GZwq).

To find this in Visual Studio Code, go to the extensions tab on the left-hand side, and type "ca65." The extension should be near the top of the list of items returned. Click on it and then the Install button (see figure A.12). You will need to accept and trust the publisher for the extension to be enabled. This extension not only adds syntax highlighting to Visual Studio Code but will also enable the build command to use the CC65 compiler/assembler to compile your code from within the editor.

Figure A.12   ca65 macro assembler extension

A.3.4 *Installing the graphics tool*

Download NES Lightbox for Mac OSX from https://github.com/kzurawel/neslightbox.

A.3.5   *Installing the music tool*

Download the macOS version of FamiStudio from https://famistudio.org/ (see figure A.13).

Figure A.13   Downloading the macOS installer of FamiStudio

Once you have the download, uncompress the file, and then launch the FamiStudio app. The demo songs are included in the contents. The app is unsigned and might require you to ignore a few warnings (see the website for more details). Also make sure you download the NES sound engine code for the CA65 Assembler (see figure A.14).

Figure A.14   Downloading the NES sound engine for the CA65 Assembler

Memory mappers

There are around 100 types of mappers for the NES. Each one usually has a name, and each usage of the mapper has been assigned a number by the iNES emulator community. These numbers are supported by most of the NES emulators. The mapper names are based on the type of hardware (chipset) the cartridge uses.

Due to the number of different mappers available, only the more popular mapper configurations will be shown in detail in this book. For more information on specific mappers from the list here, refer to the NESdev Wiki article here: https://www.nesdev.org/wiki/Mapper

B.1   Complete mapper list

At the time of writing, table B.1 represents a complete list of the mappers recorded.

Table B.1   Complete mapper list

iNES mapper	Common designation(s)	Notes
0	NROM	
1	SxROM, MMC1	
2	UxROM	
3	CNROM	
4	TxROM, MMC3, MMC6	
5	ExROM, MMC5	Contains expansion sound
7	AxROM	
9	PxROM, MMC2	
10	FxROM, MMC4	
11	Color Dreams	
13	CPROM	
15	100-in-1 Contra Function 16	Multicart
16	Bandai EPROM (24C02)	
18	Jaleco SS8806	
19	Namco 163	Contains expansion sound
21	VRC4a, VRC4c	
22	VRC2a	
23	VRC2b, VRC4e	
24	VRC6a	Contains expansion sound
25	VRC4b, VRC4d	
26	VRC6b	Contains expansion sound
34	BNROM, NINA-001	
64	RAMBO-1	MMC3 clone with extra features
66	GxROM, MxROM	
68	After Burner	ROM-based name tables
69	FME-7, Sunsoft 5B	The 5B is the FME-7 with expansion sound.
71	Camerica/Codemasters	Similar to UNROM
73	VRC3	
74	Pirate MMC3 derivative	Has both CHR ROM and CHR RAM (2K)
75	VRC1	
76	Namco 109 variant	
79	NINA-03/NINA-06	It's either 003 or 006; we don't know right now.
85	VRC7	Contains expansion sound
86	JALECO-JF-13	
94	Senjou no Ookami	
105	NES-EVENT	Similar to MMC1
113	NINA-03/NINA-06	For multicarts including mapper 79 games
118	TxSROM, MMC3	MMC3 with independent mirroring control
119	TQROM, MMC3	Has both CHR ROM and CHR RAM
159	Bandai EPROM (24C01)	
166	SUBOR	
167	SUBOR	
180	Crazy Climber	Variation of UNROM, fixed first bank at $8000
185	CNROM with protection diodes	
192	Pirate MMC3 derivative	Has both CHR ROM and CHR RAM (4K)
206	DxROM, Namco 118 / MIMIC-1	Simplified MMC3 predecessor lacking some features
210	Namco 175 and 340	Namco 163 with different mirroring
228	Action 52	
232	Camerica/Codemasters Quattro	Multicarts

B.2 NROM

The NROM mapper refers to the original memory configuration of the initial cartridges released for the NES (and Famicom). They came with either 16K or 32K of ROM, with no other special features.

B.2.1 Overview

The NROM memory mapper has the details listed in table B.2.

Table B.2 NROM overview

Item	Details
PRG ROM size	16 KiB for NROM-128, 32 KiB for NROM-256 (DIP-28 standard pinout)
PRG ROM bank size	Not bank switched
PRG RAM	2 or 4 KiB, not bank switched; only in Family Basic (but most emulators provide 8)
CHR capacity	8 KiB ROM (DIP-28 standard pinout) but most emulators support RAM
CHR bank size	Not bank switched; see CNROM
Name table mirroring	Solder pads select vertical or horizontal mirroring
Subject to bus conflicts	Yes, but irrelevant

B.2.2 Banks

All banks are fixed:

- *CPU* $6000-$7FFF—Family Basic only: PRG RAM; mirrored as necessary to fill an entire 8 KiB window; write protectable with an external switch
- *CPU* $8000-$BFFF—First 16 KB of ROM
- *CPU* $C000-$FFFF—Last 16 KB of ROM (NROM-256) or mirror of $8000-$BFFF (NROM-128)

B.3 MMC1

The Nintendo MMC1 mapper was used in quite a few titles and allows a lot of control over swapping both PRG and CHR ROM banks with up to 512K of total ROM space. In addition, an optional 8K RAM bank can be included, along with a battery to keep the contents for game saves.

B.3.1 Overview

The MMC1 memory mapper has the details listed in table B.3.

Table B.3   MMC1 overview

Item	Details
Company	Nintendo, others
Games	390
Complexity	ASIC
Boards	SKROM, SLROM, SNROM, others
Pinout	MMC1 pinout
PRG ROM capacity	256K (512K)
PRG ROM window	16K + 16K fixed or 32K
PRG RAM capacity	32K
PRG RAM window	8K
CHR capacity	128K
CHR window	4K + 4K or 8K
Name table mirroring	H, V, or 1, switchable
Bus conflicts	No
IRQ	No
Audio	No
iNES mappers	001, 105, 155

B.3.2 *Banks*

The MMC1 memory mapper divides its memory banks up as follows:

- *CPU* $6000-$7FFF—8 KB PRG RAM bank (optional)
- *CPU* $8000-$BFFF—16 KB PRG ROM bank, either switchable or fixed to the first bank
- *CPU* $C000-$FFFF—16 KB PRG ROM bank, either fixed to the last bank or switchable
- *PPU* $0000-$0FFF—4 KB switchable CHR bank
- *PPU* $1000-$1FFF—4 KB switchable CHR bank

Through writes to the MMC1 control register, it is possible for the program to swap the fixed and switchable PRG ROM banks or to set up 32 KB PRG bank switching (like BNROM), but most games use the default setup, which is like that of UxROM.

B.4   *MMC2*

The Nintendo MMC2 mapper, which is a bit simpler than MMC1, allows 128K for PRG ROM and 128K for CHR ROM. Only the first 8K of the ROM space can be switched with another block, leaving the upper 24K fixed. Each 4K of the CHR ROM can be switched with another block.

B.4.1   Overview

The MMC2 memory mapper has the details listed in table B.4.

Table B.4   MMC2 overview

Item	Details
Company	Nintendo
Games	1 (Punch Out)
Complexity	ASIC
Boards	PNROM, PEEOROM
Pinout	MMC2 pinout
PRG ROM capacity	128K
PRG ROM window	8K + 24K fixed
PRG RAM capacity	8K (PC10 ver.)
PRG RAM window	Fixed
CHR capacity	128K
CHR window	4K + 4K (triggered)
Name table mirroring	H or V, switchable
Bus conflicts	No
IRQ	No
Audio	No
iNES mappers	009

B.4.2   Banks

The MMC2 memory mapper divides its memory banks up as follows:

- *CPU* $6000-$7FFF—8 KB PRG RAM bank (Play Choice version only; contains a 6264 and 74139)
- *CPU* $8000-$9FFF—8 KB switchable PRG ROM bank
- *CPU* $A000-$FFFF—Three 8 KB PRG ROM banks, fixed to the last three banks
- *PPU* $0000-$0FFF—Two 4 KB switchable CHR ROM banks
- *PPU* $1000-$1FFF—Two 4 KB switchable CHR ROM banks

B.5   MMC3

The Nintendo MMC3 mapper arrived in 1988 and was used in several games, with the most notable being the later games in the *Mega Man* series of games.

B.5.1   Overview

The MMC3 memory mapper has the details listed in table B.5.

Table B.5   MMC3 overview

Item	Details
Company	Nintendo, others
Games	300
Complexity	ASIC
Boards	TSROM, others
Pinout	MMC3 pinout
PRG ROM capacity	512K
PRG ROM window	8K + 8K + 16K fixed
PRG RAM capacity	8K
PRG RAM window	8K
CHR capacity	256K
CHR window	2K x 2 + 1K x 4
Name table mirroring	H or V, switchable, or 4 fixed
Bus conflicts	No
IRQ	Yes
Audio	No
iNES mappers	004, 118, 119

B.5.2   *Banks*

The MMC3 memory mapper divides its memory banks up as follows:

- *CPU* $6000-$7FFF—8 KB PRG RAM bank (optional)
- *CPU* $8000-$9FFF (or $C000-$DFFF)—8 KB switchable PRG ROM bank
- *CPU* $A000-$BFFF—8 KB switchable PRG ROM bank
- *CPU* $C000-$DFFF (or $8000-$9FFF)—8 KB PRG ROM bank, fixed to the second-to-last bank
- *CPU* $E000-$FFFF—8 KB PRG ROM bank, fixed to the last bank
- *PPU* $0000-$07FF (or $1000-$17FF)—2 KB switchable CHR bank
- *PPU* $0800-$0FFF (or $1800-$1FFF)—2 KB switchable CHR bank
- *PPU* $1000-$13FF (or $0000-$03FF)—1 KB switchable CHR bank
- *PPU* $1400-$17FF (or $0400-$07FF)—1 KB switchable CHR bank
- *PPU* $1800-$1BFF (or $0800-$0BFF)—1 KB switchable CHR bank
- *PPU* $1C00-$1FFF (or $0C00-$0FFF)—1 KB switchable CHR bank

B.6 MMC5

The MMC5 is the most powerful mapper ASIC Nintendo made for the NES and Famicom. It supports many advanced features, including

- Four PRG ROM switching modes
- Four CHR ROM switching modes
- Up to 128 KB of WRAM, mappable not only at `$6000-$7FFF` but also within `$8000-$DFFF`; supports either one chip (up to 128 KB) or two chips (up to 32 KB each)
- An 8-bit by 8-bit multiplier with a 16-bit result for performing quick calculations
- Scanline detection with counter and configurable IRQ
- Frame detection with status bit
- The ability to use different CHR banks for background and 8×6 sprites (allowing 256 unique 8×16 sprite tiles, independent of the background)
- 1,024 bytes of on-chip memory, which can be used for four different purposes:
  - An extra general-use name table
  - Attribute and tile index expansion that addresses 16,384 background tiles at once and allows each individual 8×8 tile to have its own palette setting
  - Vertical split-screen
  - Extra RAM for storing program variables
- Three extra sound channels:
  - Two pulse channels, identical to those in the NES APU (except lacking pitch sweeps)
  - An 8-bit RAW PCM channel
- A fill mode name table, which can be instantly set to contain a specific tile in a specific color (useful for screen transitions)
- System reset detection:
  - Triggered by a positive or negative gap in M2 of at least 11.2 μsec.
  - Also triggered and latched by absence of AVcc.
  - After reapplying AVcc, another gap in M2 is sometimes necessary to clear the latch.
  - This feature resets some, but not all, states of the MMC5.
  - The PRG RAM +CE pin is a direct reflection of the system reset detection state.

B.6.1 Overview

The MMC5 memory mapper has the details shown in table B.6.

Table B.6   MMC5 overview

Item	Details
Company	Nintendo, Koei, others
Games	15
Complexity	ASIC
Boards	EKROM, ELROM, ETROM, EWROM
Pinout	MMC5 pinout
PRG ROM capacity	1024K
PRG ROM window	8K, 16K, or 32K
PRG RAM capacity	128K
PRG RAM window	8K ($6000-$DFFF), 16K (only $8000-$BFFF at PRG mode 1/2)
CHR capacity	1024K
CHR window	1K, 2K, 4K, or 8K
Name table mirroring	Arbitrary, up to three source name tables (plus fill mode)
Bus conflicts	No
IRQ	Yes
Audio	Yes
iNES mappers	005

B.6.2   Banks

The MMC5 provides four distinct banking modes for both PRG ROM and CHR ROM:

- PRG mode 0:
    - *CPU* $6000-$7FFF—8 KB switchable PRG RAM bank
    - *CPU* $8000-$FFFF—32 KB switchable PRG ROM bank
- PRG mode 1:
    - *CPU* $6000-$7FFF—8 KB switchable PRG RAM bank
    - *CPU* $8000-$BFFF—16 KB switchable PRG ROM/RAM bank
    - *CPU* $C000-$FFFF—16 KB switchable PRG ROM bank
- PRG mode 2:
    - *CPU* $6000-$7FFF—8 KB switchable PRG RAM bank
    - *CPU* $8000-$BFFF—16 KB switchable PRG ROM/RAM bank
    - *CPU* $C000-$DFFF—8 KB switchable PRG ROM/RAM bank
    - *CPU* $E000-$FFFF—8 KB switchable PRG ROM bank
- PRG mode 3:
    - *CPU* $6000-$7FFF—8 KB switchable PRG RAM bank
    - *CPU* $8000-$9FFF—8 KB switchable PRG ROM/RAM bank
    - *CPU* $A000-$BFFF—8 KB switchable PRG ROM/RAM bank

- – *CPU* $C000-$DFFF—8 KB switchable PRG ROM/RAM bank
- – *CPU* $E000-$FFFF—8 KB switchable PRG ROM bank
- CHR mode 0:
  - – *PPU* $0000-$1FFF—8 KB switchable CHR bank
- CHR mode 1:
  - – *PPU* $0000-$0FFF—4 KB switchable CHR bank
  - – *PPU* $1000-$1FFF—4 KB switchable CHR bank
- CHR mode 2:
  - – *PPU* $0000-$07FF—2 KB switchable CHR bank
  - – *PPU* $0800-$0FFF—2 KB switchable CHR bank
  - – *PPU* $1000-$17FF—2 KB switchable CHR bank
  - – *PPU* $1800-$1FFF—2 KB switchable CHR bank
- CHR mode 3:
  - – *PPU* $0000-$03FF—1 KB switchable CHR bank
  - – *PPU* $0400-$07FF—1 KB switchable CHR bank
  - – *PPU* $0800-$0BFF—1 KB switchable CHR bank
  - – *PPU* $0C00-$0FFF—1 KB switchable CHR bank
  - – *PPU* $1000-$13FF—1 KB switchable CHR bank
  - – *PPU* $1400-$17FF—1 KB switchable CHR bank
  - – *PPU* $1800-$1BFF—1 KB switchable CHR bank
  - – *PPU* $1C00-$1FFF—1 KB switchable CHR bank

B.7 UxROM

Another Nintendo memory mapper is UxROM, with quite a large possible ROM size of up to 4096K and CHR RAM, along with a very simple memory mapping scheme.

B.7.1 Overview

The UxROM memory mapper has the details shown in table B.7.

Table B.7 UxROM overview

Item	Details
Company	Nintendo, others
Games	155
Complexity	Discrete logic
Boards	UNROM, UOROM
PRG ROM capacity	256K/4096K
PRG ROM window	16K + 16K fixed
PRG RAM capacity	None
CHR capacity	8K

(continued)

Item	Details
CHR window	n/a
Name table mirroring	Fixed H or V, controlled by solder pads
Bus conflicts	Yes/No
IRQ	No
Audio	No
iNES mappers	002, 094, 180

B.7.2   Banks

The UxROM memory mapper divides its memory banks up as follows:

- *CPU* $8000-$BFFF—16 KB switchable PRG ROM bank
- *CPU* $C000-$FFFF—16 KB PRG ROM bank, fixed to the last bank

B.8   VRC1

VRC1 is an early Konami mapper used mostly for Famicom releases in Japan from Konami and Jaleco. It enables 128K of PRG ROM and CHR ROM.

B.8.1   Overview

The VRC1 memory mapper has the details shown in table B.8.

Table B.8   VRC1 overview

Item	Details
Company	Konami
Games	6
Complexity	ASIC
Boards	JF-20, JF-22, 4036, 302114A, 350459
Pinout	VRC1 pinout
PRG ROM capacity	128K
PRG ROM window	8K
PRG RAM capacity	none
PRG RAM window	n/a
CHR capacity	128K
CHR window	4K
Name table mirroring	H or V, switchable
Bus conflicts	No
IRQ	No
Audio	No
iNES mappers	075

B.8.2 Banks

The VRC1 memory mapper divides its memory banks up as follows:

- *CPU* $8000-$9FFF—8 KiB switchable PRG ROM bank
- *CPU* $A000-$BFFF—8 KiB switchable PRG ROM bank
- *CPU* $C000-$DFFF—8 KiB switchable PRG ROM bank
- *CPU* $E000-$FFFF—8 KiB PRG ROM bank, fixed to the last bank
- *PPU* $0000-$0FFF—4 KiB switchable CHR bank
- *PPU* $1000-$1FFF—4 KiB switchable CHR bank

B.9   VRC2 and VRC4

These are two very similar mappers used by earlier releases from Konami that extend both PRG and CHR ROM, supply 8K of PRG RAM, and have an interrupt that triggers after a certain number of CPU cycles.

B.9.1 Overview

The details of the VRC2 and VRC4 memory mappers are shown in table B.9 (differences are highlighted in bold in the VRC4 column).

Table B.9   VRC2 and VRC4 overview

Item	VRC2 details	VRC4 details
Company	Konami	Konami
Complexity	ASIC	ASIC
Boards	VRC2a-c	**VRC4a-f**
Pinout	VRC2 pinout	VRC2 pinout
PRG ROM capacity	256K	256K
PRG ROM window	8K	8K
PRG RAM capacity	8K	8K
PRG RAM window	8K	8K
CHR capacity	256K	**512K**
CHR window	1K	1K
Name table mirroring	H, V switchable	**H, V, 1 switchable**
Bus conflicts	No	No
IRQ	Yes	Yes
Audio	No	No
iNES mappers	021, 022, 023, 025	021, 022, 023, 025

B.9.2 Banks

The VRC2 and VRC4 memory mapper divides its memory banks up as follows:

- VRC2:
  - *PPU* $0000-$03FF—1 KiB switchable CHR bank
  - *PPU* $0400-$07FF—1 KiB switchable CHR bank
  - *PPU* $0800-$0BFF—1 KiB switchable CHR bank
  - *PPU* $0C00-$0FFF—1 KiB switchable CHR bank
  - *PPU* $1000-$13FF—1 KiB switchable CHR bank
  - *PPU* $1400-$17FF—1 KiB switchable CHR bank
  - *PPU* $1800-$1BFF—1 KiB switchable CHR bank
  - *PPU* $1C00-$1FFF—1 KiB switchable CHR bank
  - *CPU* $6000-$6FFF—1-bit latch, or
  - *CPU* $6000-$7FFF—Optional 8 KiB RAM
  - *CPU* $8000-$9FFF—8 KiB switchable PRG ROM bank
  - *CPU* $A000-$BFFF—8 KiB switchable PRG ROM bank
  - *CPU* $C000-$FFFF—16 KiB PRG ROM bank, fixed to the last 16 KB
- VRC4:
  - *PPU* $0000-$03FF—1 KiB switchable CHR bank
  - *PPU* $0400-$07FF—1 KiB switchable CHR bank
  - *PPU* $0800-$0BFF—1 KiB switchable CHR bank
  - *PPU* $0C00-$0FFF—1 KiB switchable CHR bank
  - *PPU* $1000-$13FF—1 KiB switchable CHR bank
  - *PPU* $1400-$17FF—1 KiB switchable CHR bank
  - *PPU* $1800-$1BFF—1 KiB switchable CHR bank
  - *PPU* $1C00-$1FFF—1 KiB switchable CHR bank
  - *CPU* $6000-$6FFF—Optional 2 KiB PRG RAM bank (mirrored once), or
  - *CPU* $6000-$7FFF—Optional 8 KiB PRG RAM bank
  - *CPU* $8000-$9FFF ($C000-$DFFF)—8 KiB switchable PRG ROM bank
  - *CPU* $A000-$BFFF—8 KiB switchable PRG ROM bank
  - *CPU* $C000-$DFFF (*or* $8000-$9FFF)—8 KiB PRG ROM bank, fixed to the second-last bank
  - *CPU* $E000-$FFFF—8 KiB PRG ROM bank, fixed to the last bank

B.10 VRC

This is a much later Konami mapper that includes an FM (frequency modulation) sound processor, like that used in several synthesizer keyboards.

B.10.1 Overview

The VRC7 memory mapper has the details shown in table B.10.

Table B.10   VRC7 overview

Items	Details
Company	Konami
Games	2
Complexity	ASIC
Boards	352402, 353429
Pinout	VRC7 pinout
PRG ROM capacity	512K
PRG ROM window	8K x 3 + 8K fixed
PRG RAM capacity	8K
PRG RAM window	8K fixed
CHR capacity	256K
CHR window	1K x 8
Name table mirroring	H, V, or 1, switchable
Bus conflicts	No
IRQ	Yes
Audio	VRC7a only
iNES mappers	085

B.10.2 *Banks*

The VRC7 memory mapper divides its memory banks up as follows:

- CPU memory banks:
    - `$600-0$7FFF`—8 KB PRG-RAM bank, fixed
    - `$8000-$9FFF`—8 KB switchable PRG-ROM bank
    - `$A000-$BFFF`—8 KB switchable PRG-ROM bank
    - `$C000-$DFFF`—8 KB switchable PRG-ROM bank
    - `$E000-$FFFF`—8 KB PRG-ROM bank, fixed to the last bank
- PPU memory banks:
    - `$0000-$03FF`—1 KB switchable CHR-ROM bank
    - `$0400-$07FF1`—KB switchable CHR-ROM bank
    - `$0800-$0BFF`—1 KB switchable CHR-ROM bank
    - `$0C00-$0FFF`—1 KB switchable CHR-ROM bank
    - `$1000-$13FF`—1 KB switchable CHR-ROM bank
    - `$1400-$17FF`—1 KB switchable CHR-ROM bank
    - `$1800-$1BFF`—1 KB switchable CHR-ROM bank
    - `$1C00-$1FFF`—1 KB switchable CHR-ROM bank

If CHR-RAM is used instead of CHR-ROM, the banking feature is still functional.

Memory and IO map

The NES architecture is based on the 8-bit 6502 CPU, which can access 64K of memory at any one time. The 6502 processor does not have specific instructions to access external ports but instead uses dedicated memory locations to read and write to external devices. This appendix will show the memory map in more detail and list all the memory-mapped ports built into the original hardware.

C.1 Memory map

The NES's 64K memory space is split into multiple sections. The lower 4K of memory contains all of the dedicated sections for the CPU, and the next section, the PPU memory-mapped registers. The upper 48K of space is split up into areas that are provided by the game cartridge (see figure C.1).

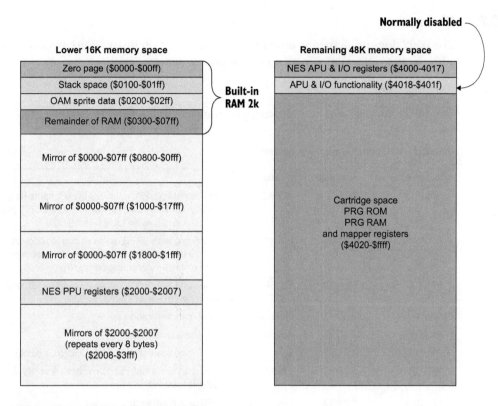

Figure C.1 NES/Famicom memory map

The cartridge space from `$4020-$ffff` can be used for any purpose, such as ROM, RAM, and memory-mapped registers. Many common mappers place ROM and save/work RAM in these locations:

- `$6000-$7fff`—Battery-backed save or work RAM (commonly referred to as WRAM or PRG-RAM)
- `$8000-$ffff`—ROM and mapper memory mapped registers

If using DPCM 1-bit digital samples, the sample's data needs to be located from `$c000` to `$fff1`. The CPU expects the interrupt vectors to be in a fixed position at the end of the cartridge space:

- `$fffa-$fffb`—NMI vector
- `$fffc-$fffd`—Reset vector
- `$fffe-$ffff`—IRQ/BRK vector

C.2 IO map

The 6502 does not have any direct port communication instructions; instead, memory addresses are allocated as read and write port addresses.

C.2.1 PPU registers

The PPU exposes eight memory-mapped registers to the CPU (see table C.1).

Table C.1 PPU memory-mapped registers

Common Name	Address	Bits	Notes
PPUCTRL	$2000	VPHB SINN	NMI enable (V), PPU master/slave (P), sprite height (H), background tile select (B), sprite tile select (S), increment mode (I), name table select (NN)
PPUMASK	$2001	BGRs bMmG	Color emphasis (BGR), sprite enable (s), background enable (b), sprite left column enable (M), background left column enable (m), greyscale (G)
PPUSTATUS	$2002	VSO- —	vBlank (V), sprite 0 hit (S), sprite overflow (O); read resets write pair for $2005/$2006
OAMADDR	$2003	aaaa aaaa	OAM read/write address
OAMDATA	$2004	dddd dddd	OAM data read/write
PPUSCROLL	$2005	xxxx xxxx	Fine scroll position (two writes: X scroll, Y scroll)
PPUADDR	$2006	aaaa aaaa	PPU read/write address (two writes: most significant byte, least significant byte)
PPUDATA	$2007	dddd dddd	PPU data read/write
OAMDMA	$4014	aaaa aaaa	OAM DMA high address

C.2.2 APU registers

The APU exposes 21 memory-mapped registers to the CPU. They are all write-only except $4015, which is read/write (see table C.2)

Table C.2 APU memory-mapped registers

Address	Bits	Function
Pulse 1 channel (write)		
$4000	DDLC NNNN	Duty, loop envelope/disable length counter, constant volume, envelope period/volume
$4001	EPPP NSSS	Sweep unit: enabled, period, negative, shift count
$4002	LLLL LLLL	Timer low
$4003	LLLL LHHH	Length counter load, timer high (also resets duty and starts envelope)

(continued)

Address	Bits	Function
Pulse 2 channel (write)		
$4004	DDLC NNNN	Duty, loop envelope/disable length counter, constant volume, envelope period/volume
$4005	EPPP NSSS	Sweep unit: enabled, period, negative, shift count
$4006	LLLL LLLL	Timer low
$4007	LLLL LHHH	Length counter load, timer high (also resets duty and starts envelope)
Triangle channel (write)		
$4008	CRRR RRRR	Length counter disable/linear counter control, linear counter reload value
$400A	LLLL LLLL	Timer low
$400B	LLLL LHHH	Length counter load, timer high (also reloads linear counter)
Noise channel (write)		
$400C	--LC NNNN	Loop envelope/disable length counter, constant volume, envelope period/volume
$400E	L--- PPPP	Loop noise, noise period
$400F	LLLL L---	Length counter load (also starts envelope)
DMC channel (write)		
$4010	IL-- FFFF	IRQ enable, loop sample, frequency index
$4011	-DDD DDDD	Direct load
$4012	AAAA AAAA	Sample address %11AAAAAA.AA000000
$4013	LLLL LLLL	Sample length %0000LLLL.LLLL0001
$4015	---D NT21	Control: DMC enable, length counter enables: noise, triangle, pulse 2, pulse 1 (write)
$4016	IF-D NT21	Status: DMC interrupt, frame interrupt, length counter status: noise, triangle, pulse 2, pulse 1 (read)
$4017	SD-- ---	Frame counter: 5-frame sequence, disable frame interrupt (write)

The NES and Famicom have a set of I/O ports used for controllers and other peripherals, consisting of the following:

- One output port, 3 bits wide, accessible by writing the bottom 3 bits of $4016.
- The values latched by $4016/write appear on the OUT0-OUT2 output pins of the 2A03/07, where OUT0 is routed to the controller ports and OUT0-OUT2 to the expansion port on the NES.

- Two input ports, each 5 bits wide, accessible by reading the bottom 5 bits of $4016 and $4017. Reading $4016 and $4017 activates the /OE1 and /OE2 signals, respectively, which are routed to the controller ports and the expansion port.

- On the NES, only D0, D3, and D4 are connected to both controller ports, while all of D0-D4 are connected to the expansion port.

- On the original Famicom, the two ports differ: $4016 D0 and D2 and $4017 D0 are permanently connected to both controllers, while $4016 D1 and all of $4017's D0-D4 are connected to the expansion port.

- On the AV Famicom, only D0 is connected to the controller ports. The expansion port is unchanged.

index